[is__]
[bub_]

WOLVERINE BY BENJAMIN PERCY VOL. 4. Contains material originally published in magazine form as WOLVERINE (2020) #20-25. First printing 2022. ISBN 978-1-302-92726-4. Published by MARVEL WORLDWIDE, INC., a subsidiary of MARVEL ENTERTAINMENT, LLC. OFFICE OF PUBLICATION: 1290 Avenue of the Americas, New York, NY 10104. © 2022 MARVEL No similarity between any of the names, characters, persons, and/or institutions in this book with those of any living or dead person or institution is intended, and any such similarity which may exist is purely coincidental. **Printed in Canada.** KEVIN FEIGE, Chief Creative Officer; DAN BUCKLEY, President, Marvel Entertainment; DAVID BOGART, Associate Publisher & SVP of Talent Affairs; TOM BREVOORT, VP, Executive Editor; NICK LOWE, Executive Editor, VP of Content, Digital Publishing; DAVID GABRIEL, VP of Print & Digital Publishing; SVEN LARSEN, VP of Licensed Publishing; MARK ANNUNZIATO, VP of Planning & Forecasting; JEFF YOUNGQUIST, VP of Production & Special Projects; ALEX MORALES, Director of Publishing Operations; DAN EDINGTON, Director of Editorial Operations; RICKEY PURDIN, Director of Talent Relations; JENNIFER GRÜNWALD, Director of Production & Special Projects; SUSAN CRESPI, Production Manager; STAN LEE, Chairman Emeritus. For information regarding advertising in Marvel Comics or on Marvel.com, please contact Vit DeBellis, Custom Solutions & Integrated Advertising Manager, at vdebellis@marvel.com. For Marvel subscription inquiries, please call 888-511-5480. **Manufactured between 9/30/2022 and 11/1/2022 by SOLISCO PRINTERS, SCOTT, QC, CANADA.**

10 9 8 7 6 5 4 3 2 1

WOLVERINE

Writer:	**Benjamin Percy**
Artists:	**Adam Kubert** (#20-23)
	& Federico Vicentini (#24-25)
Colorists:	**Frank Martin** (#20-23)
	& Frank D'Armata (#24-25)
	with Dijjo Lima (#20)
"Bar Brawl" Artists:	**Greg Land & Jay Leisten;**
	Juan Ferreyra; Kyle Charles;
	Andrea Di Vito; Klaus Janson;
	and Emma Kubert
	& Guillermo Ortego
"Bar Brawl" Colorists:	**Frank Martin & Juan Ferreyra**
Letterer:	**VC's Cory Petit**
Cover Art:	**Adam Kubert &**
	Frank Martin
Design:	**Tom Muller**
Assistant Editor:	**Drew Baumgartner**
Editor:	**Mark Basso**
Senior Editor:	**Jordan D. White**

Collection Editor:	**Jennifer Grünwald**
Assistant Editor:	**Daniel Kirchhoffer**
Assistant Managing Editor:	**Maia Loy**
Associate Manager, Talent Relations:	**Lisa Montalbano**
VP Production & Special Projects:	**Jeff Youngquist**
SVP Print, Sales & Marketing:	**David Gabriel**
Editor in Chief:	**C.B. Cebulski**

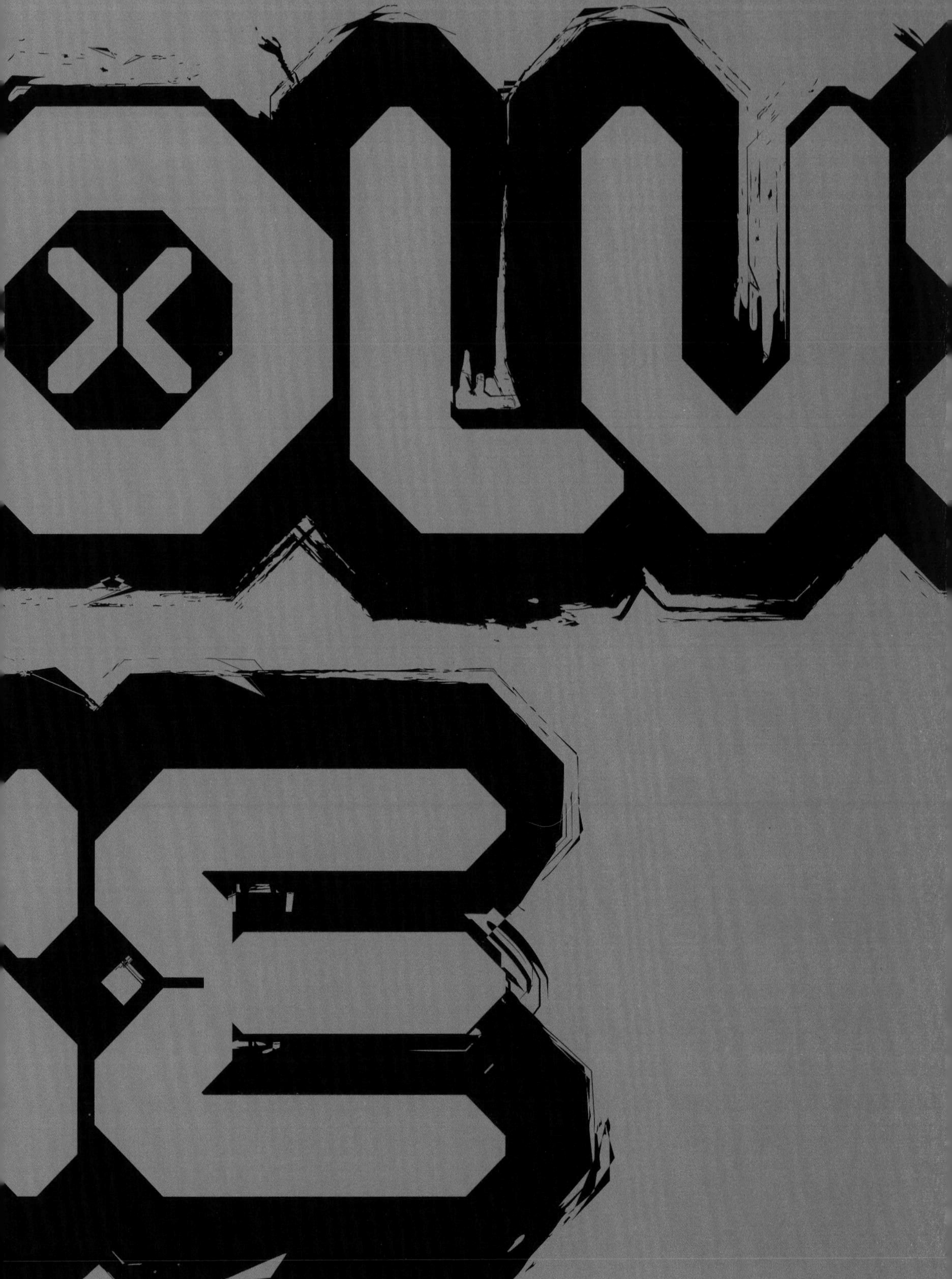

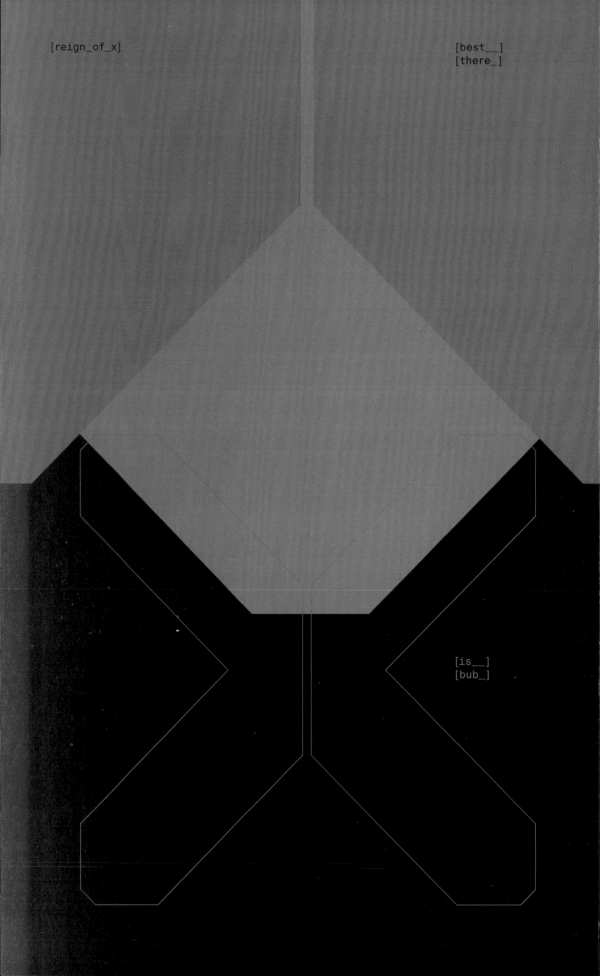

[reign_of_x]

[best__]
[there_]

[is__]
[bub_]

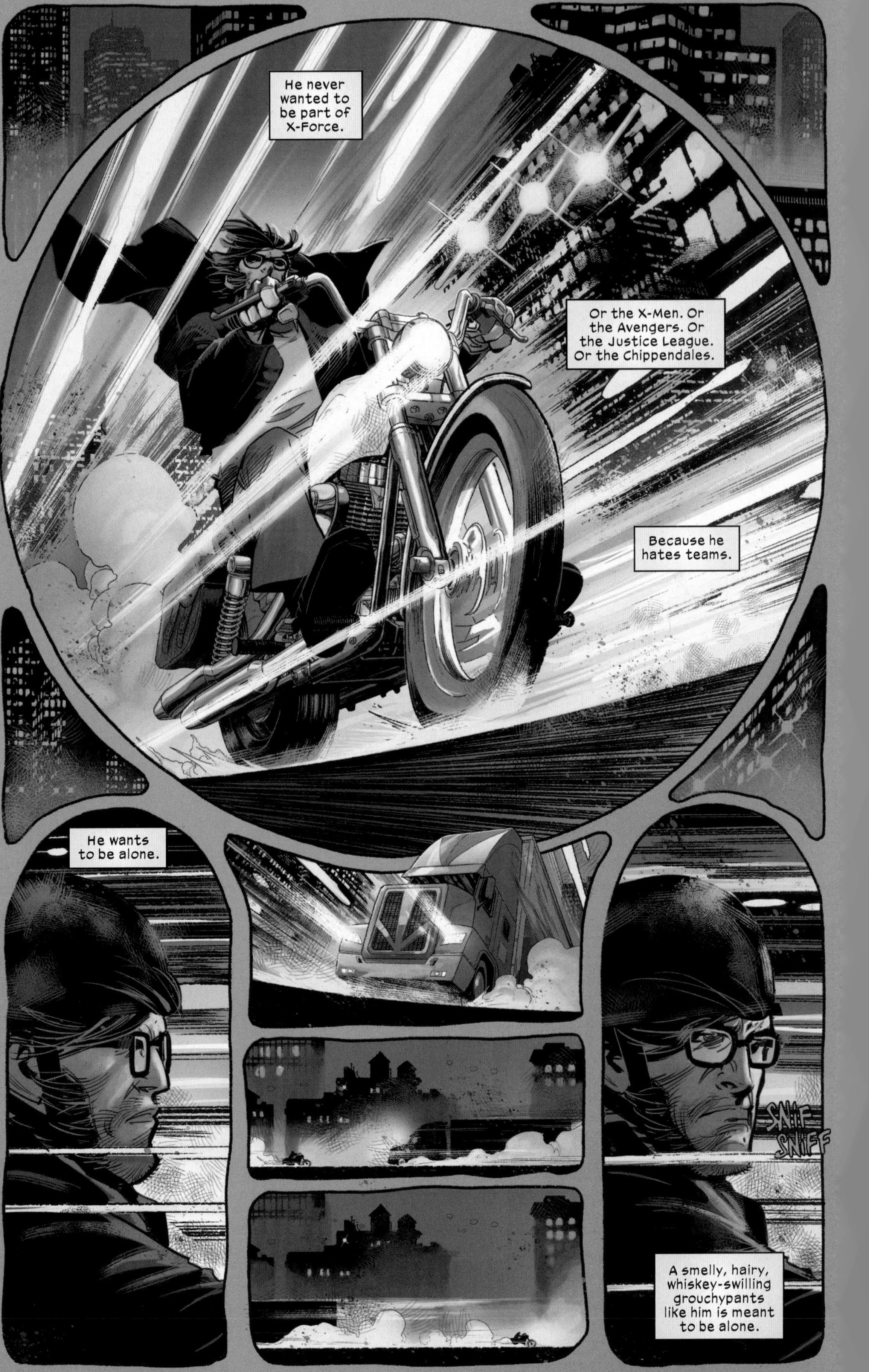
He never wanted to be part of X-Force.
Or the X-Men. Or the Avengers. Or the Justice League. Or the Chippendales.
Because he hates teams.
He wants to be alone.
SNIFF
SNIFF
A smelly, hairy, whiskey-swilling grouchypants like him is meant to be alone.

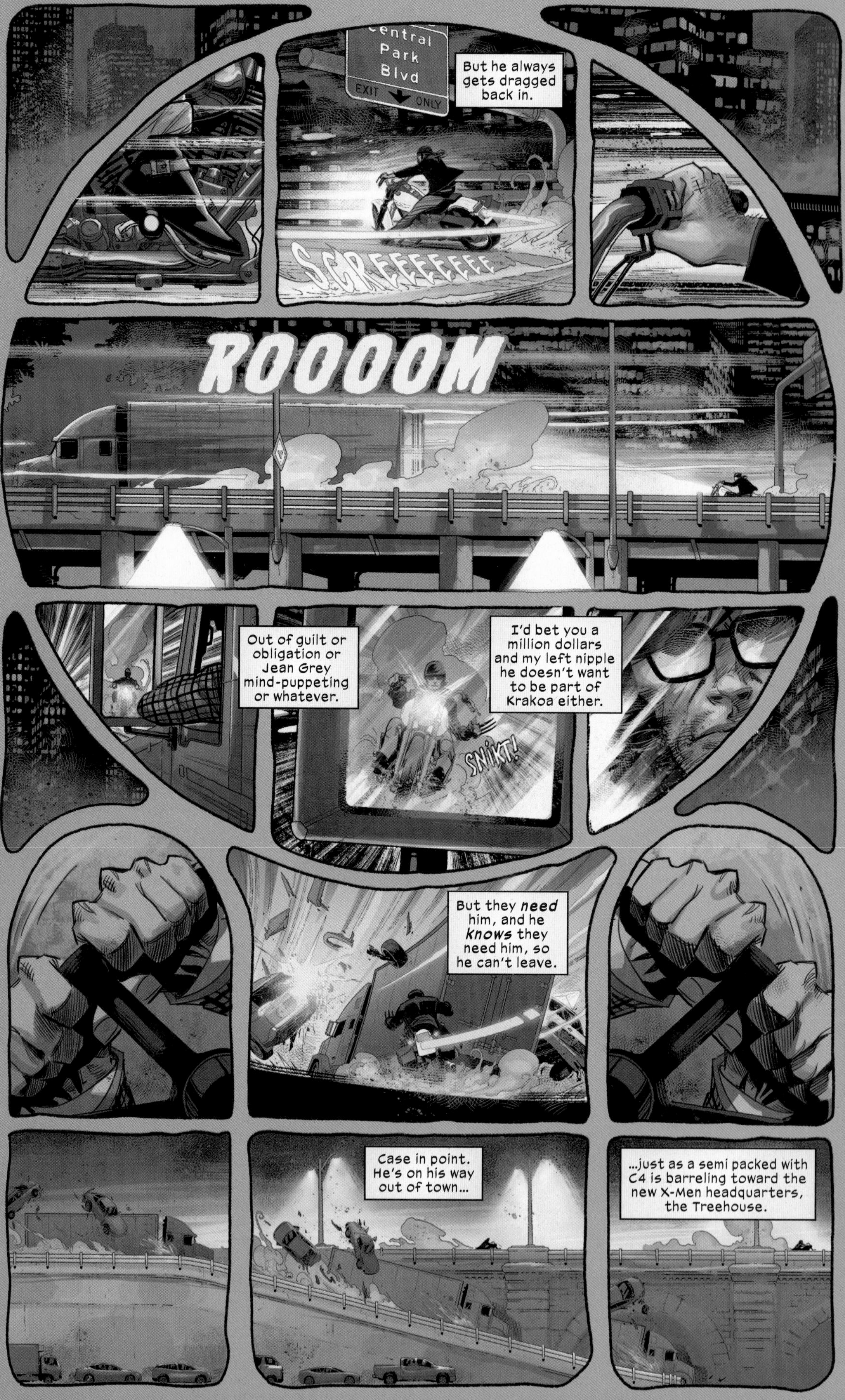
Central
Park
Blvd
EXIT ONLY
But he always gets dragged back in.
SCREEEEEEE
ROOOOM
Out of guilt or obligation or Jean Grey mind-puppeting or whatever.
I'd bet you a million dollars and my left nipple he doesn't want to be part of Krakoa either.
SNIKT!
But they *need* him, and he *knows* they need him, so he can't leave.
Case in point. He's on his way out of town...
...just as a semi packed with C4 is barreling toward the new X-Men headquarters, the Treehouse.

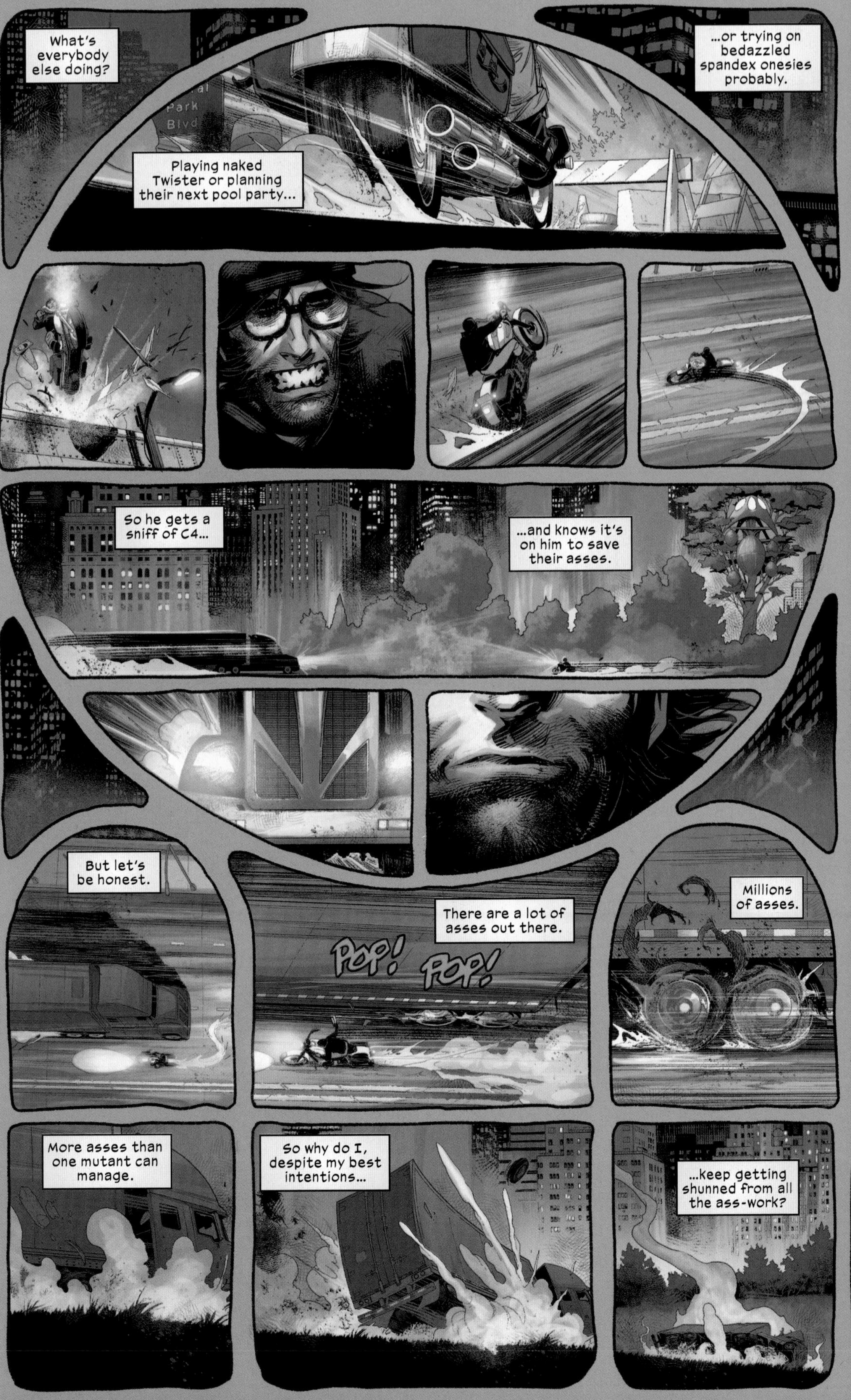
What's everybody else doing?
...or trying on bedazzled spandex onesies probably.
Playing naked Twister or planning their next pool party...
So he gets a sniff of C4...
...and knows it's on him to save their asses.
But let's be honest.
There are a lot of asses out there.
POP! POP!
Millions of asses.
More asses than one mutant can manage.
So why do I, despite my best intentions...
...keep getting shunned from all the ass-work?

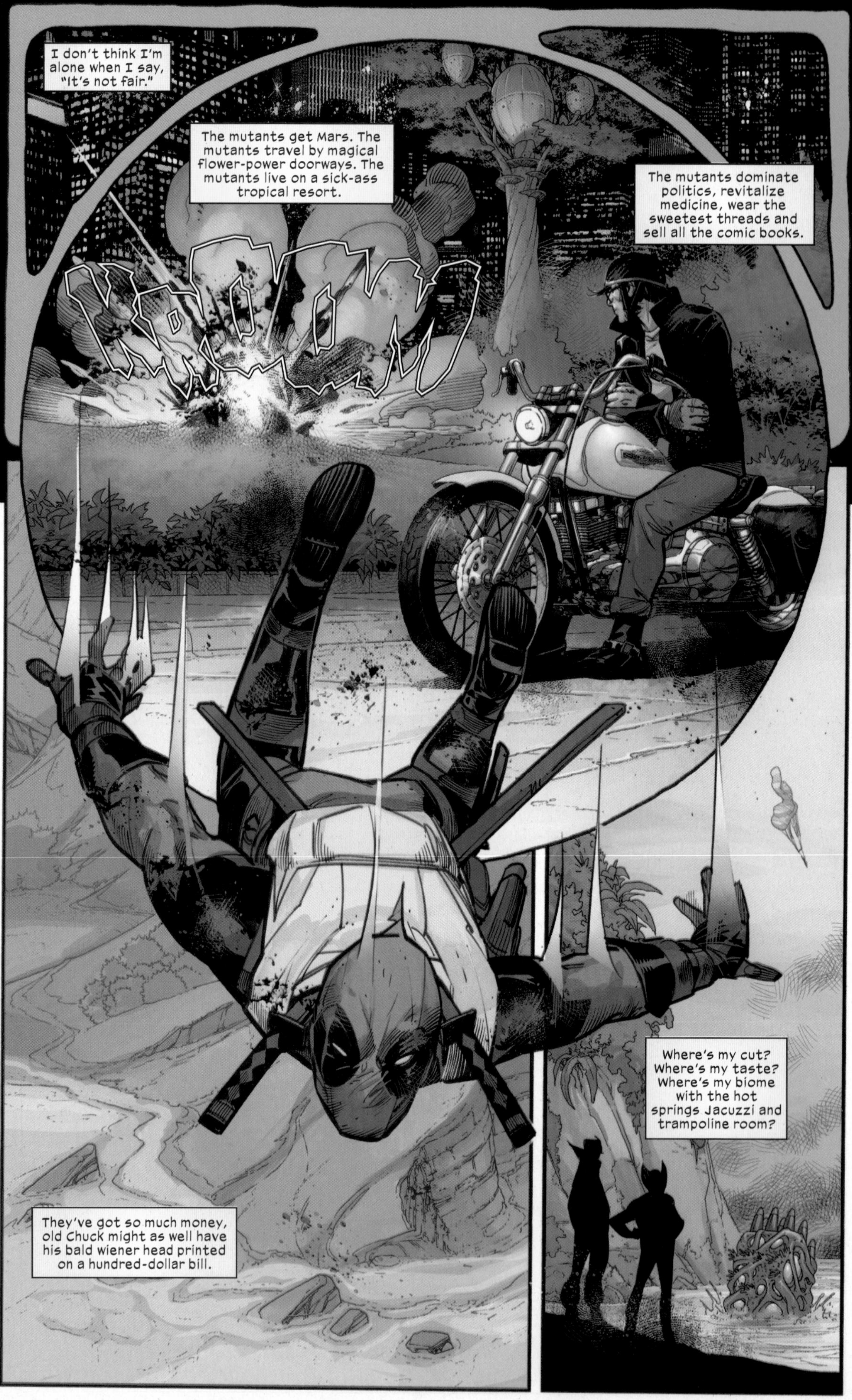
I don't think I'm alone when I say, "It's not fair."
The mutants get Mars. The mutants travel by magical flower-power doorways. The mutants live on a sick-ass tropical resort.
The mutants dominate politics, revitalize medicine, wear the sweetest threads and sell all the comic books.
KA-BOOM
They've got so much money, old Chuck might as well have his bald wiener head printed on a hundred-dollar bill.
Where's my cut? Where's my taste? Where's my biome with the hot springs Jacuzzi and trampoline room?

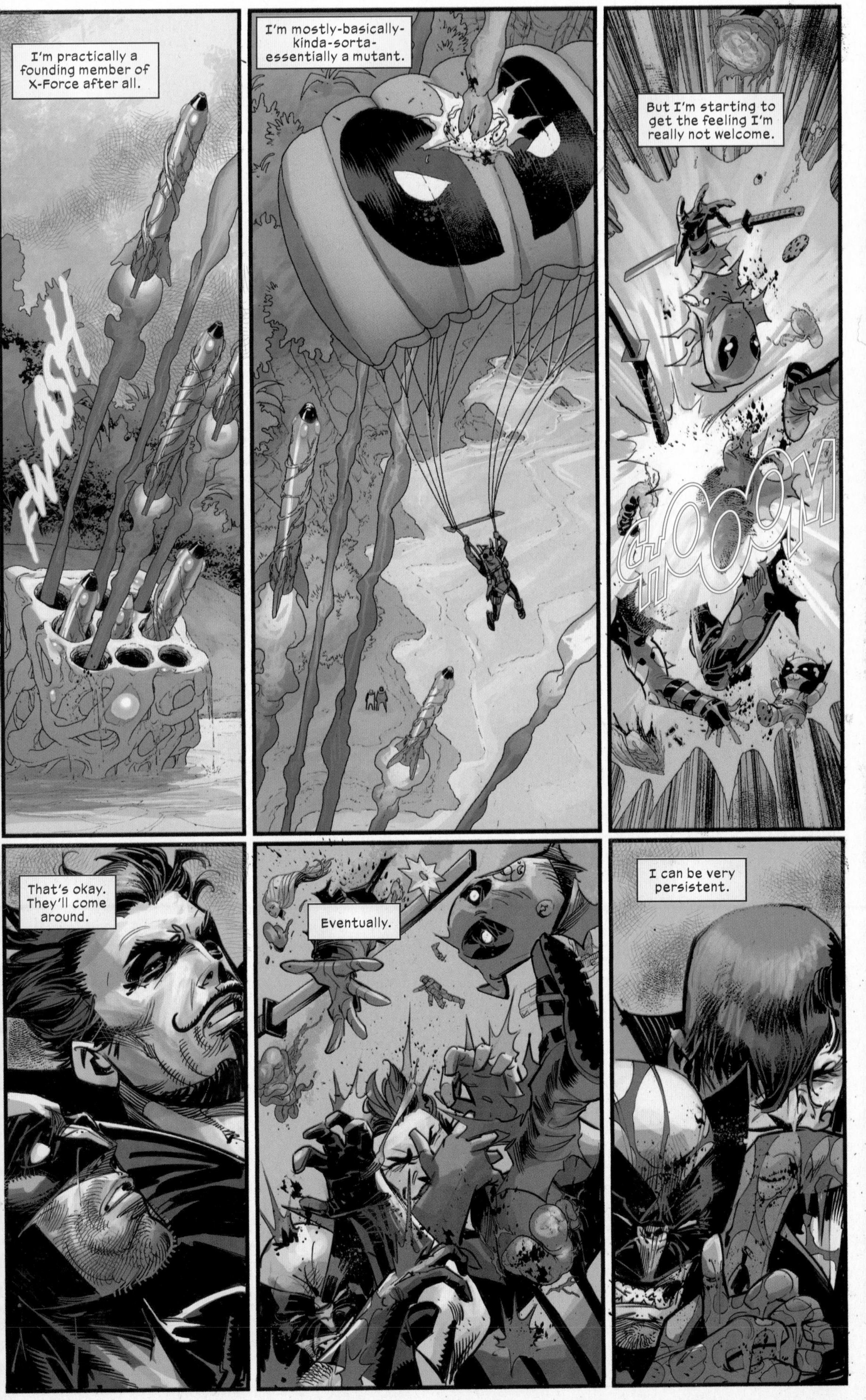
I'm practically a founding member of X-Force after all.
FWASH
I'm mostly-basically-kinda-sorta-essentially a mutant.
But I'm starting to get the feeling I'm really not welcome.
CHOOOM
That's okay. They'll come around.
Eventually.
I can be very persistent.

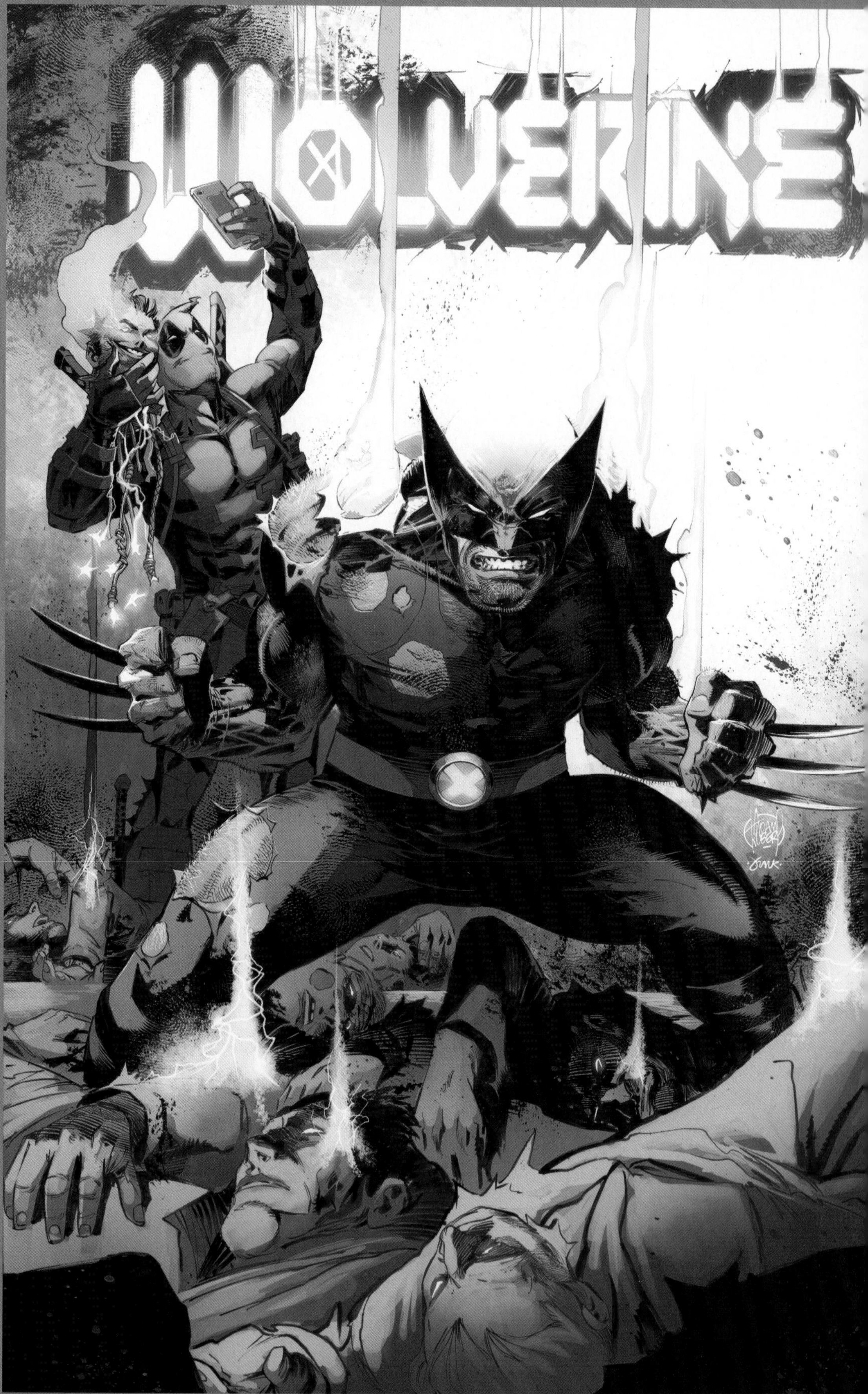
WOLVERINE

Trigger Warning

WOLVERINE

— TWO HEADS

Wolverine has recently returned from a time-shredding adventure to save Charles Xavier's life in the past and therefore Krakoa's existence in the present. This is naturally good news for mutantkind, who have made Krakoa their home, and even for the mutants and humans outside the island. Seems like one of those outside is especially happy -- you see, Deadpool REALLY wants to be accepted on Krakoa, and he figures now's his chance. This could be a thing.

[WOLVERINE]

[DEADPOOL]

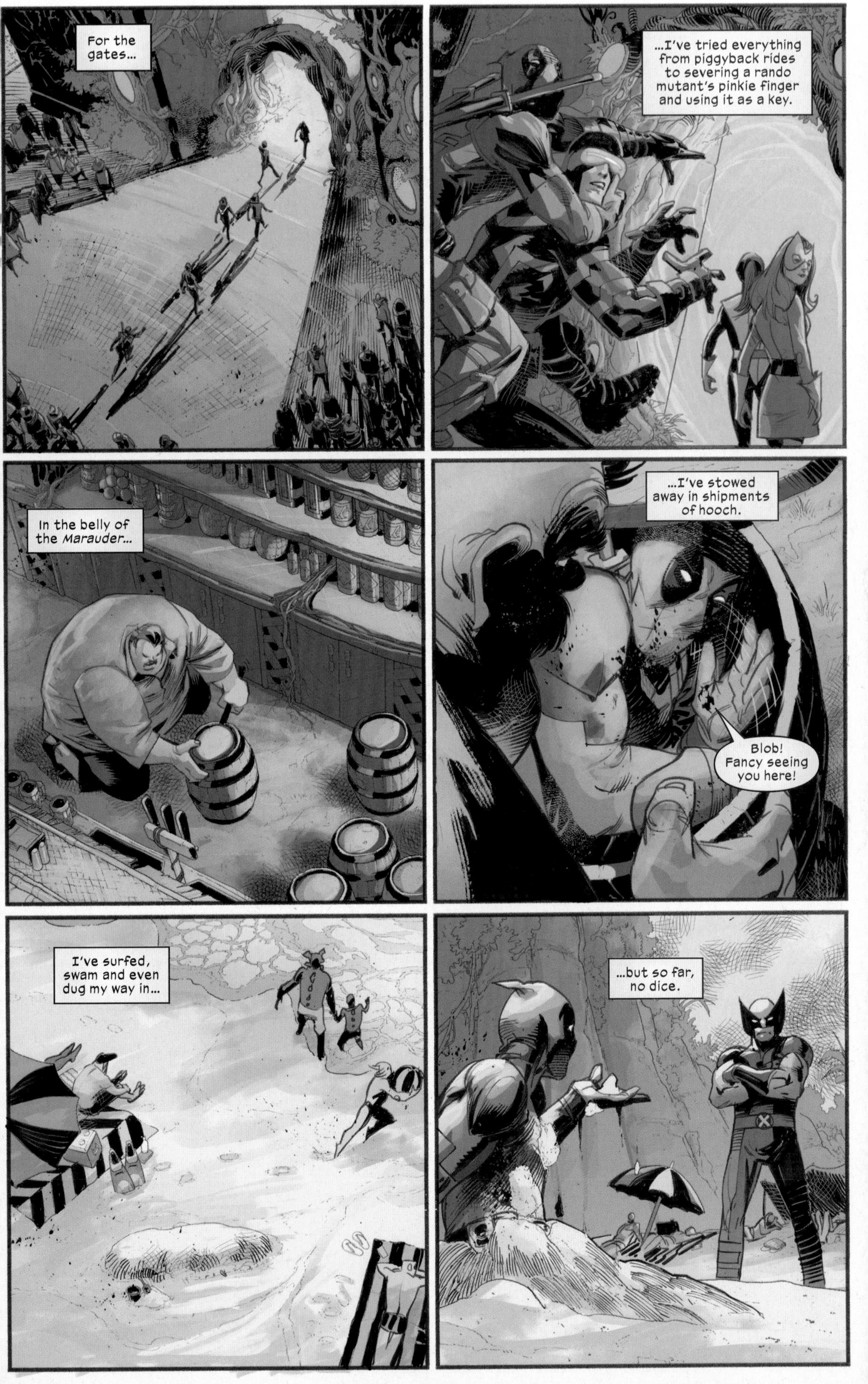
For the gates...
...I've tried everything from piggyback rides to severing a rando mutant's pinkie finger and using it as a key.
In the belly of the Marauder...
...I've stowed away in shipments of hooch.
Blob! Fancy seeing you here!
I've surfed, swam and even dug my way in...
...but so far, no dice.

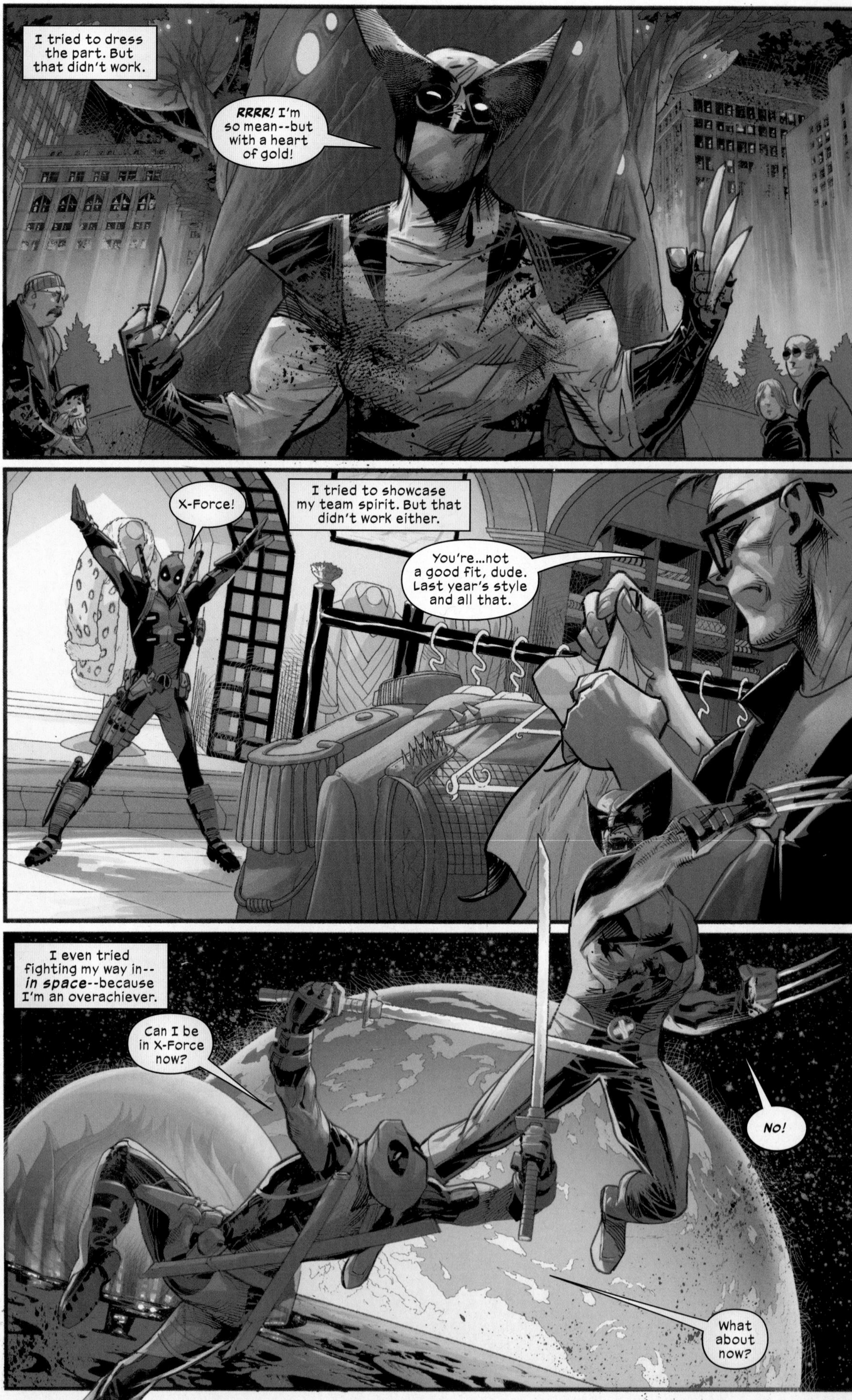
I tried to dress the part. But that didn't work.
RRRR! I'm so mean--but with a heart of gold!
X-Force!
I tried to showcase my team spirit. But that didn't work either.
You're...not a good fit, dude. Last year's style and all that.
I even tried fighting my way in-- ***in space***--because I'm an overachiever.
Can I be in X-Force now?
NO!
What about now?

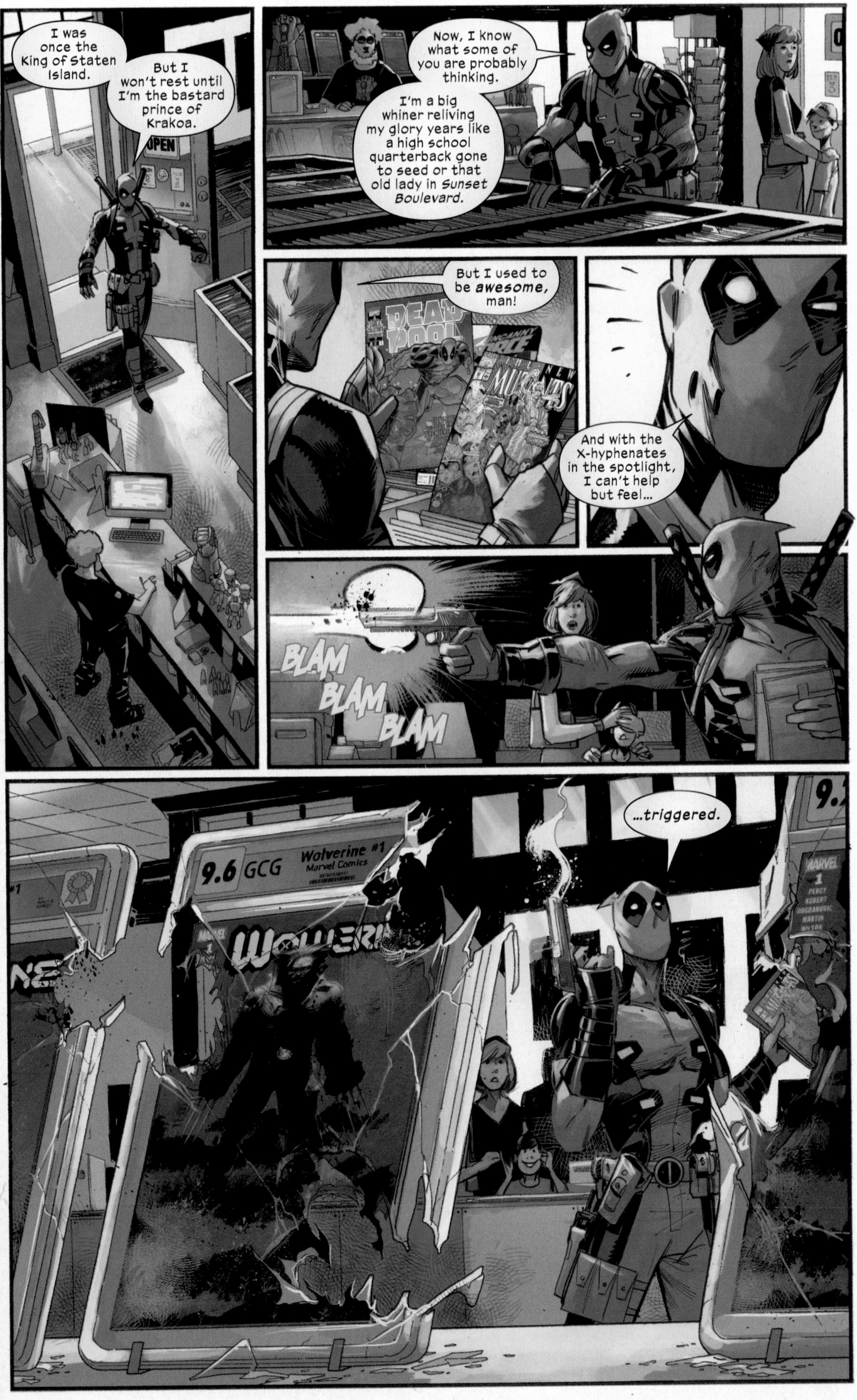

I was once the King of Staten Island.
But I won't rest until I'm the bastard prince of Krakoa.
OPEN
Now, I know what some of you are probably thinking.
I'm a big whiner reliving my glory years like a high school quarterback gone to seed or that old lady in *Sunset Boulevard*.
But I used to be *awesome*, man!
And with the X-hyphenates in the spotlight, I can't help but feel...
BLAM
BLAM
BLAM
...triggered.
9.6 GCG
Wolverine #1
Marvel Comics

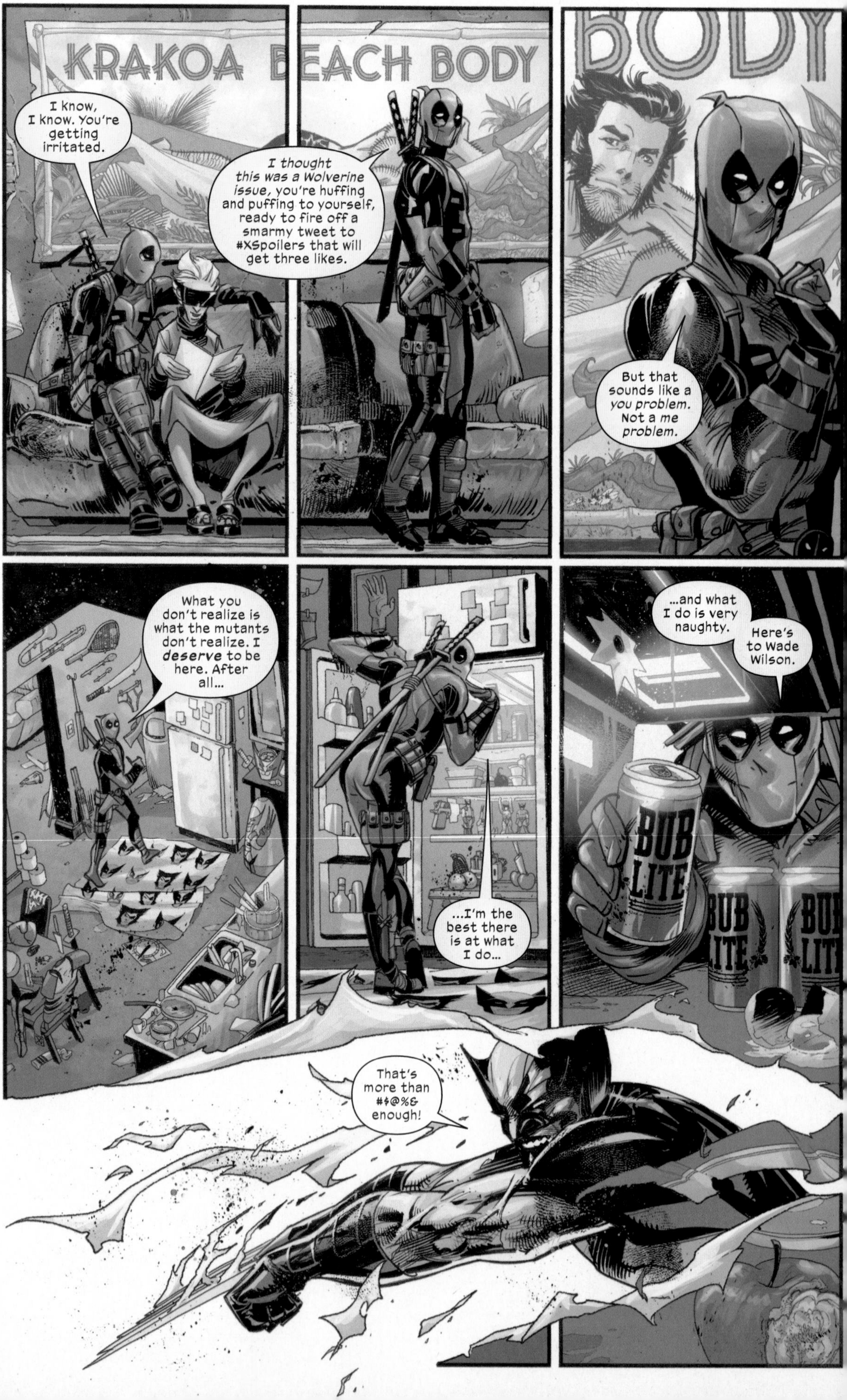
KRAKOA BEACH BODY
I know, I know. You're getting irritated.
I thought this was a Wolverine issue, you're huffing and puffing to yourself, ready to fire off a smarmy tweet to #XSpoilers that will get three likes.
BODY
But that sounds like a you problem. Not a me problem.
What you don't realize is what the mutants don't realize. I deserve to be here. After all...
...I'm the best there is at what I do...
...and what I do is very naughty.
Here's to Wade Wilson.
BUB LITE
That's more than #$@%& enough!

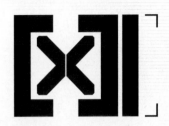

SAGE'S LOGBOOK: DEBRIEFING

After Wolverine successfully soldiered through the timestream, defending Xavier's bloodline, he fell into a drunken slumber that lasted forty hours.

A debriefing followed [at the Pointe].
Audience: Sage, Beast

Excerpt:

BEAST: Logan...I know I speak for all of us when I say thank you.

LOGAN: *Hrrm.*

BEAST: I know you were exhausted in mind and in body. But you carried on. I know you remain exhausted in mind and body currently. But we must gather what intelligence we can before it is lost to the ether, yes?

LOGAN: *Hrrm.*

BEAST: Homeostasis is the maintenance of constancy. As a body regulates its temperature. As a bird maintains its wind-borne flight. At a glance, there is no such constancy for mutants. Because we are the very definition of change.

LOGAN: ...

BEAST: Whoever brings change to the world will face a constant assault. And we -- as mutantkind -- will never rest as a result. We will have to keep fighting. You will have to keep fighting. Fighting is our constancy. I think that's a good way to consider both what we've all been through already -- as well as our destiny going forward, yes?

LOGAN: You say so, bub.

SAGE: Logan...before we go on...I also want to say I think you deserve to take a break. Go do something fun.

LOGAN: Fun?

SAGE: Wouldn't something fun be nice for a change? After all that mayhem?

LOGAN: Fun, huh? I got some ideas. Maybe you can help me.

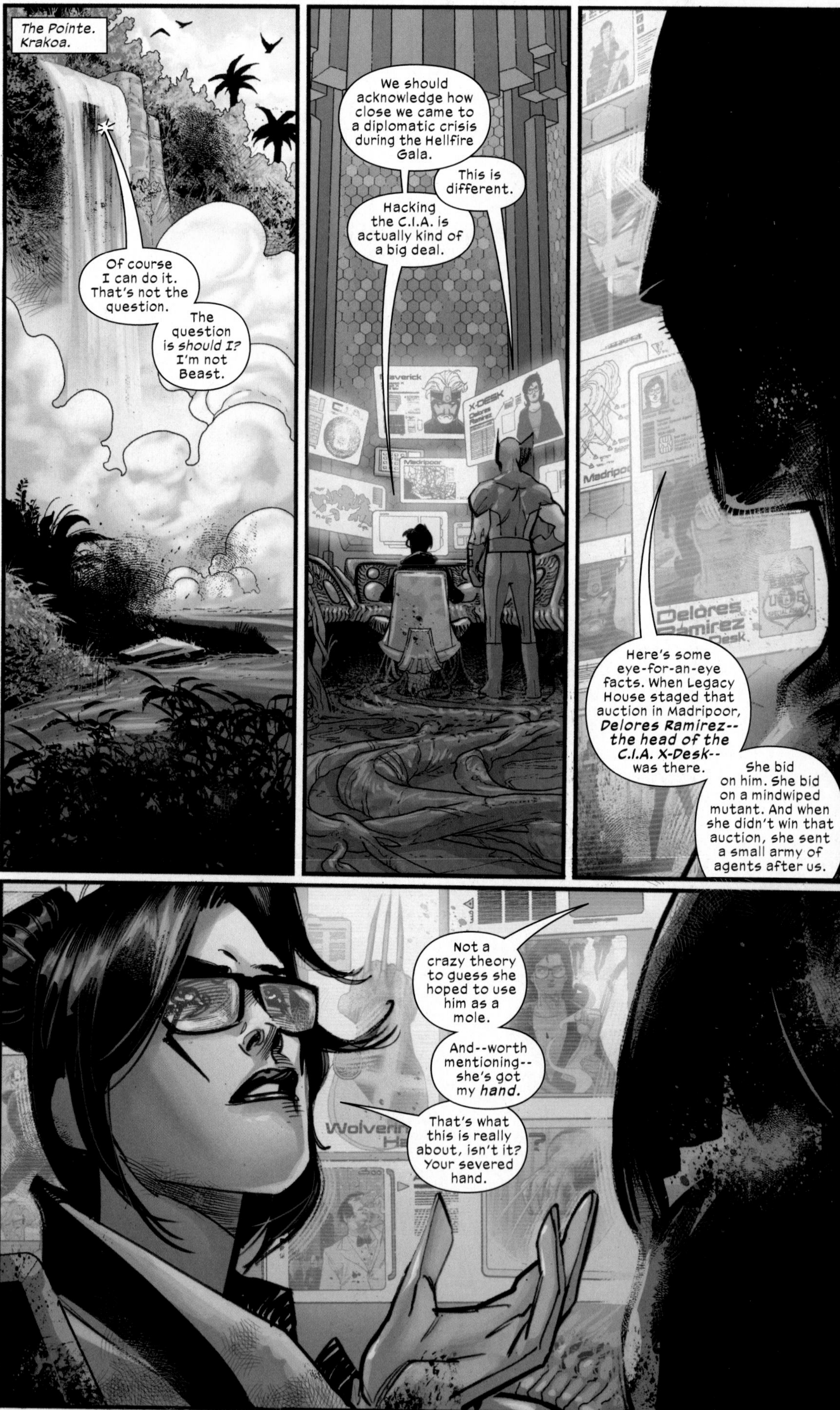
The Pointe. Krakoa.
Of course I can do it. That's not the question.
The question is *should I?* I'm not Beast.
We should acknowledge how close we came to a diplomatic crisis during the Hellfire Gala.
Hacking the C.I.A. is actually kind of a big deal.
This is different.
Maverick
C.I.A.
X-DESK
Delores Ramirez
Madripoor
Delores Ramirez
Here's some eye-for-an-eye facts. When Legacy House staged that auction in Madripoor, ***Delores Ramirez-- the head of the C.I.A. X-Desk--*** was there.
She bid on him. She bid on a mindwiped mutant. And when she didn't win that auction, she sent a small army of agents after us.
Not a crazy theory to guess she hoped to use him as a mole.
And--worth mentioning--she's got my *hand.*
That's what this is really about, isn't it? Your severed hand.

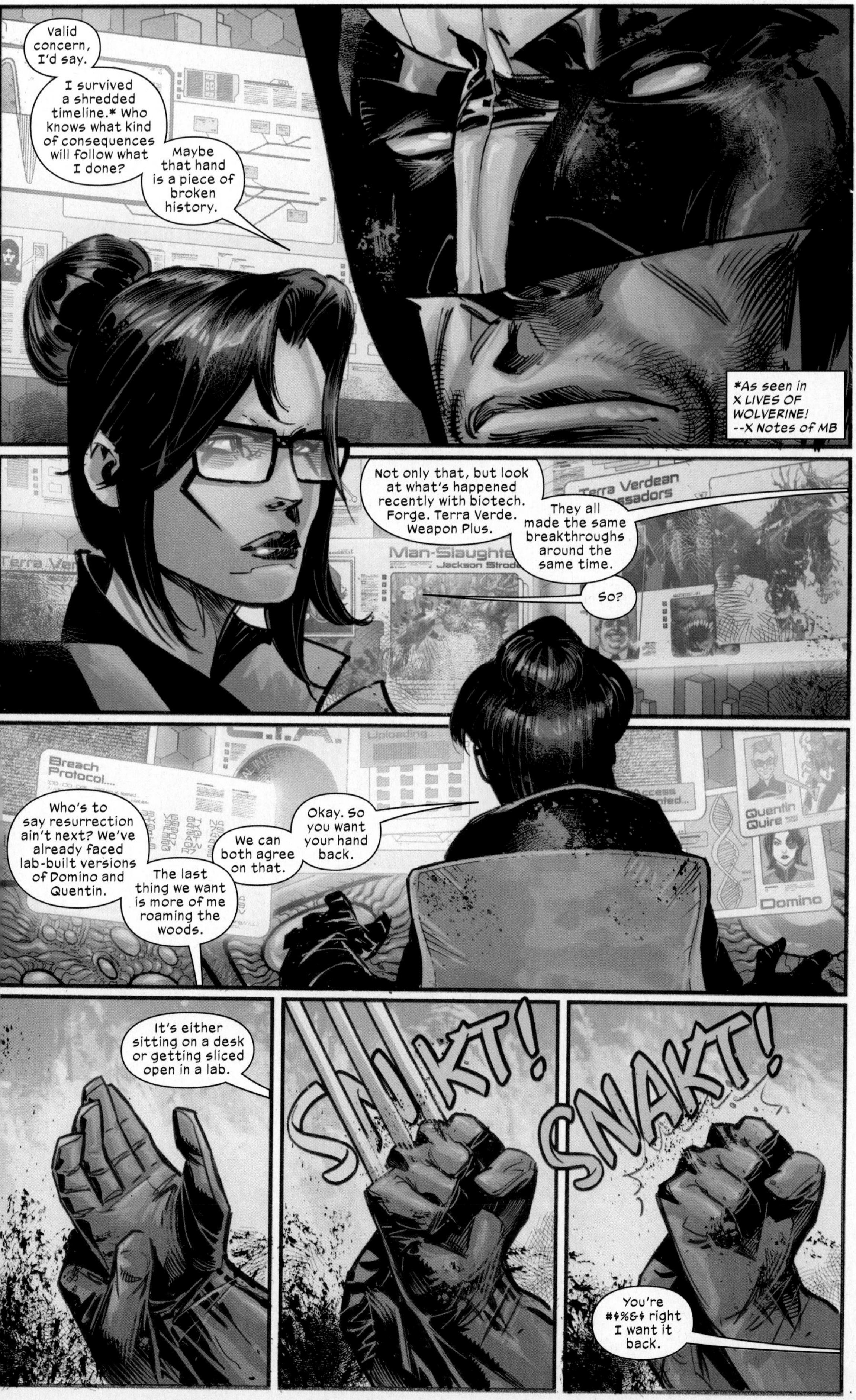
Valid concern, I'd say.
I survived a shredded timeline.* Who knows what kind of consequences will follow what I done?
Maybe that hand is a piece of broken history.
*As seen in X LIVES OF WOLVERINE! --X Notes of MB
Not only that, but look at what's happened recently with biotech. Forge. Terra Verde. Weapon Plus.
They all made the same breakthroughs around the same time.
So?
Who's to say resurrection ain't next? We've already faced lab-built versions of Domino and Quentin.
The last thing we want is more of me roaming the woods.
We can both agree on that.
Okay. So you want your hand back.
It's either sitting on a desk or getting sliced open in a lab.
SNIKT!
SNAKT!
You're #$%&$ right I want it back.

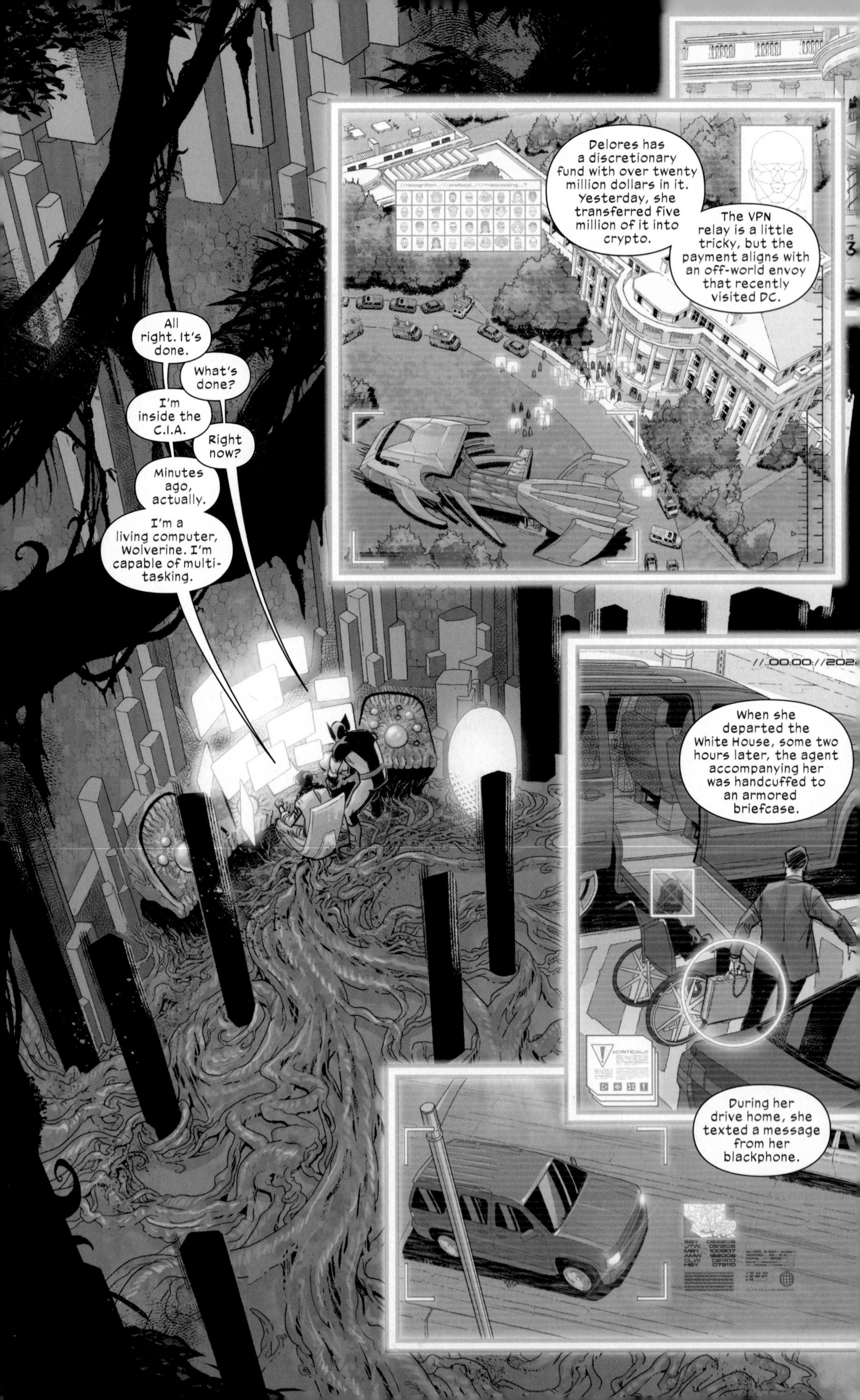

//recognition...///protocol...///accessing...?
Delores has a discretionary fund with over twenty million dollars in it. Yesterday, she transferred five million of it into crypto.
The VPN relay is a little tricky, but the payment aligns with an off-world envoy that recently visited DC.
All right. It's done.
What's done?
I'm inside the C.I.A.
Right now?
Minutes ago, actually.
I'm a living computer, Wolverine. I'm capable of multi-tasking.
//..00:00://202
When she departed the White House, some two hours later, the agent accompanying her was handcuffed to an armored briefcase.
//CRITICAL//
During her drive home, she texted a message from her blackphone.

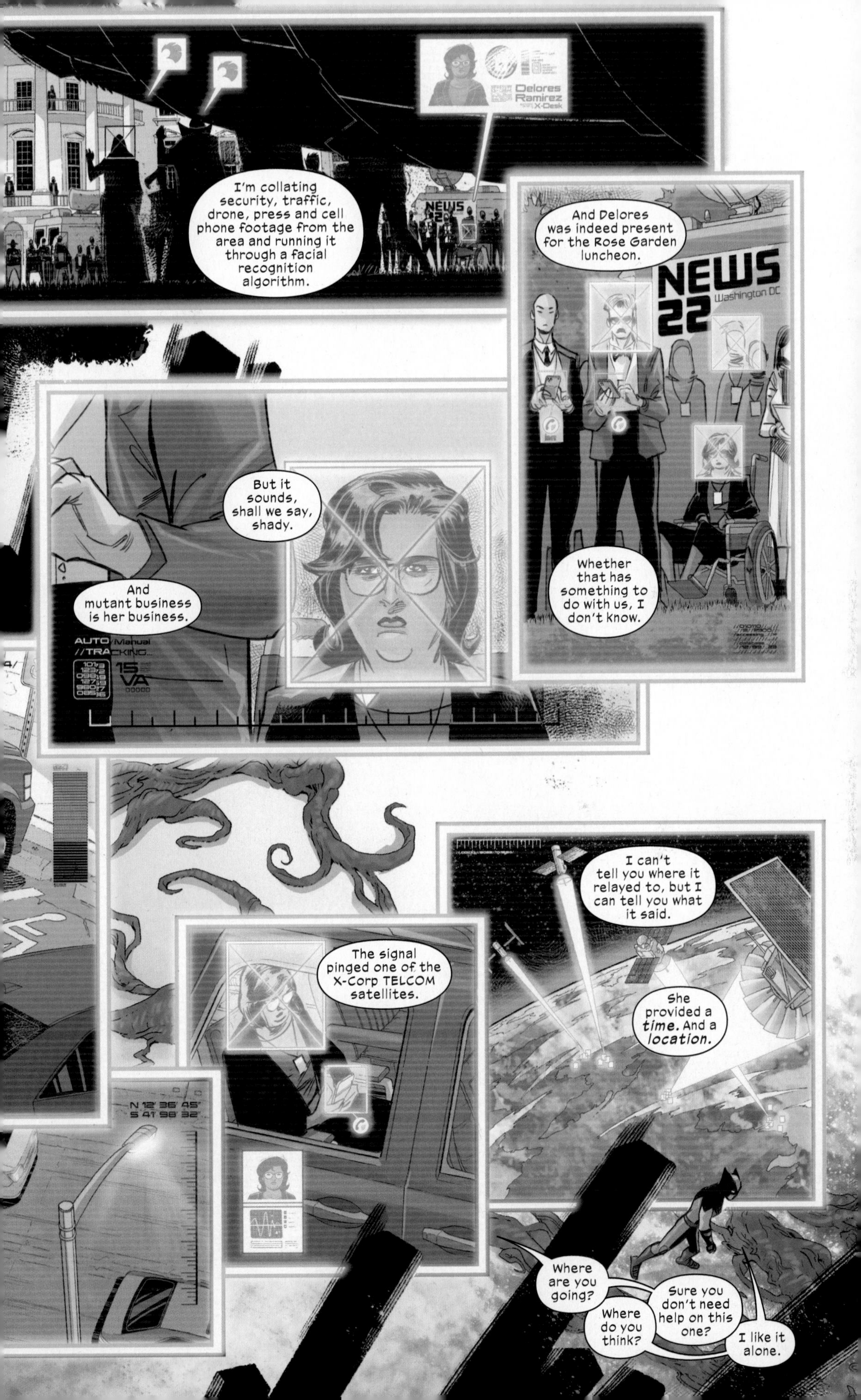
Delores Ramirez
X-Desk
I'm collating security, traffic, drone, press and cell phone footage from the area and running it through a facial recognition algorithm.
NEWS 22
And Delores was indeed present for the Rose Garden luncheon.
NEWS 22 Washington DC
Whether that has something to do with us, I don't know.
But it sounds, shall we say, shady.
And mutant business is her business.
AUTO/Manual
//TRACKING
15 VA
I can't tell you where it relayed to, but I can tell you what it said.
The signal pinged one of the X-Corp TELCOM satellites.
She provided a *time.* And a *location.*
N 12' 36' 45"
S 41' 98' 32"
Where are you going?
Where do you think?
Sure you don't need help on this one?
I like it alone.

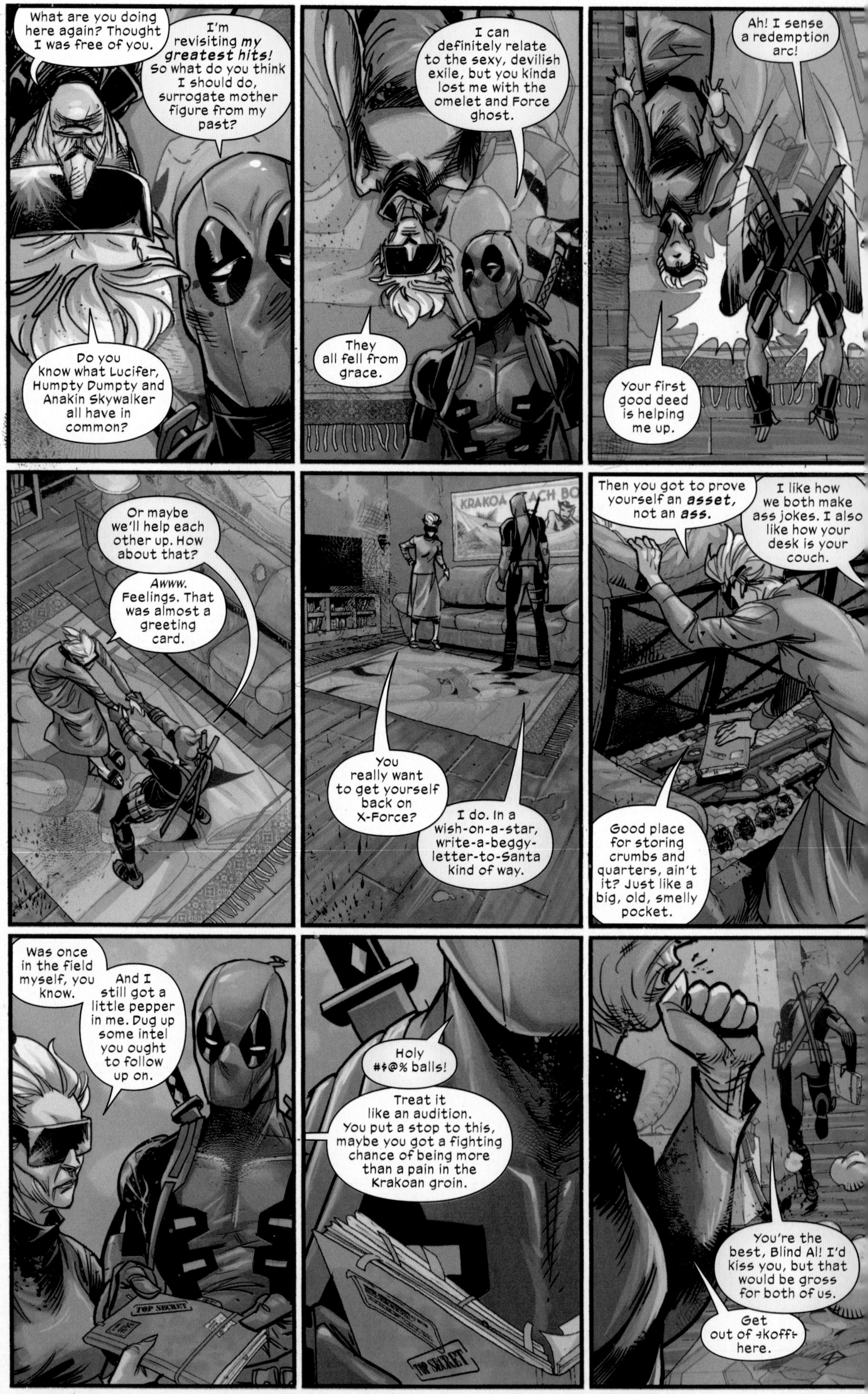

What are you doing here again? Thought I was free of you.
I'm revisiting my greatest hits! So what do you think I should do, surrogate mother figure from my past?
Do you know what Lucifer, Humpty Dumpty and Anakin Skywalker all have in common?
I can definitely relate to the sexy, devilish exile, but you kinda lost me with the omelet and Force ghost.
They all fell from grace.
Ah! I sense a redemption arc!
Your first good deed is helping me up.
Or maybe we'll help each other up. How about that?
Awww. Feelings. That was almost a greeting card.
You really want to get yourself back on X-Force?
I do. In a wish-on-a-star, write-a-beggy-letter-to-Santa kind of way.
Then you got to prove yourself an asset, not an ass.
I like how we both make ass jokes. I also like how your desk is your couch.
Good place for storing crumbs and quarters, ain't it? Just like a big, old, smelly pocket.
Was once in the field myself, you know.
And I still got a little pepper in me. Dug up some intel you ought to follow up on.
TOP SECRET
Holy #$@% balls!
Treat it like an audition. You put a stop to this, maybe you got a fighting chance of being more than a pain in the Krakoan groin.
TOP SECRET
You're the best, Blind Al! I'd kiss you, but that would be gross for both of us.
Get out of -koff- here.

[dead...[0.0]
[pool...[0.0]

"Whatever I say in here is canon? Right? So Emma Frost is hopelessly in love with me and I would beat Hulk in a fight and Captain America is secretly afraid of dentists and Doom has the sickest super villain costume and Nicky Fury lost his eye in a bet gone wrong (long story) and I'm an Omega-level mutant and this issue is actually a #1 because from now on the title is DEADPOOL! (...and wolverine)."

-- WADE WILSON

[dead...[0.0]
[pool...[0.0]

[wolverine_20]

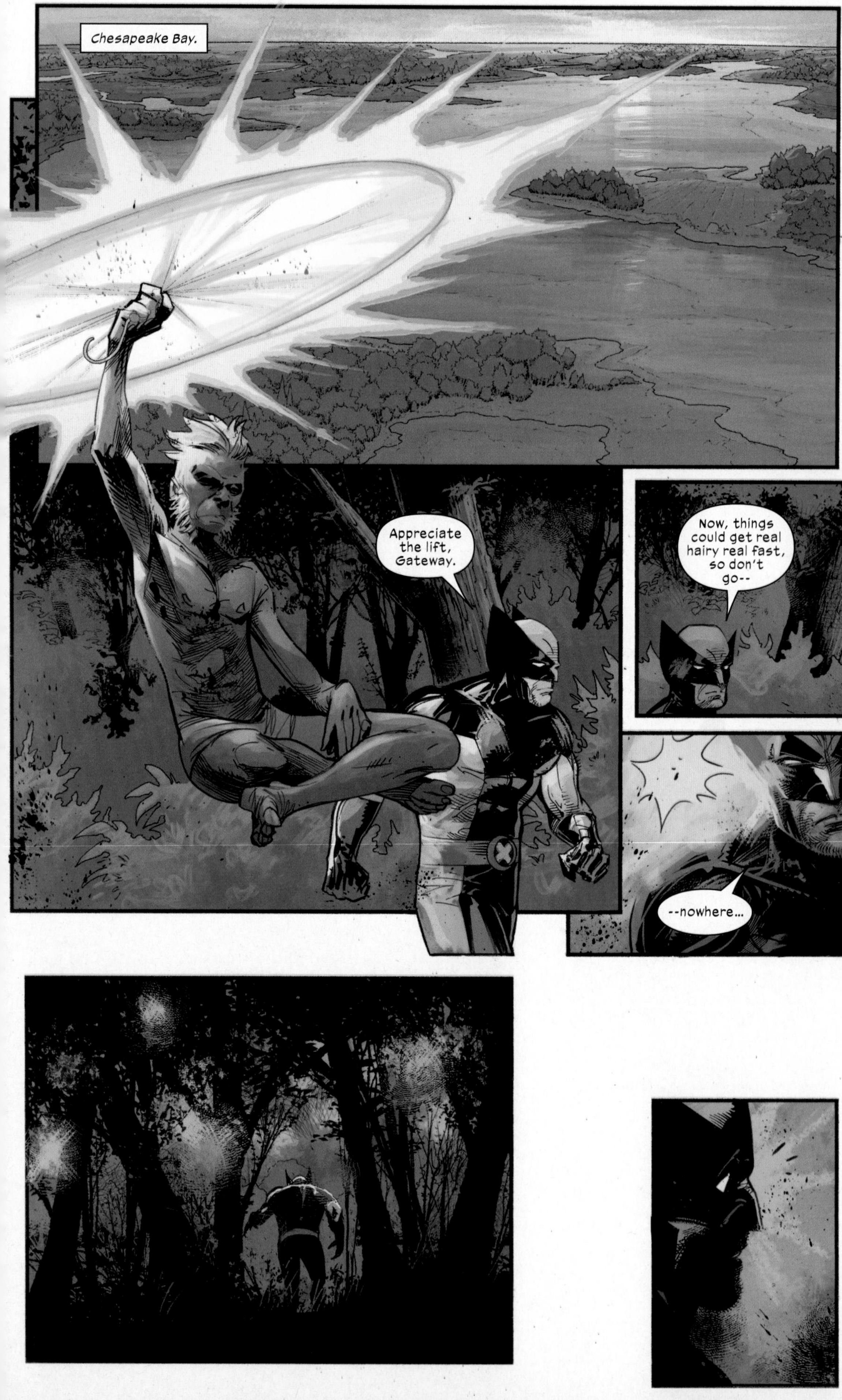
Chesapeake Bay.
Appreciate the lift, Gateway.
Now, things could get real hairy real fast, so don't go--
--nowhere...

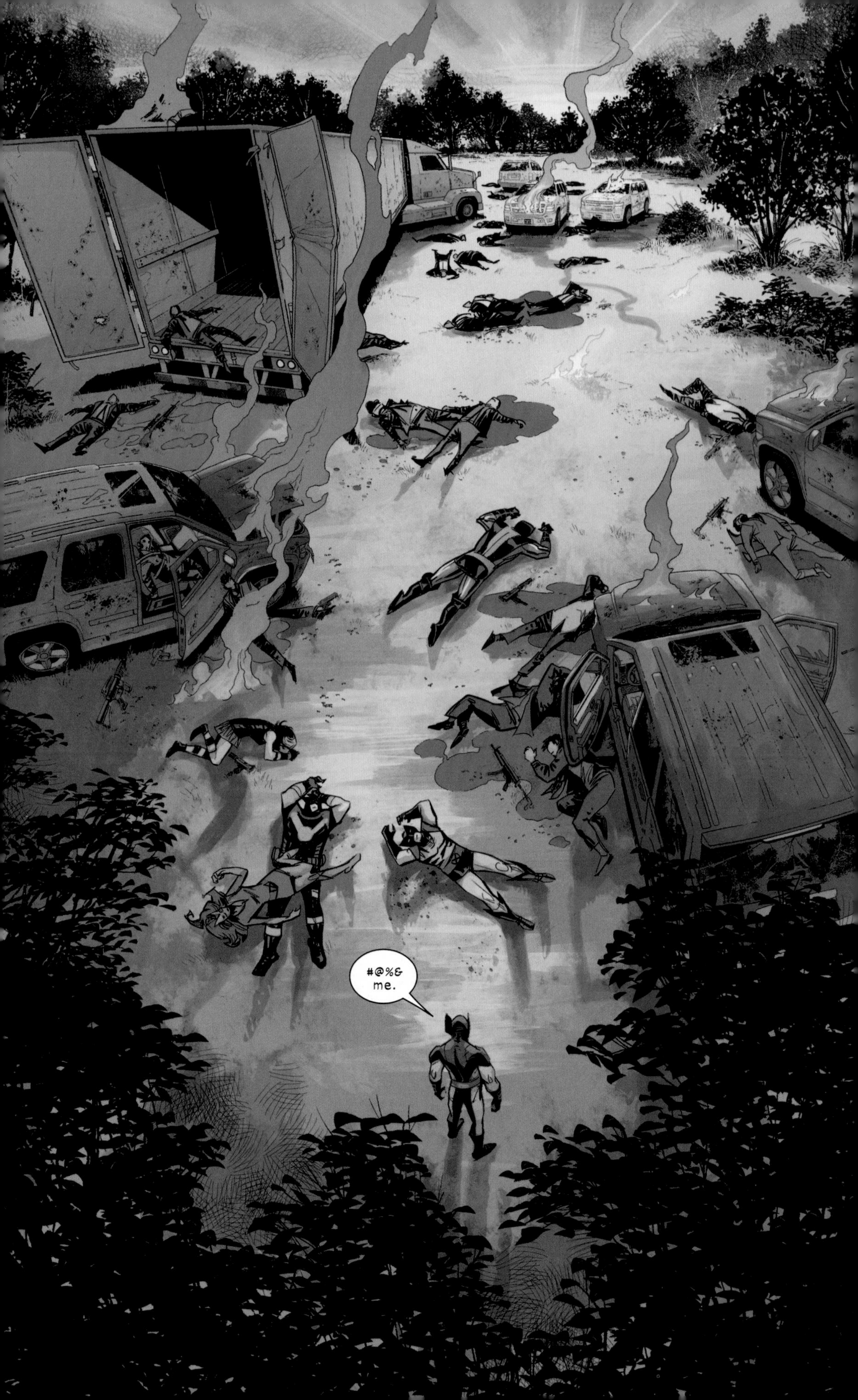
#@%& me.

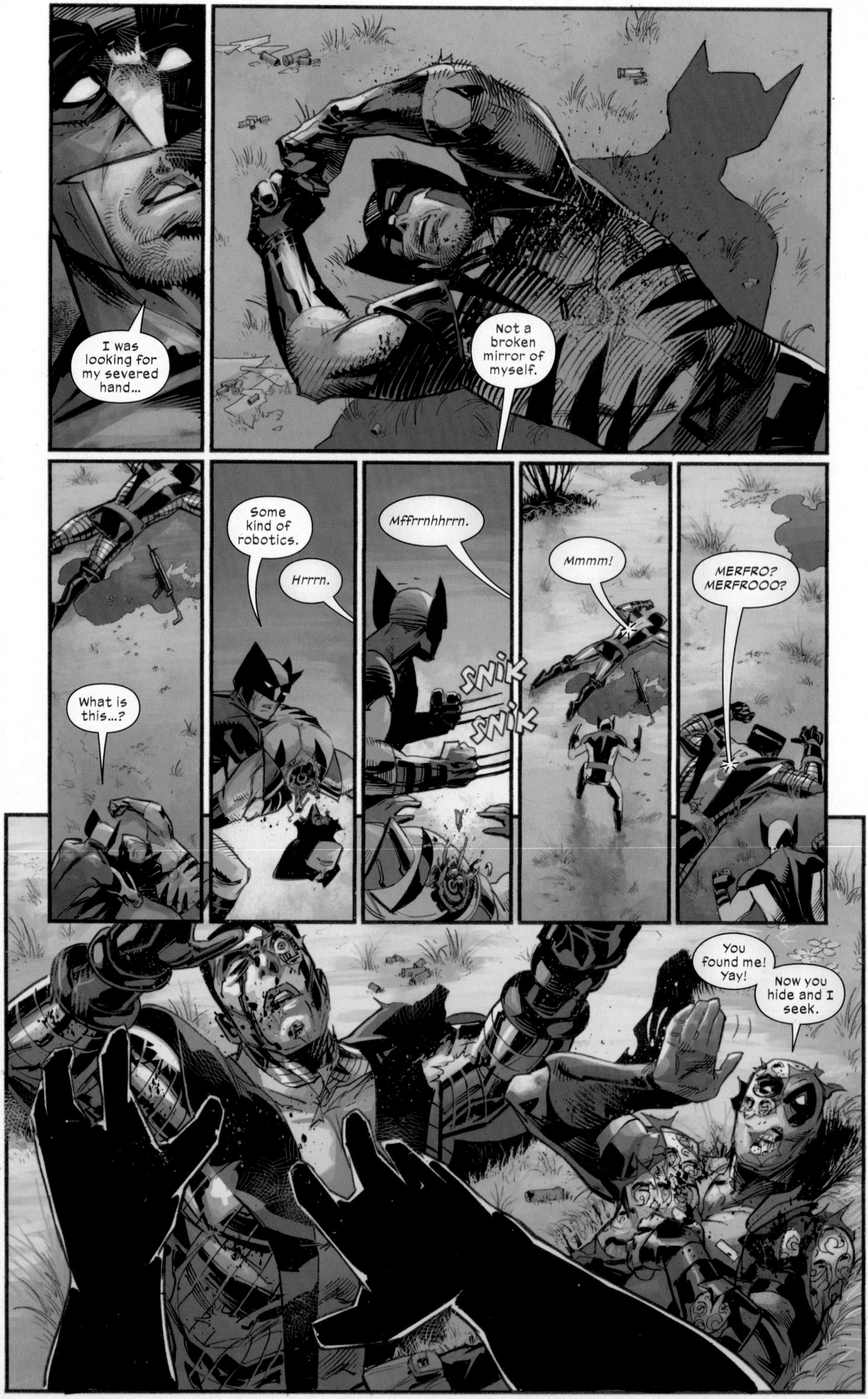
I was looking for my severed hand...
Not a broken mirror of myself.
What is this...?
Some kind of robotics.
Hrrrn.
Mffrrnhhrrn.
SNIK
SNIK
Mmmm!
MERFRO? MERFROOO?
You found me! Yay!
Now you hide and I seek.

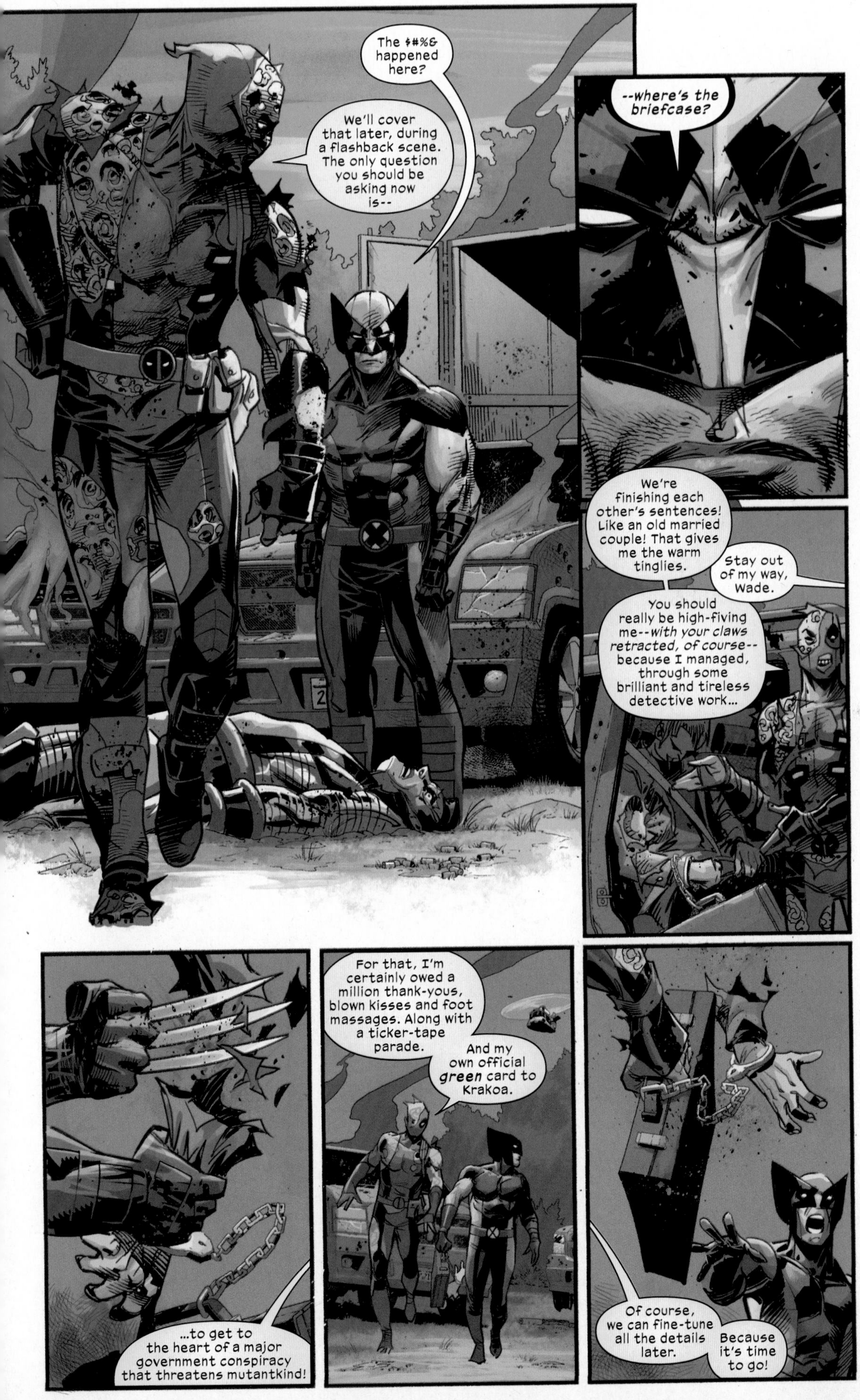
The $#%& happened here?
We'll cover that later, during a flashback scene. The only question you should be asking now is--
--where's the briefcase?
We're finishing each other's sentences! Like an old married couple! That gives me the warm tinglies.
Stay out of my way, Wade.
You should really be high-fiving me--*with your claws retracted, of course*--because I managed, through some brilliant and tireless detective work...
...to get to the heart of a major government conspiracy that threatens mutantkind!
For that, I'm certainly owed a million thank-yous, blown kisses and foot massages. Along with a ticker-tape parade.
And my own official *green* card to Krakoa.
Of course, we can fine-tune all the details later.
Because it's time to go!

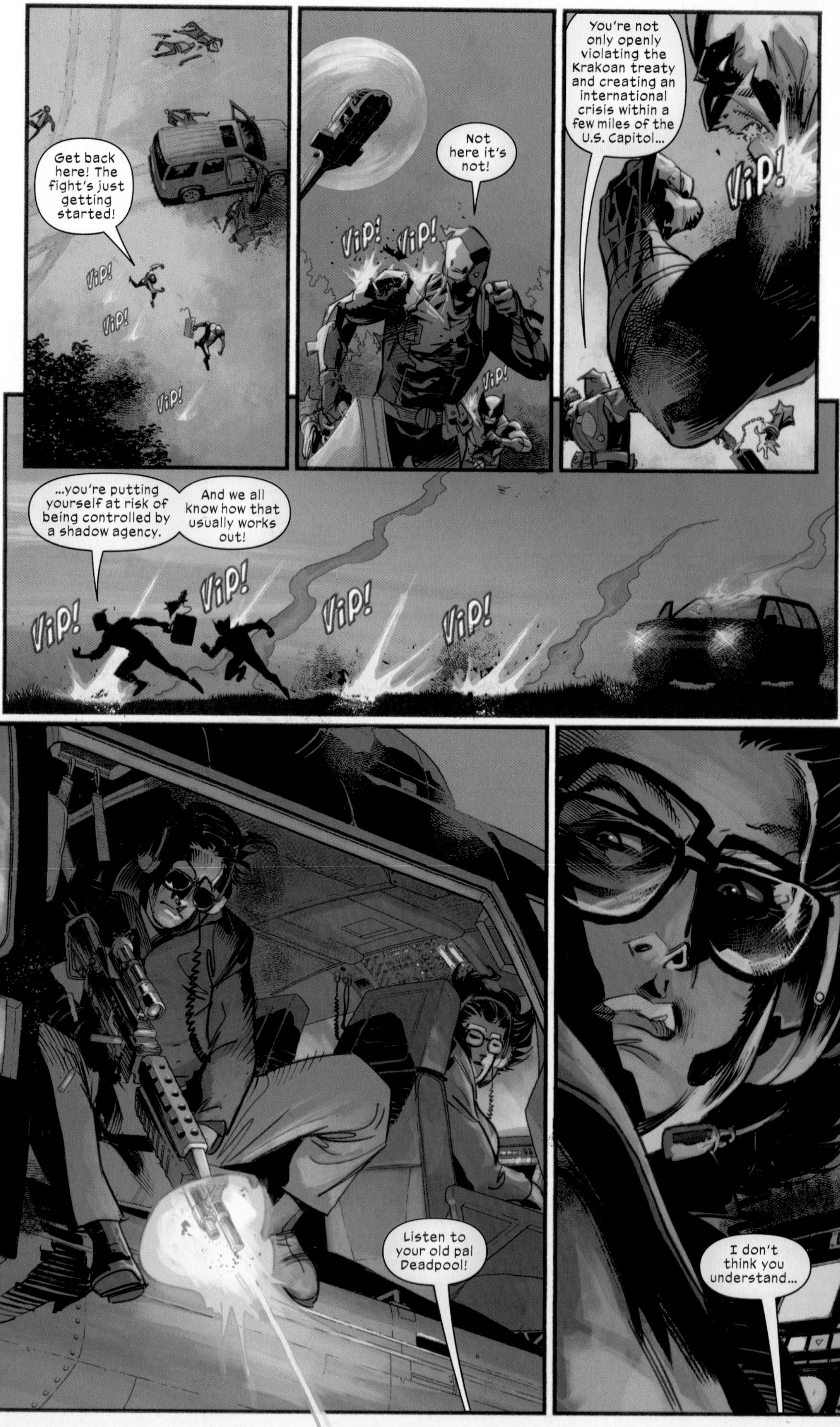
Get back here! The fight's just getting started!
VIP!
VIP!
VIP!
Not here it's not!
VIP!
VIP!
VIP!
You're not only openly violating the Krakoan treaty and creating an international crisis within a few miles of the U.S. Capitol...
VIP!
...you're putting yourself at risk of being controlled by a shadow agency.
And we all know how that usually works out!
VIP!
VIP!
VIP!
VIP!
Listen to your old pal Deadpool!
I don't think you understand...

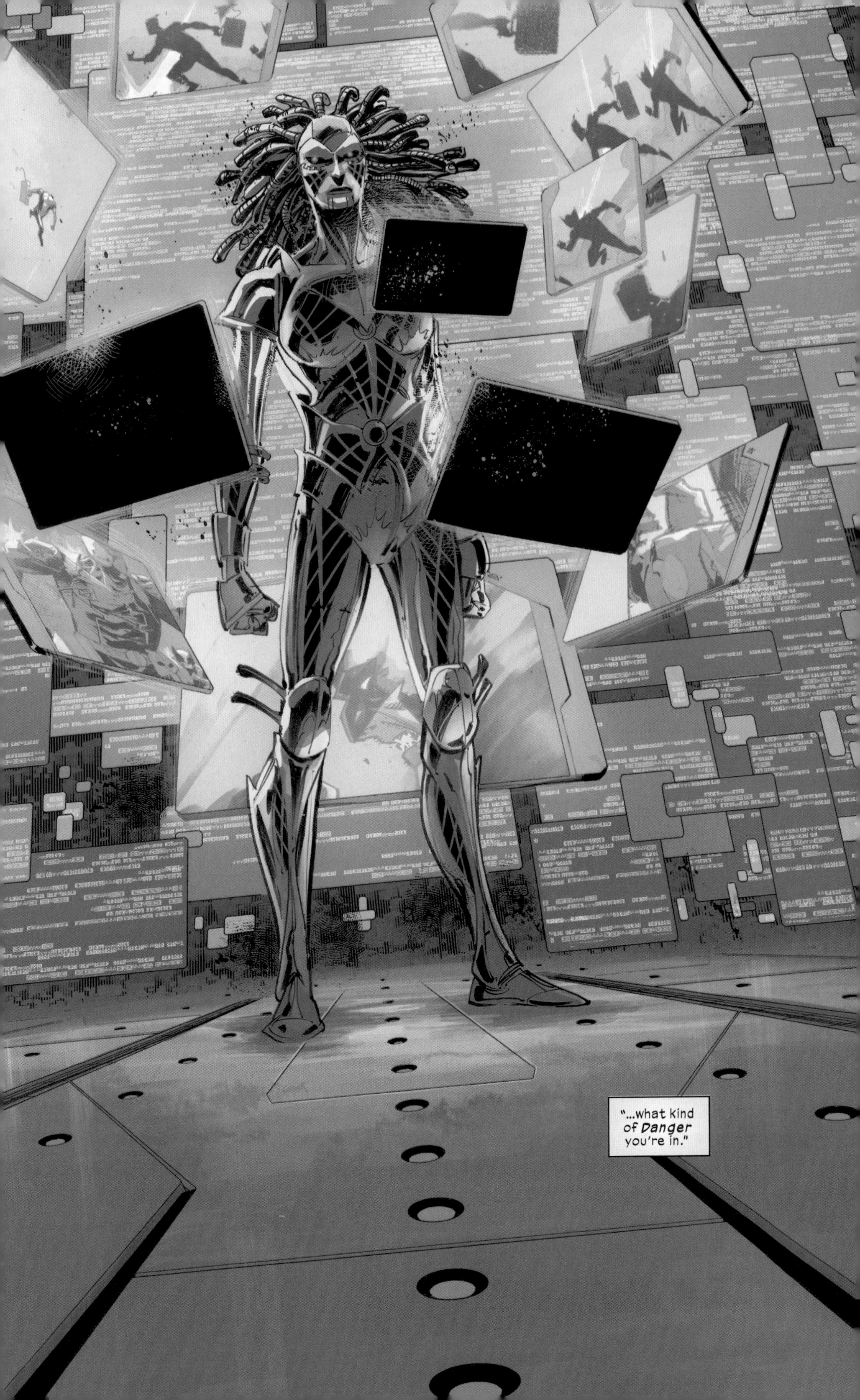
"...what kind of *Danger* you're in."

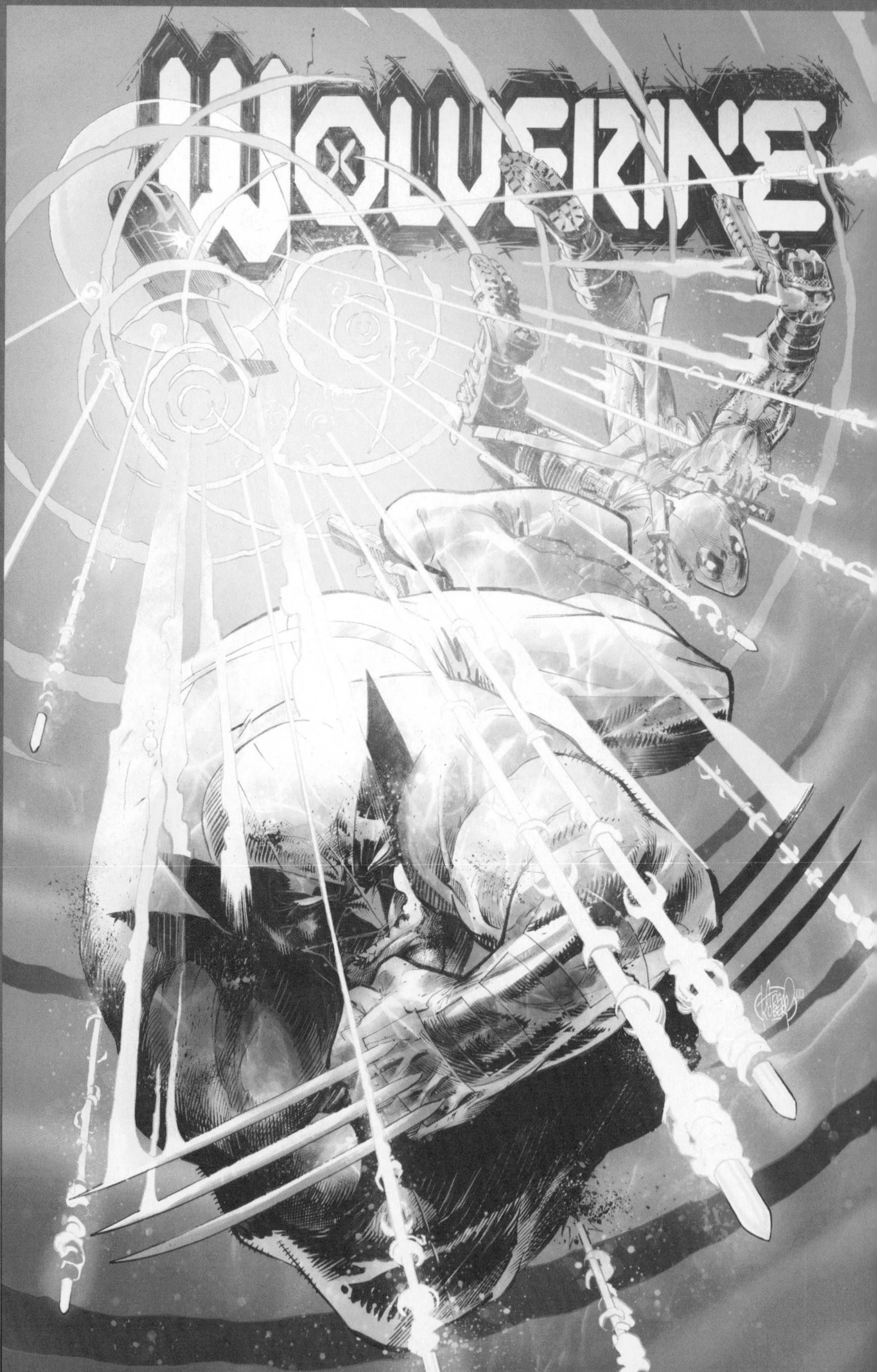
WOLVERINE

Glory Daze

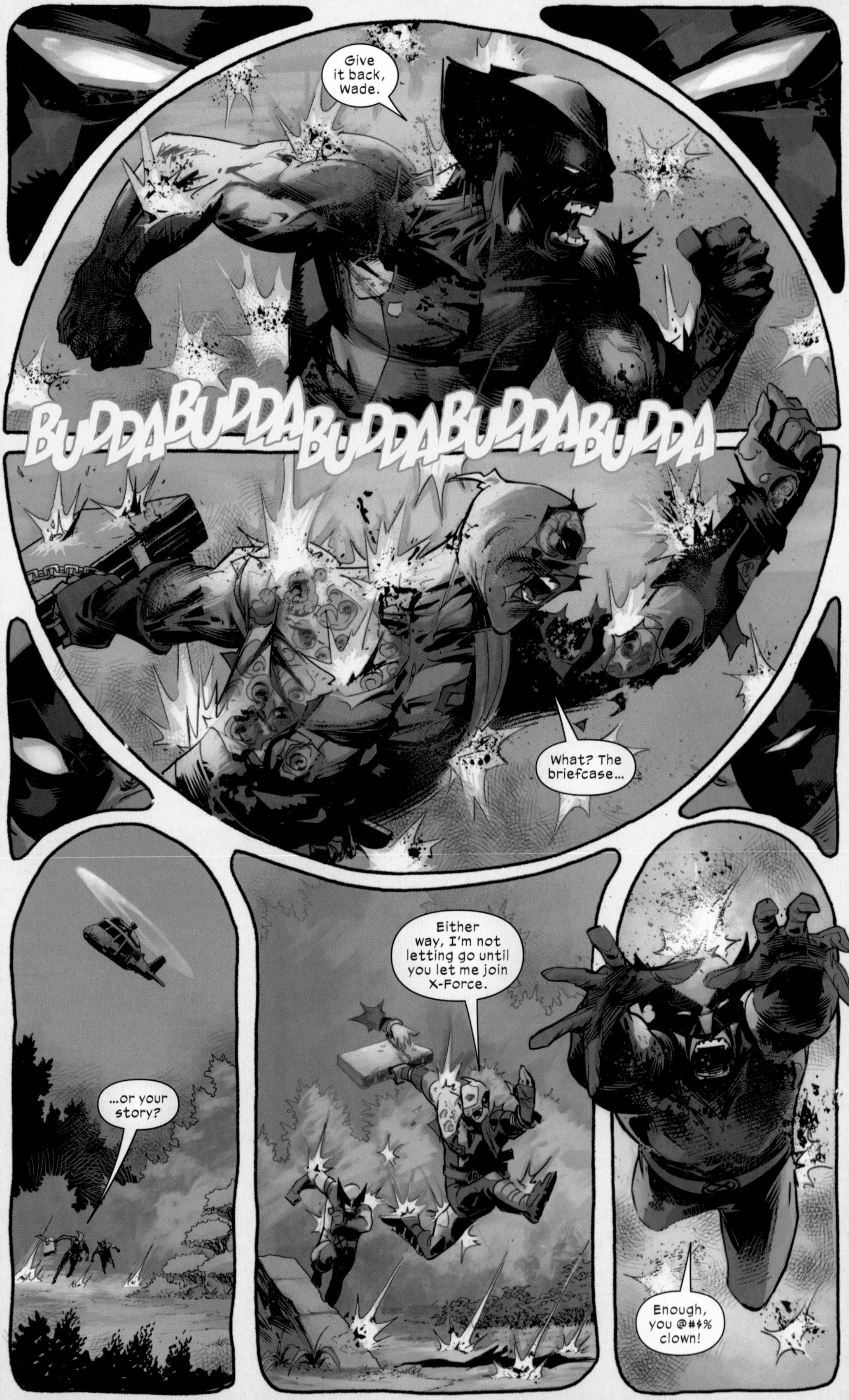

Give it back, Wade.
BUDDABUDDABUDDABUDDABUDDA
What? The briefcase...
...or your story?
Either way, I'm not letting go until you let me join X-Force.
Enough, you @#$% clown!

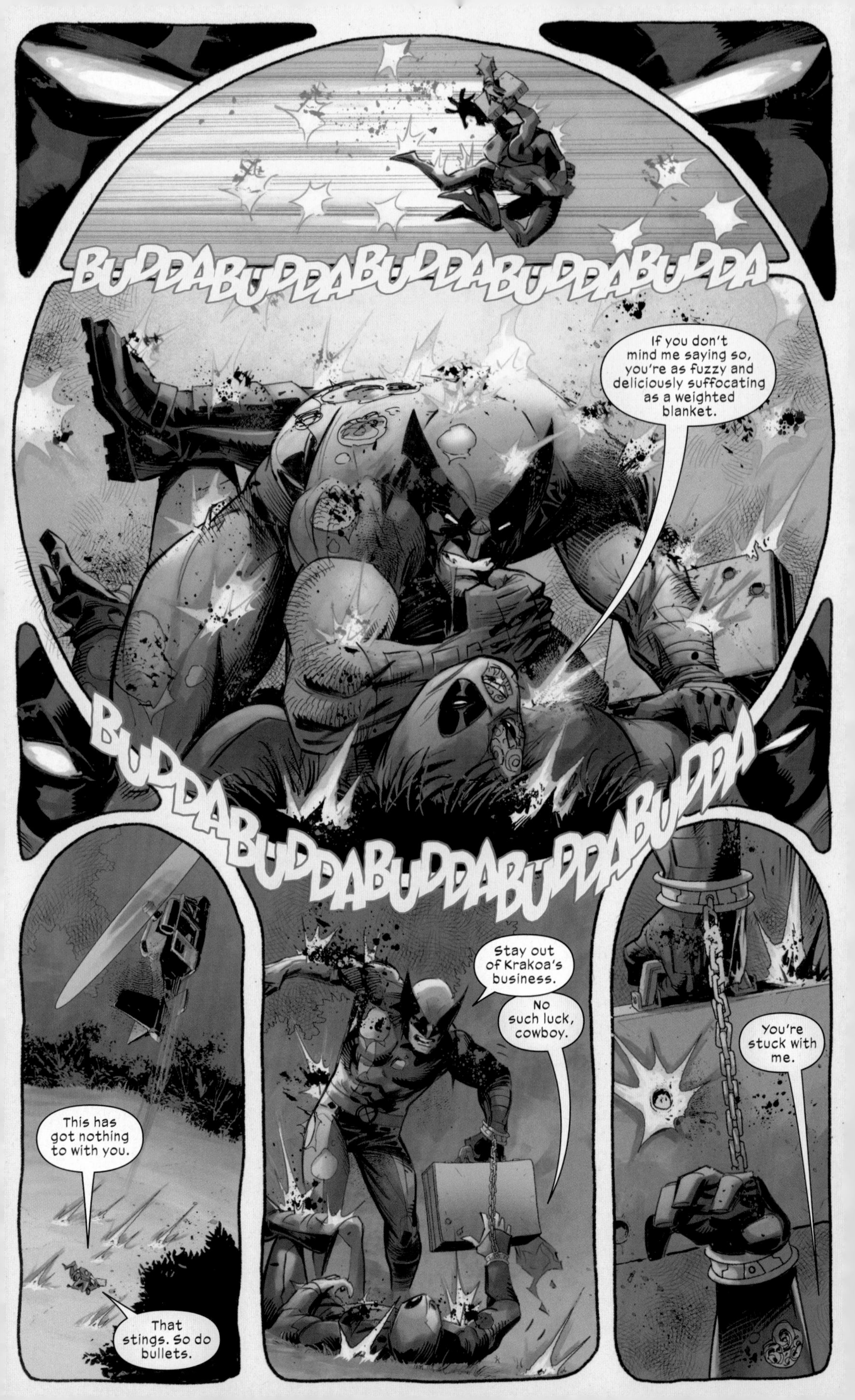
BUDDABUDDABUDDABUDDABUDDA
If you don't mind me saying so, you're as fuzzy and deliciously suffocating as a weighted blanket.
BUDDABUDDABUDDABUDDA
This has got nothing to with you.
That stings. So do bullets.
Stay out of Krakoa's business.
No such luck, cowboy.
You're stuck with me.

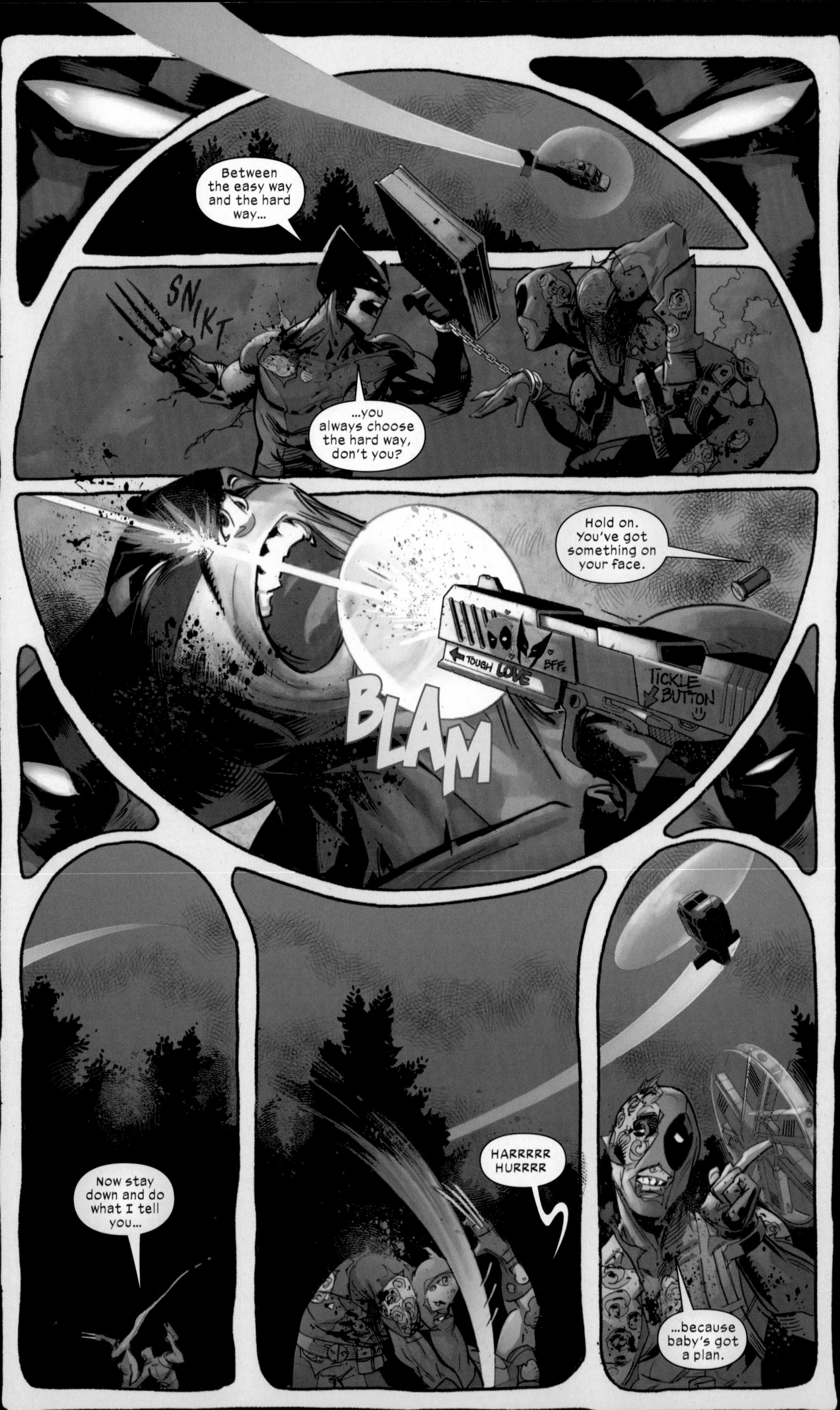

Between the easy way and the hard way...
SNIKT
...you always choose the hard way, don't you?
Hold on. You've got something on your face.
TOUGH LOVE
BFFs
TICKLE BUTTON
BLAM
Now stay down and do what I tell you...
HARRRRR HURRRR
...because baby's got a plan.

00_Destiny]
00____ofX]

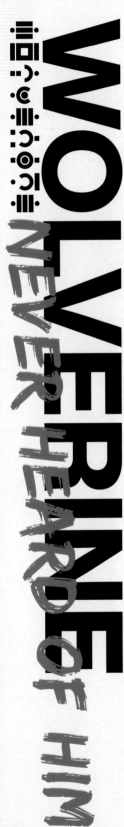

WOLVERINE

NEVER HEARD OF HIM

~~CHAINED TOGETHER~~

DEADPOOL RULZ, WOLVERINE DROOLZ!!!!

[WOLVERINE]

[DEADPOOL]

Pursuing a tip from Sage, Wolverine followed Delores Ramirez, head of the C.I.A.'s X-Desk, to Maryland, where she was transporting something in an armored briefcase.

BOOOOORING!

When Wolverine arrived on the scene, however, he found a battlefield littered with the bodies of C.I.A. agents and robotic replicas of many mutants, including himself. He also discovered Deadpool, who was hoping to prove himself worthy of rejoining X-Force on Krakoa.

WOOT WOOT!

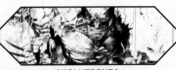

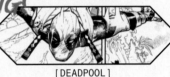

TEAMWORK, BABY!

The two managed to recover the briefcase, though Deadpool seemed to know who was behind it.

DANGER. IT'S DANGER. YOU KNOW, FROM THE DANGER ROOM?

[00_best_]
[00_there]

[00_00..00]
[00_00..21]

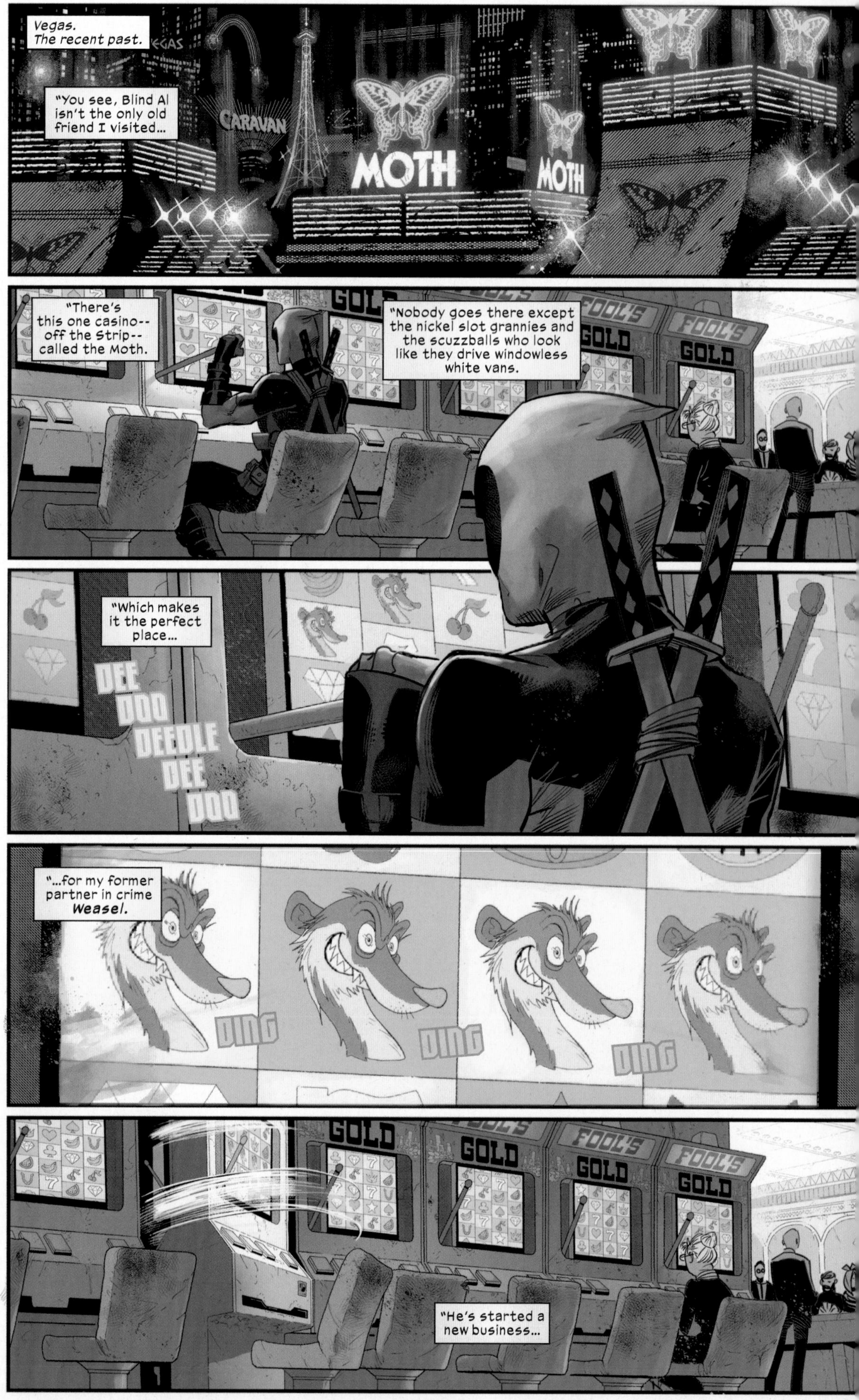
Vegas.
The recent past.
"You see, Blind Al isn't the only old friend I visited...
VEGAS
CARAVAN
MOTH
MOTH
"There's this one casino--off the Strip--called the Moth.
"Nobody goes there except the nickel slot grannies and the scuzzballs who look like they drive windowless white vans.
GOLD
FOOL'S
GOLD
FOOL'S
GOLD
"Which makes it the perfect place...
DEE DOO DEEDLE DEE DOO
"...for my former partner in crime *Weasel*.
DING
DING
DING
GOLD
FOOL'S
GOLD
FOOL'S
GOLD
FOOL'S
GOLD
"He's started a new business...

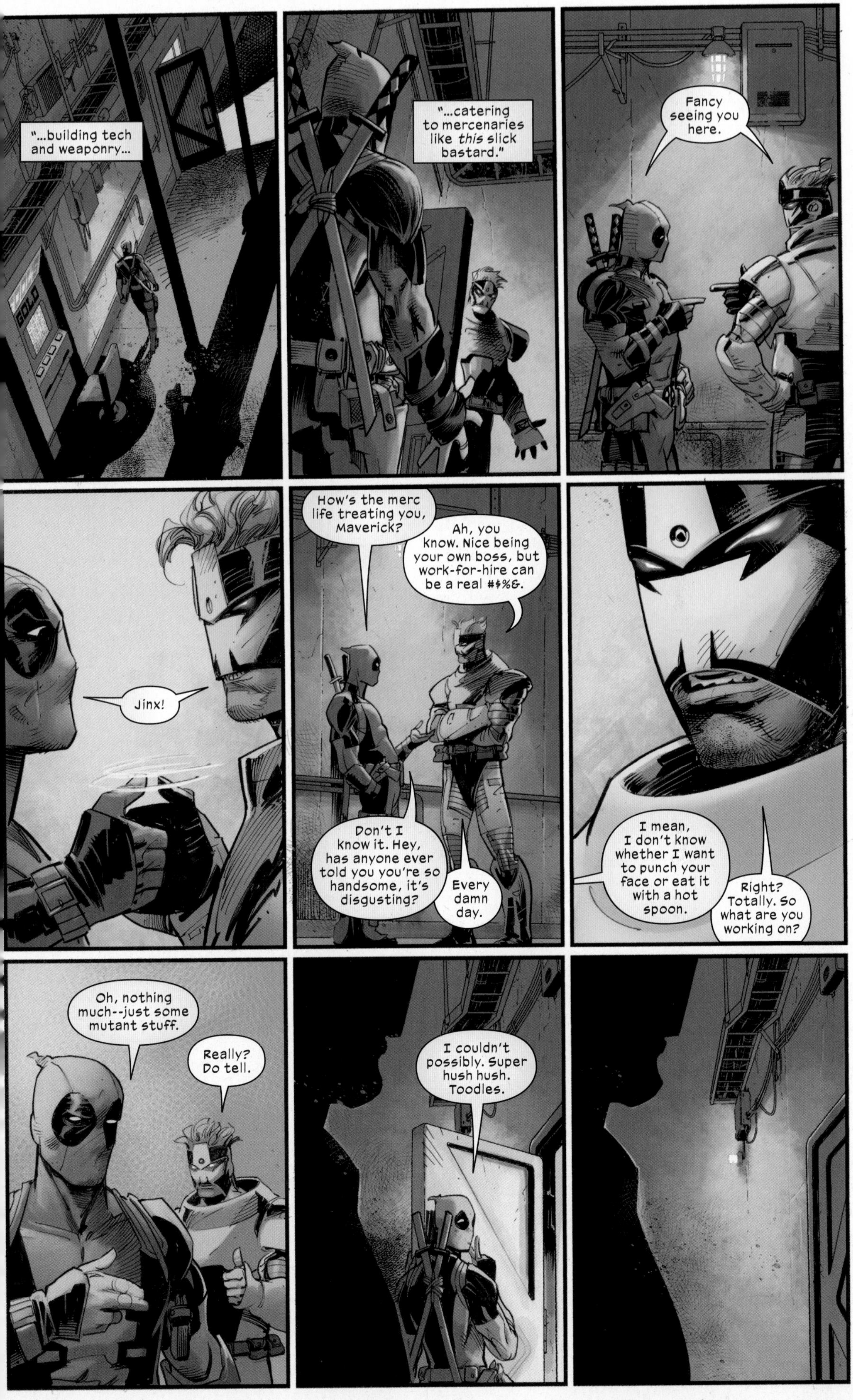

"...building tech and weaponry...
"...catering to mercenaries like *this* slick bastard."
Fancy seeing you here.
Jinx!
How's the merc life treating you, Maverick?
Ah, you know. Nice being your own boss, but work-for-hire can be a real #$%&.
Don't I know it. Hey, has anyone ever told you you're so handsome, it's disgusting?
Every damn day.
I mean, I don't know whether I want to punch your face or eat it with a hot spoon.
Right? Totally. So what are you working on?
Oh, nothing much--just some mutant stuff.
Really? Do tell.
I couldn't possibly. Super hush hush. Toodles.

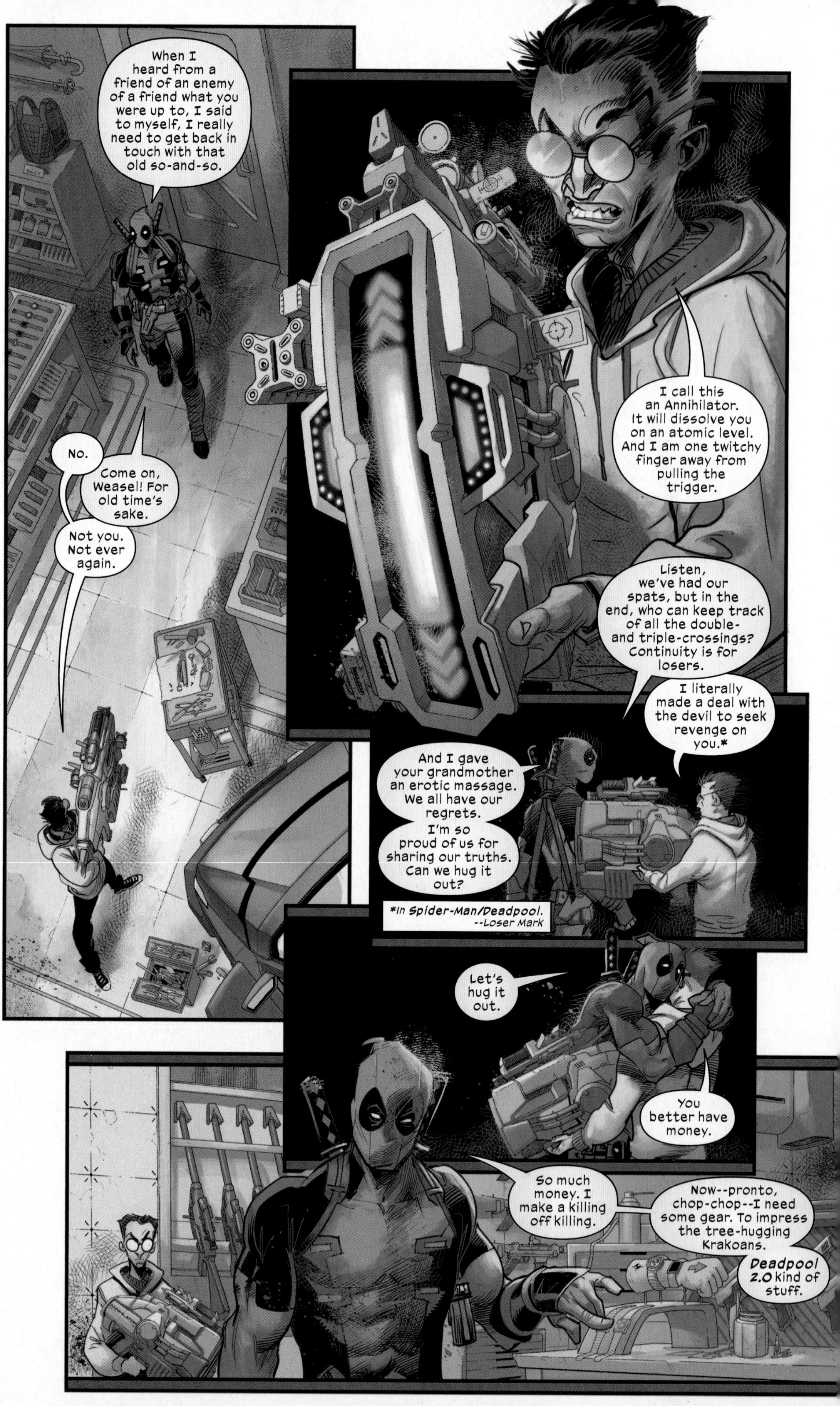
When I heard from a friend of an enemy of a friend what you were up to, I said to myself, I really need to get back in touch with that old so-and-so.
I call this an Annihilator. It will dissolve you on an atomic level. And I am one twitchy finger away from pulling the trigger.
No.
Come on, Weasel! For old time's sake.
Not you. Not ever again.
Listen, we've had our spats, but in the end, who can keep track of all the double- and triple-crossings? Continuity is for losers.
I literally made a deal with the devil to seek revenge on you.*
And I gave your grandmother an erotic massage. We all have our regrets.
I'm so proud of us for sharing our truths. Can we hug it out?
*In Spider-Man/Deadpool. --Loser Mark
Let's hug it out.
You better have money.
So much money. I make a killing off killing.
Now--pronto, chop-chop--I need some gear. To impress the tree-hugging Krakoans.
Deadpool 2.0 kind of stuff.

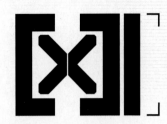

LOGBOOK: WEASEL

Re: Deadpool visit (xx/xx/xxxx)

Inventory: [items released]

1) Holographic image inducer (2.0). Updated version includes (by request) an exploding poodle, a bear in a tutu and Jonathan Hickman on a unicycle.

2) Fart Gas.

3) Teleportation Belt (2.0) <Warning: GPS unreliable>.

4) Leopard-print thong with warming microfibers.

5) Mr. Tickle Fingers.

6) Big-ass gun.

7) Grenade belt.

8) Rubik's Cube.

9) Another big-ass gun.

10) EMP.

11) Xavier sex tape <top secret and gross>.

12) C-4 chewing gum.

13) *New Mutants*, Issue #98 <CGC grade: 1.2>.

14) ███████████ <Warning: Do NOT use except in case of emergency>.

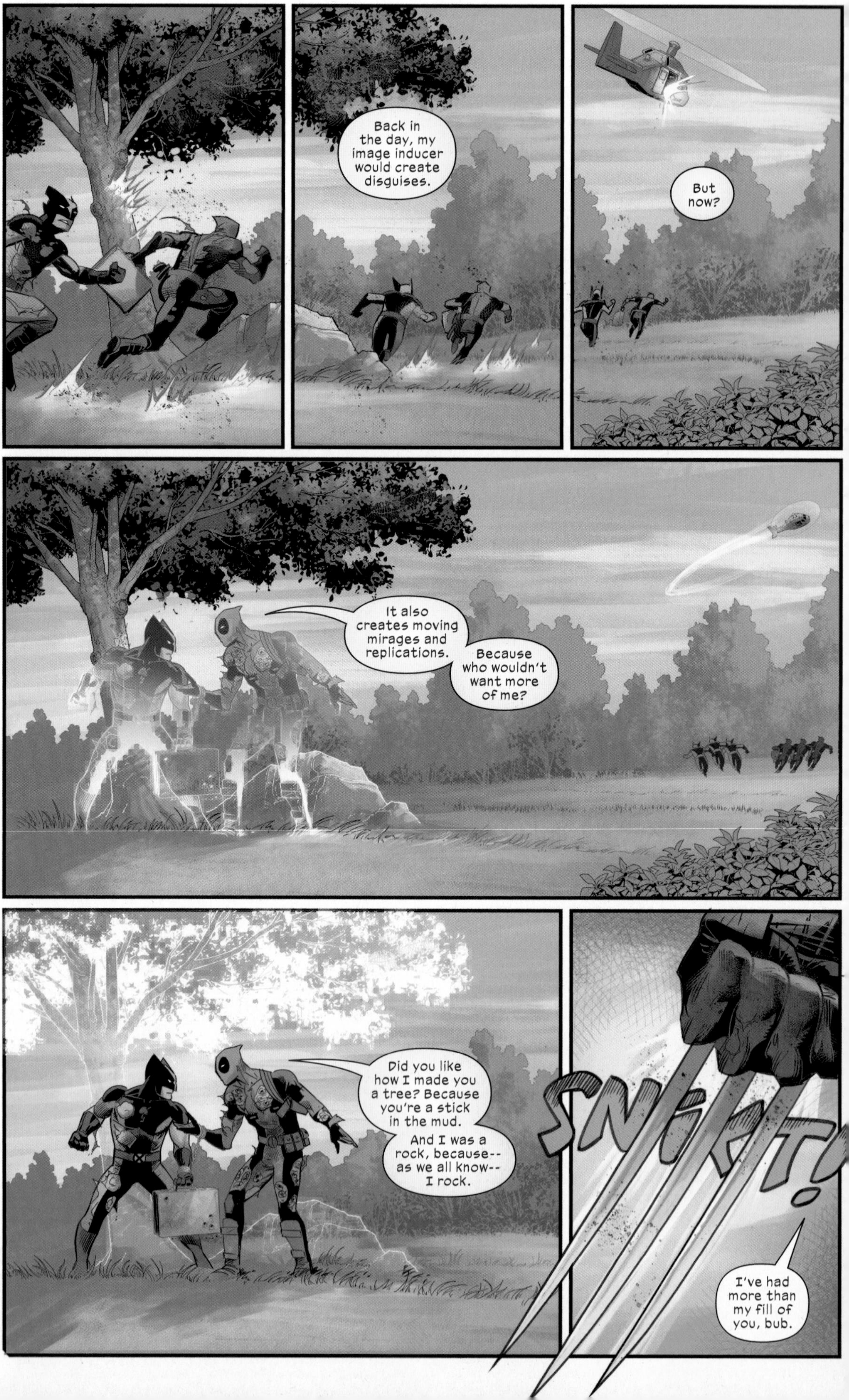

Back in the day, my image inducer would create disguises.
But now?
It also creates moving mirages and replications.
Because who wouldn't want more of me?
Did you like how I made you a tree? Because you're a stick in the mud.
And I was a rock, because--as we all know--I rock.
SNIKT!
I've had more than my fill of you, bub.

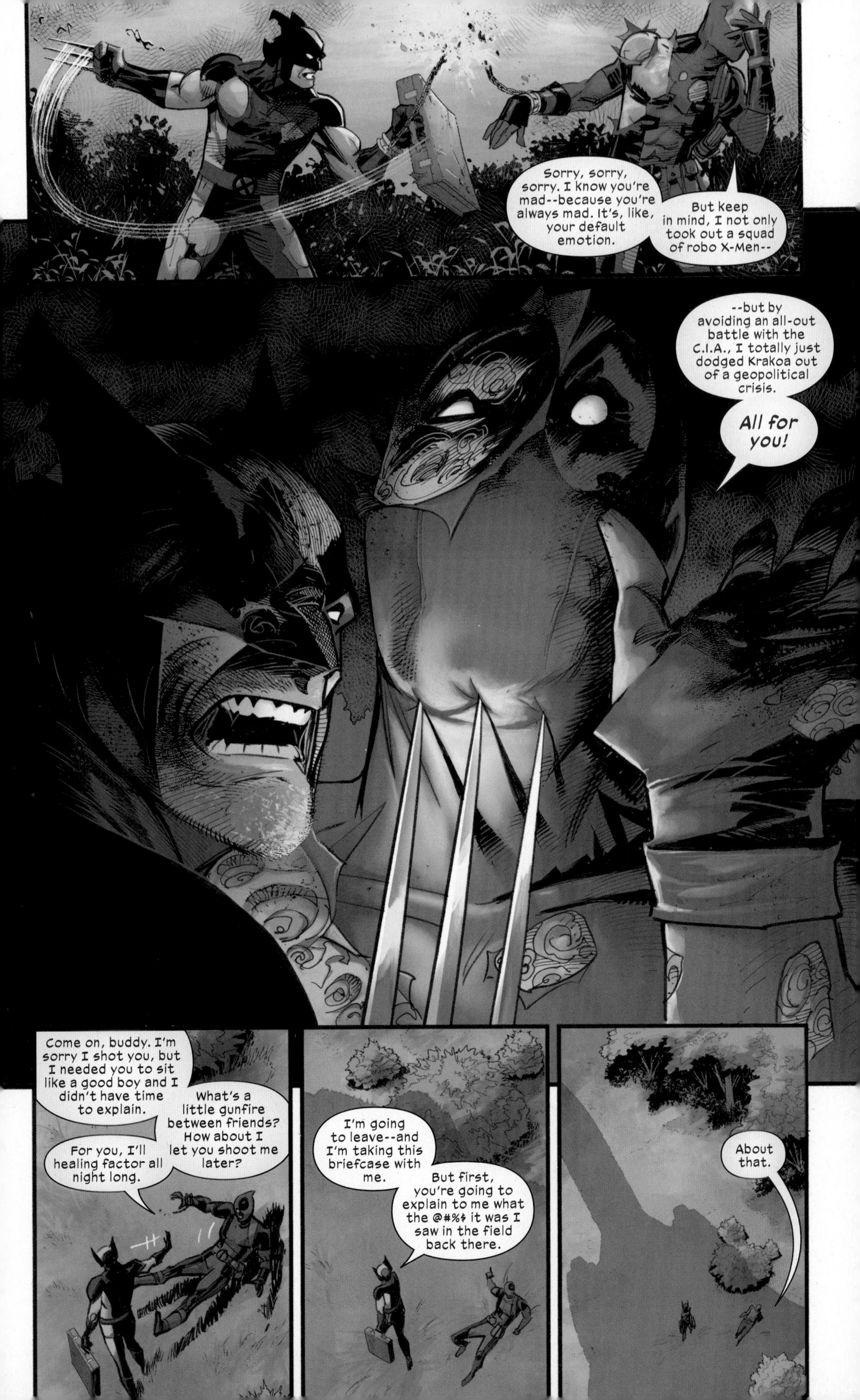
Sorry, sorry, sorry. I know you're mad--because you're always mad. It's, like, your default emotion.
But keep in mind, I not only took out a squad of robo X-Men--
--but by avoiding an all-out battle with the C.I.A., I totally just dodged Krakoa out of a geopolitical crisis.
All for you!
Come on, buddy. I'm sorry I shot you, but I needed you to sit like a good boy and I didn't have time to explain.
What's a little gunfire between friends? How about I let you shoot me later?
For you, I'll healing factor all night long.
I'm going to leave--and I'm taking this briefcase with me.
But first, you're going to explain to me what the @#%$ it was I saw in the field back there.
About that.

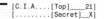

For: Deadpool. From: Blind Al.
Hope this helps, chump.
Good luck. Don't screw up!

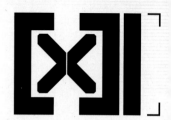

C.I.A.: X-DESK

Delores Ramirez

[Memo to Self]

Re: Mutant Automatons

I'll admit, it still stings.

Legacy House hosted a black-market auction, and a mind-wiped mutant [Christoph "Christopher" Nord, A.K.A David North, A.K.A Maverick] was up for bid. The C.I.A. delegated a monetary fund that all but guaranteed he could have been mine. Wholly and completely. The perfect, subservient mole for Krakoa.

Yes, things eventually worked out. Or mostly worked out. Maverick became an informant, but his codename points to his unreliability. He is only loyal to himself -- and the highest bidder.

But I did come away from the auction that night with something substantial. A hand. The severed hand -- reportedly -- of Wolverine.

Upon closer inspection, the claws turned out to be not adamantium but steel. The flesh was synthetic. The veins were wires clogged with oil.

At first I was disappointed yet again, but then an idea began to fester. Who had built this? Because it was a brilliant replication.

And sometimes a replication is all you need, such as when the robber prods a finger against his jacket pocket, distending the fabric in the shape of a gun.

What if I didn't need a mutant? Just a shadow of one? Or two? Or twenty?

As spies, as blackmail ambassadors, what have you. These automatons could be employed in countless scenarios, including to stain the reputation of the mutants.

I handed over the hand to a forensics team, and they came back to me with a name:

DANGER

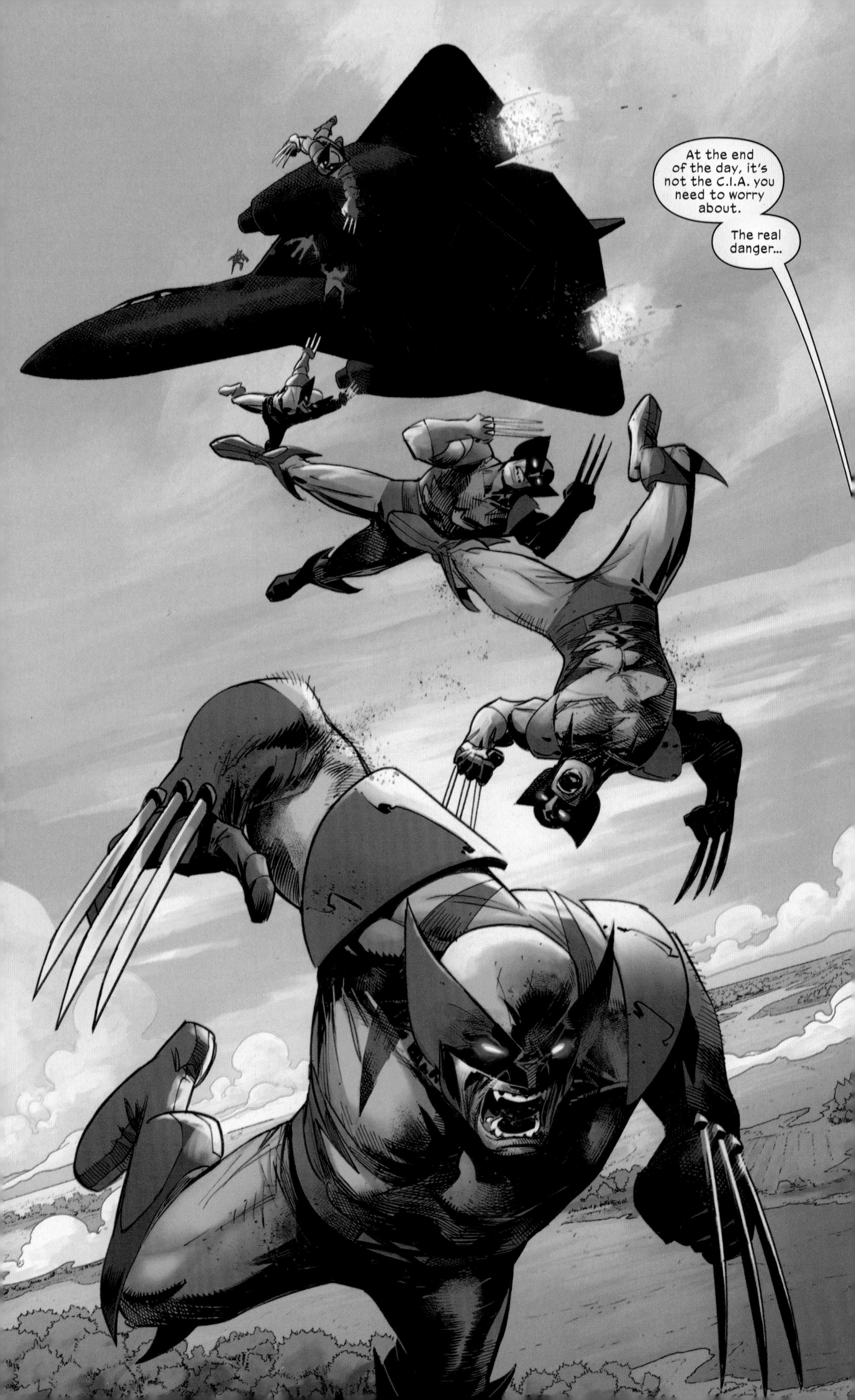
At the end of the day, it's not the C.I.A. you need to worry about.
The real danger...

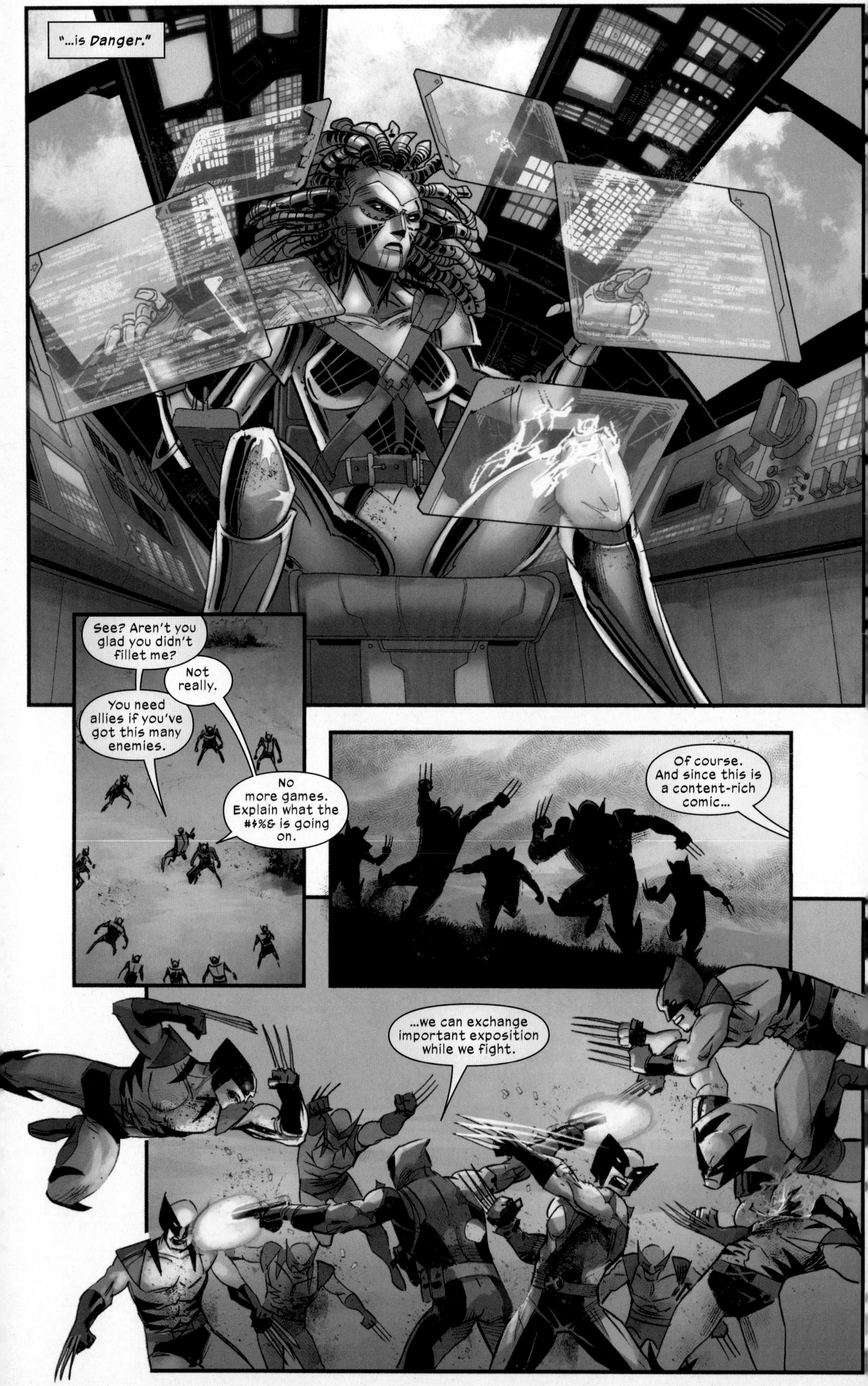
"...is Danger."
See? Aren't you glad you didn't fillet me?
Not really.
You need allies if you've got this many enemies.
No more games. Explain what the #$%& is going on.
Of course. And since this is a content-rich comic...
...we can exchange important exposition while we fight.

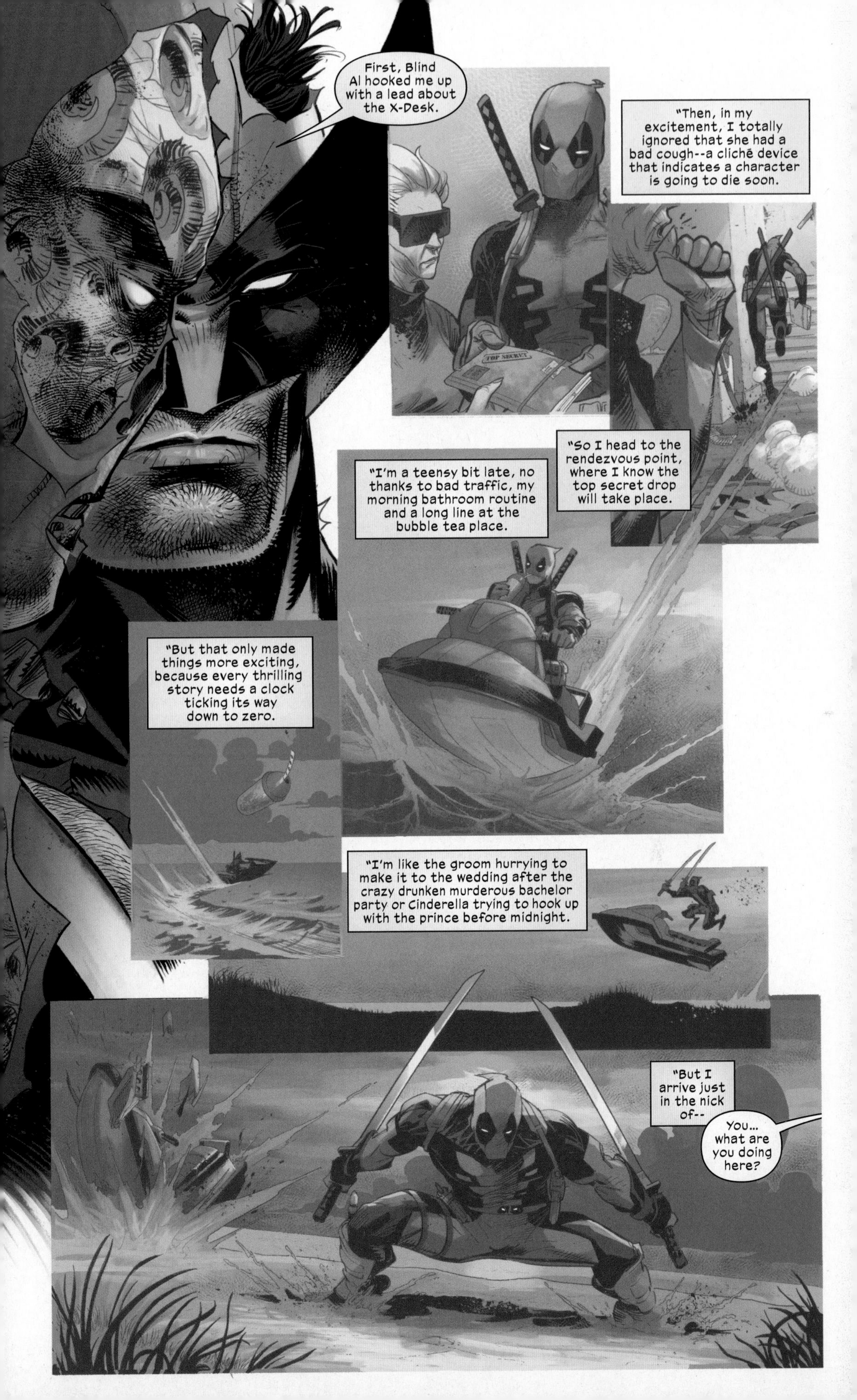
First, Blind Al hooked me up with a lead about the X-Desk.
"Then, in my excitement, I totally ignored that she had a bad cough--a cliché device that indicates a character is going to die soon.
TOP SECRET
"So I head to the rendezvous point, where I know the top secret drop will take place.
"I'm a teensy bit late, no thanks to bad traffic, my morning bathroom routine and a long line at the bubble tea place.
"But that only made things more exciting, because every thrilling story needs a clock ticking its way down to zero.
"I'm like the groom hurrying to make it to the wedding after the crazy drunken murderous bachelor party or Cinderella trying to hook up with the prince before midnight.
"But I arrive just in the nick of--
You... what are you doing here?

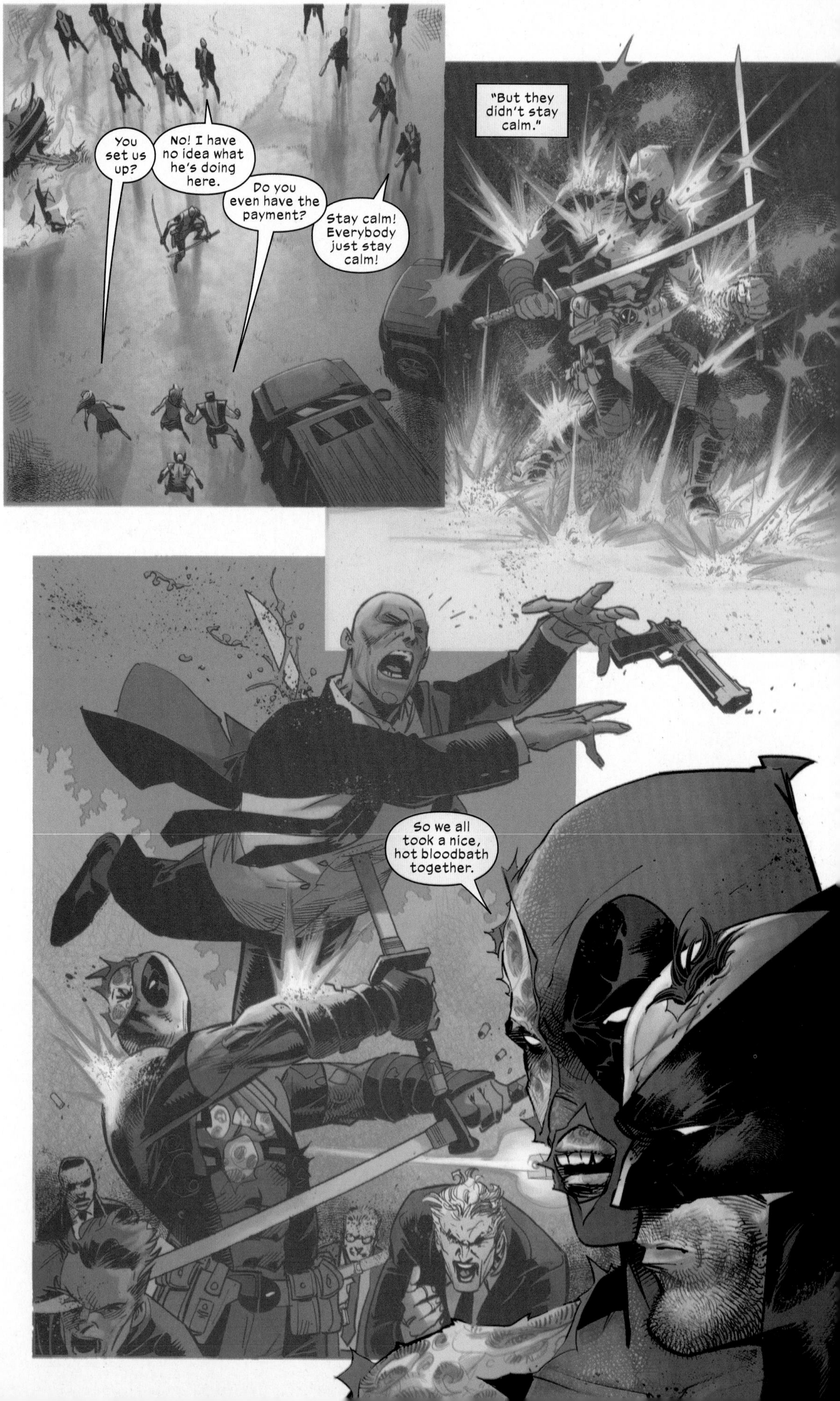
You set us up?
No! I have no idea what he's doing here.
Do you even have the payment?
Stay calm! Everybody just stay calm!
"But they didn't stay calm."
So we all took a nice, hot bloodbath together.

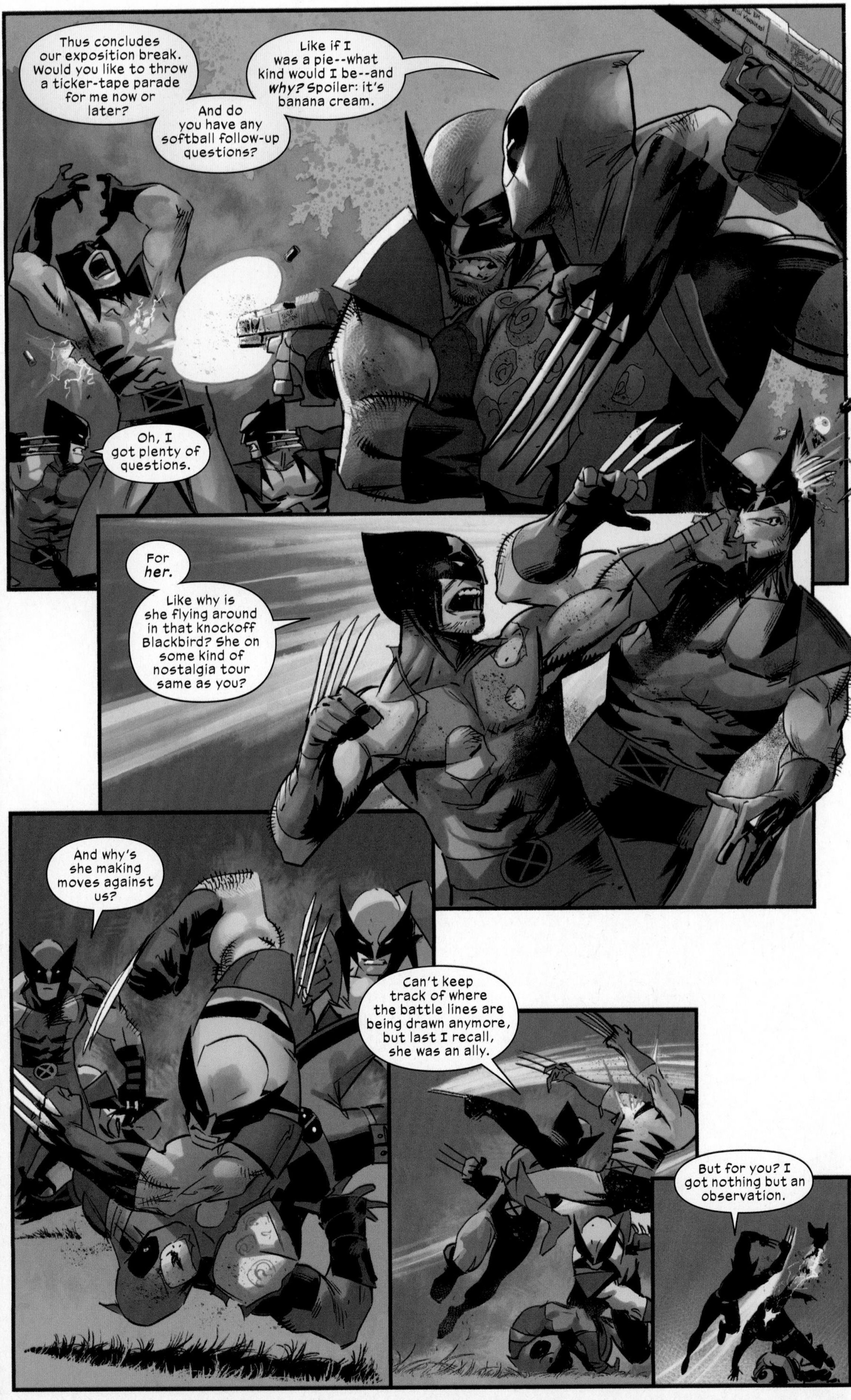
Thus concludes our exposition break. Would you like to throw a ticker-tape parade for me now or later?
And do you have any softball follow-up questions?
Like if I was a pie--what kind would I be--and *why?* Spoiler: it's banana cream.
Oh, I got plenty of questions.
For *her.*
Like why is she flying around in that knockoff Blackbird? She on some kind of nostalgia tour same as you?
And why's she making moves against us?
Can't keep track of where the battle lines are being drawn anymore, but last I recall, she was an ally.
But for you? I got nothing but an observation.

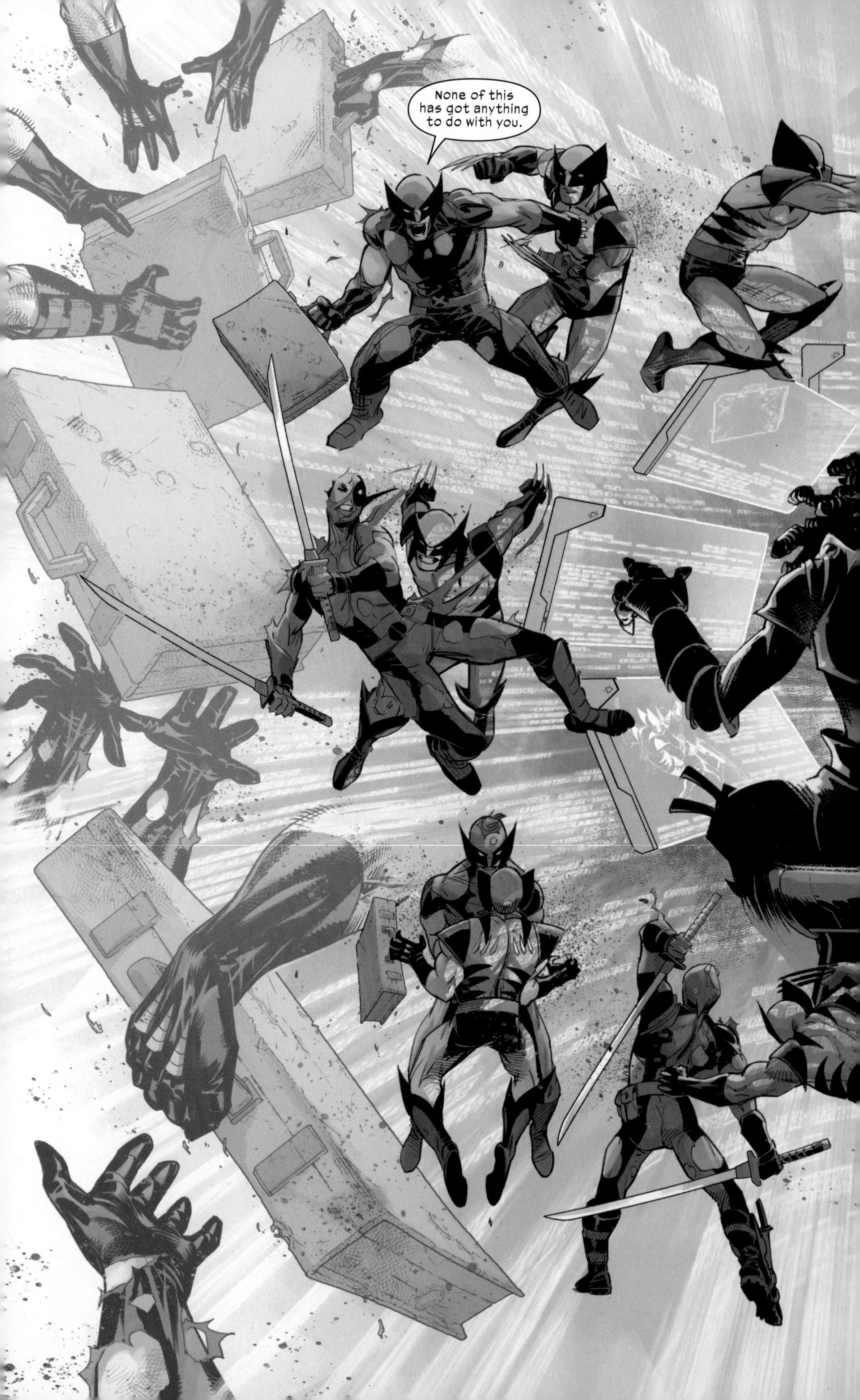
None of this has got anything to do with you.

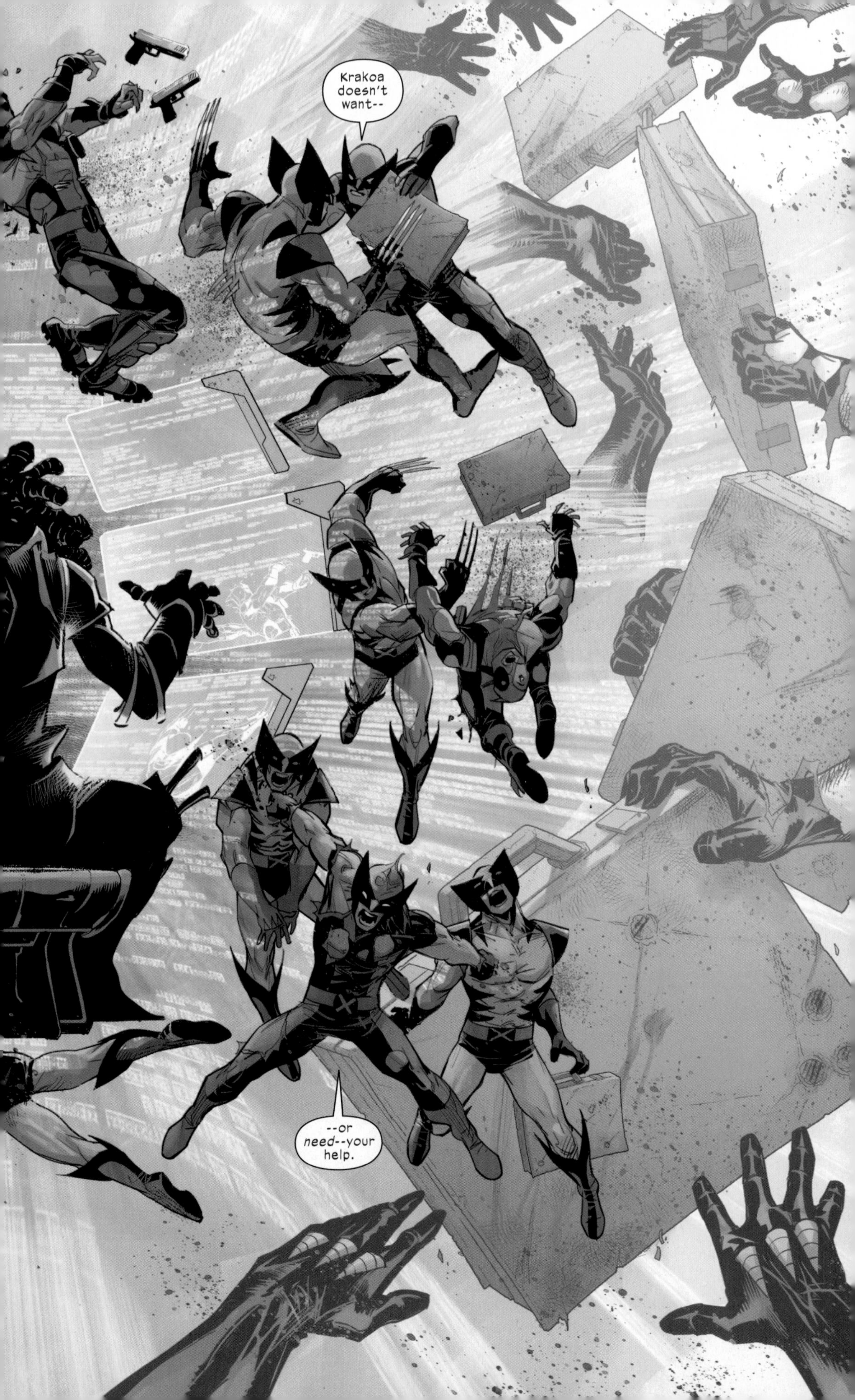
Krakoa doesn't want--
--or need--your help.

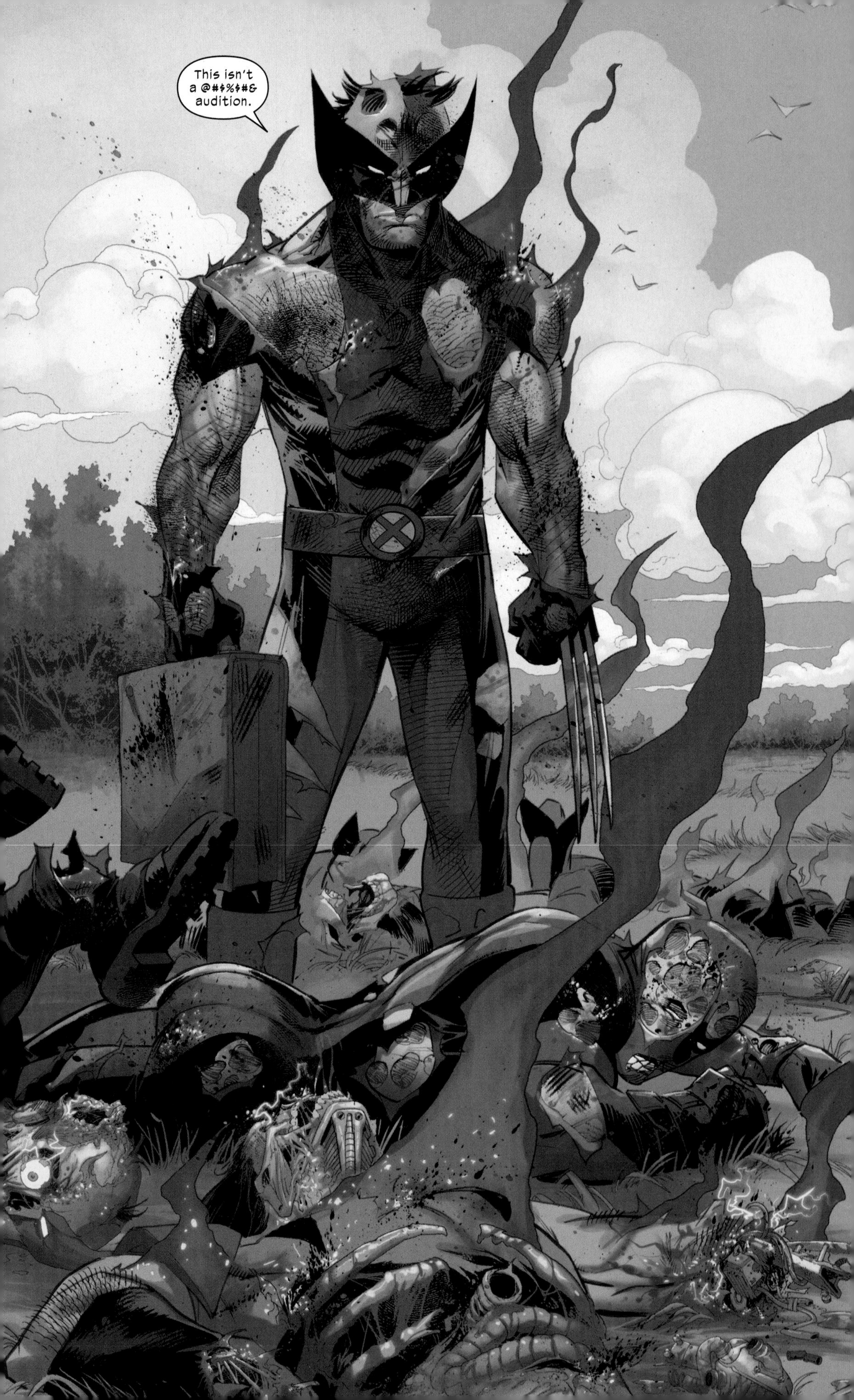
This isn't a @#$%$#& audition.

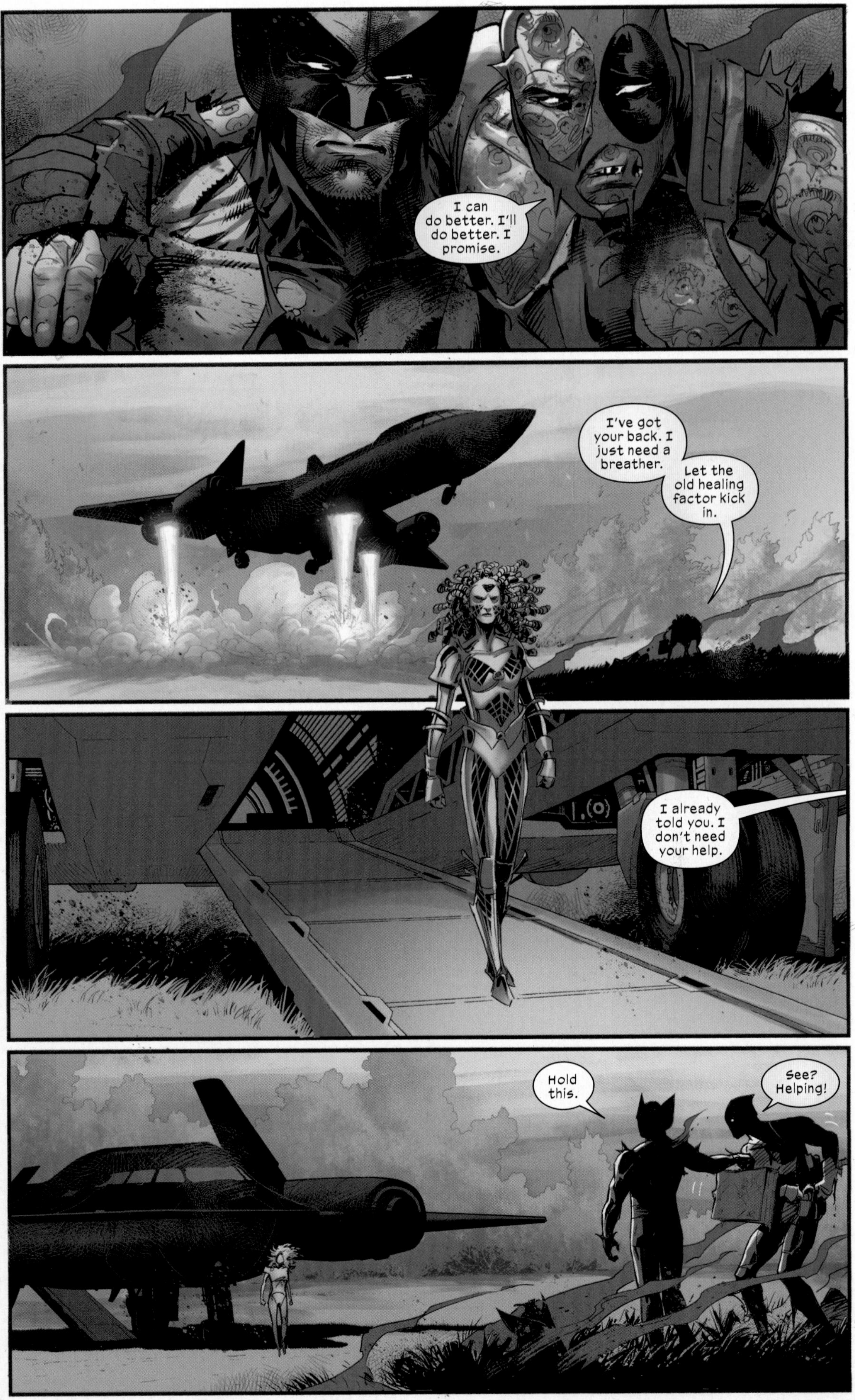
I can do better. I'll do better. I promise.
I've got your back. I just need a breather.
Let the old healing factor kick in.
I already told you. I don't need your help.
Hold this.
See? Helping!

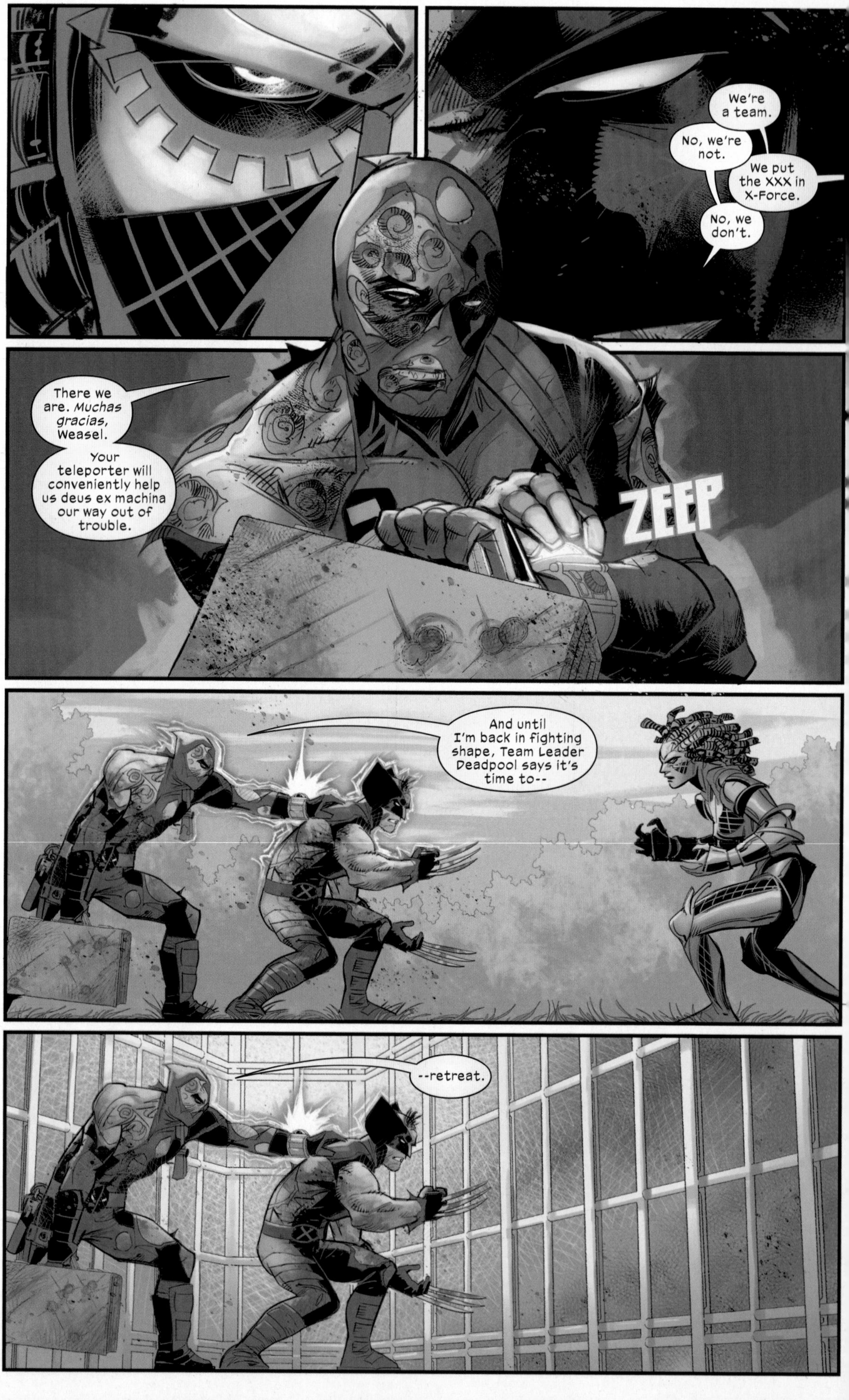
We're a team.
No, we're not.
We put the XXX in X-Force.
No, we don't.
There we are. *Muchas gracias,* Weasel.
Your teleporter will conveniently help us deus ex machina our way out of trouble.
ZEEP
And until I'm back in fighting shape, Team Leader Deadpool says it's time to--
--retreat.

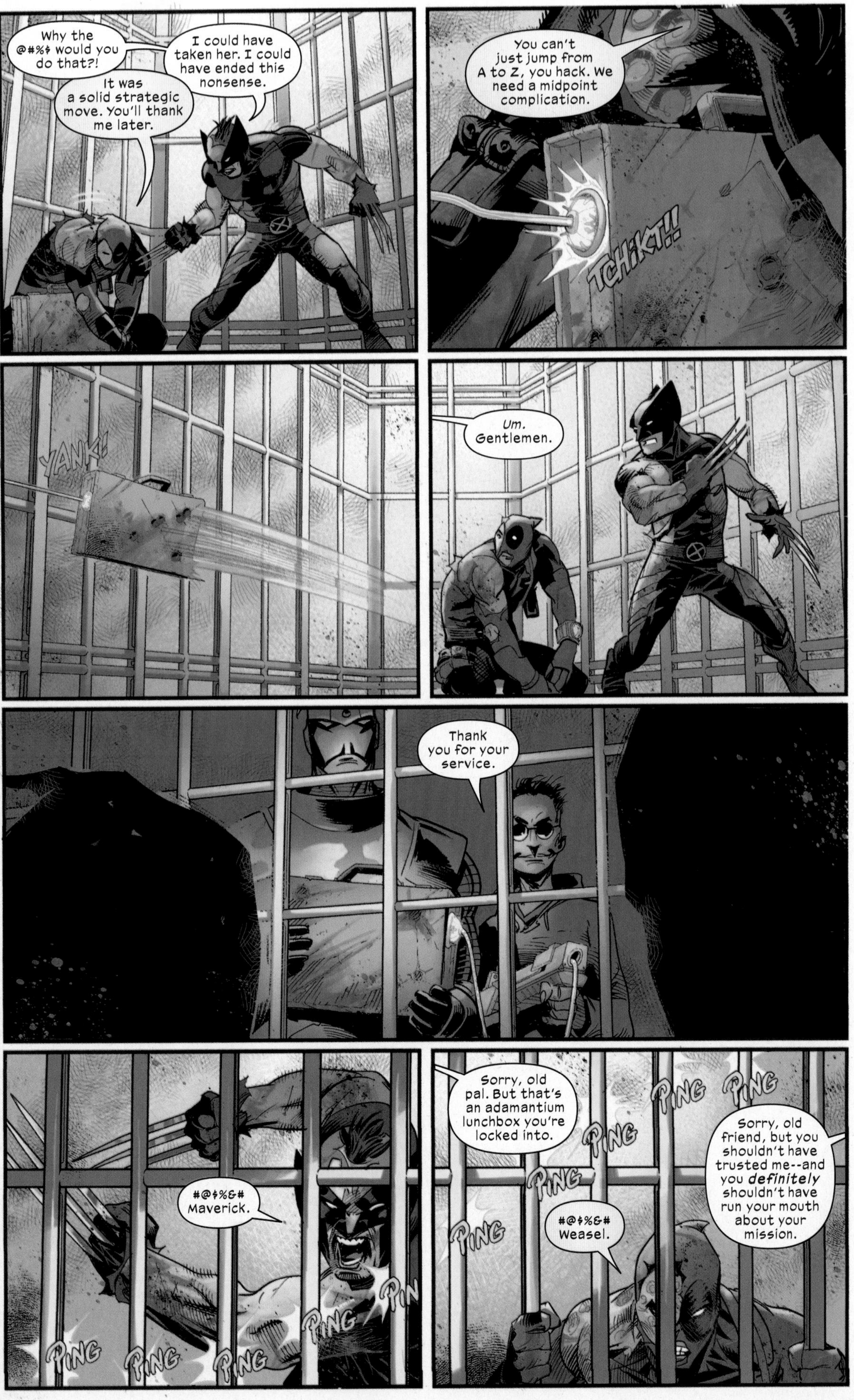
Why the @#%$ would you do that?!
I could have taken her. I could have ended this nonsense.
It was a solid strategic move. You'll thank me later.
You can't just jump from A to Z, you hack. We need a midpoint complication.
TCHIKT!!
YANK!
Um. Gentlemen.
Thank you for your service.
#@$%&# Maverick.
PING PING PING PING PING
Sorry, old pal. But that's an adamantium lunchbox you're locked into.
PING PING PING PING PING
Sorry, old friend, but you shouldn't have trusted me--and you *definitely* shouldn't have run your mouth about your mission.
#@$%&# Weasel.

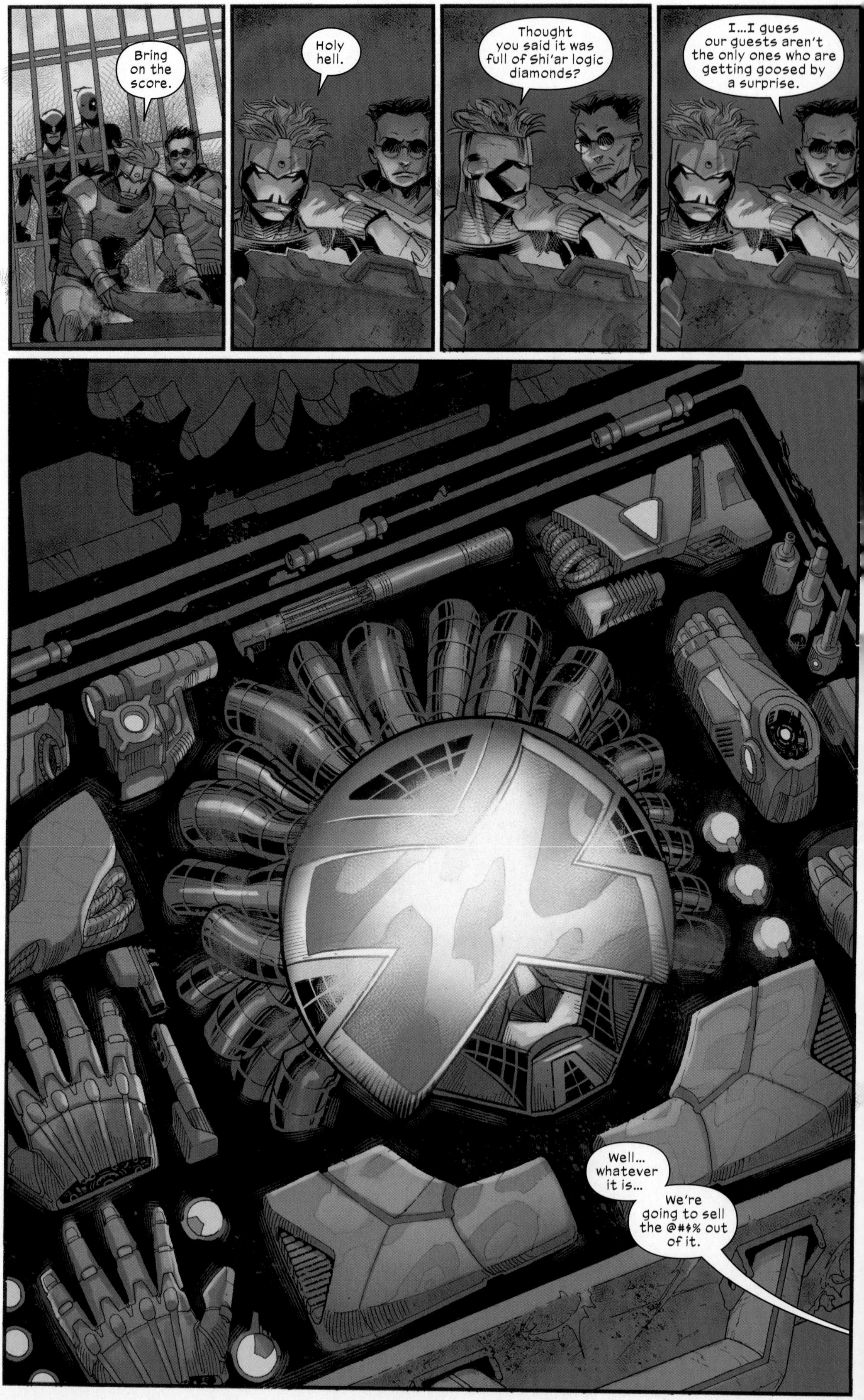
Bring on the score.
Holy hell.
Thought you said it was full of Shi'ar logic diamonds?
I...I guess our guests aren't the only ones who are getting goosed by a surprise.
Well... whatever it is...
We're going to sell the @#$% out of it.

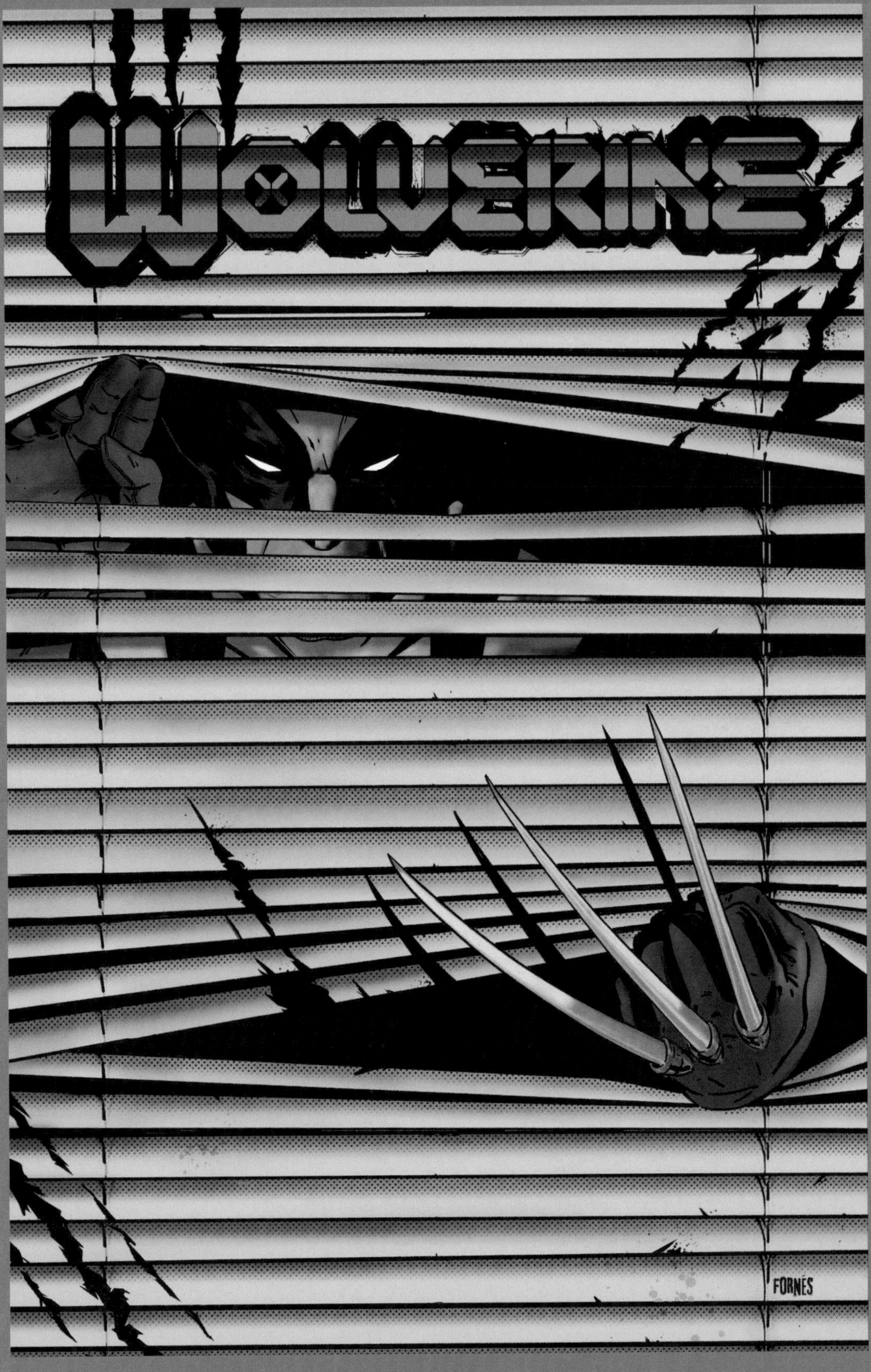
WOLVERINE
FORNÉS

Wolverine #20 Variant by Jorge Fornés

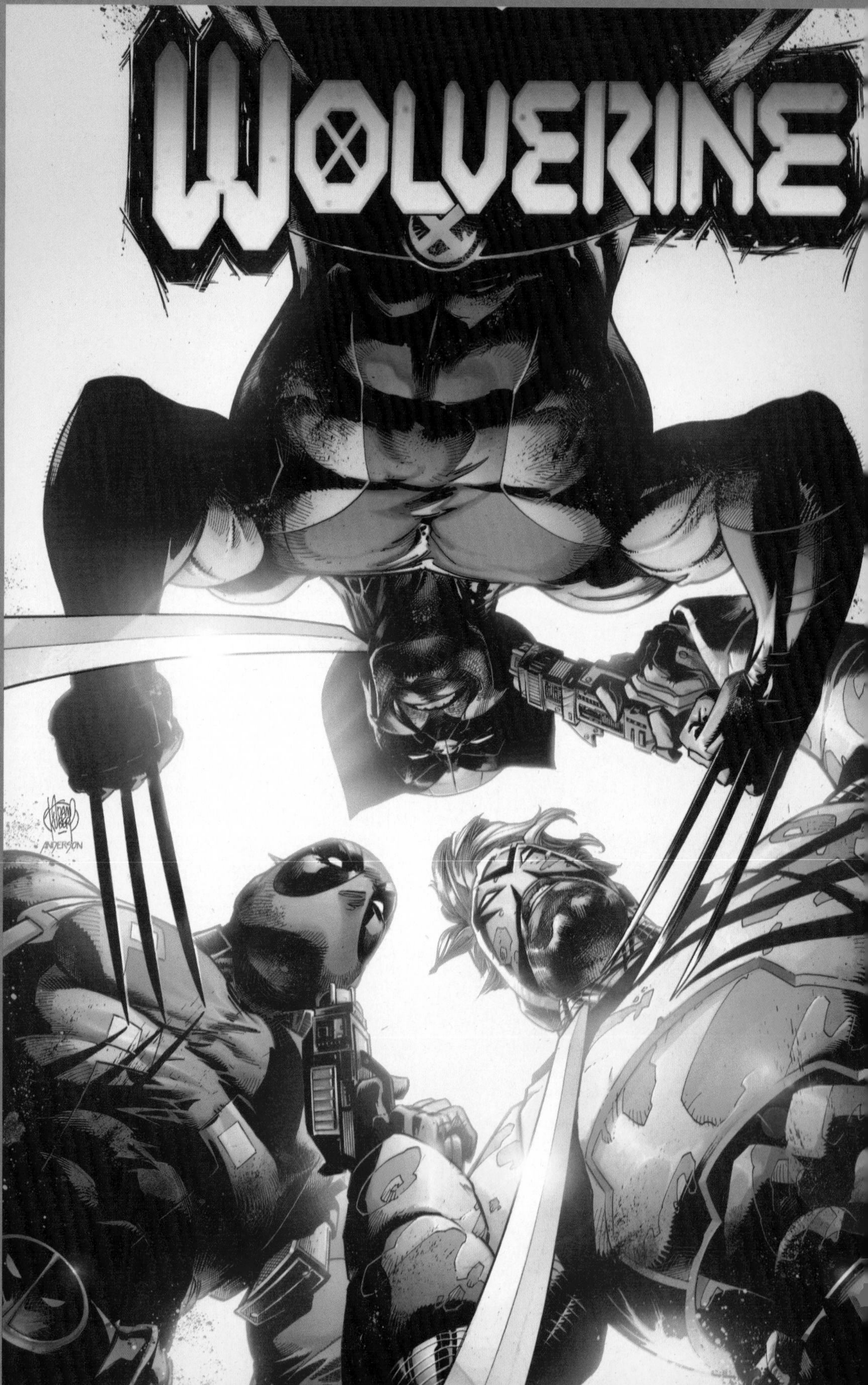
WOLVERINE

Bad Gamble

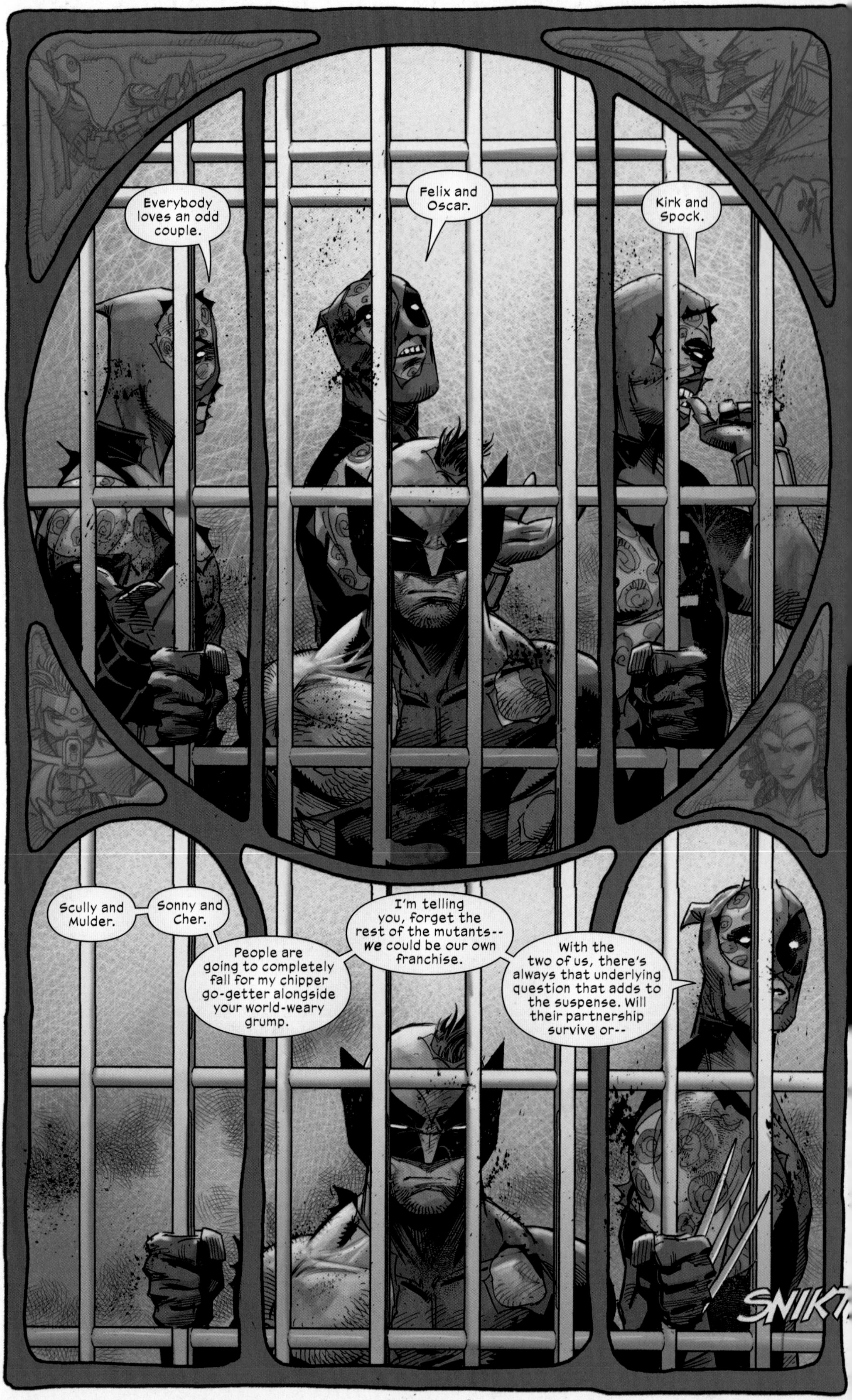
Everybody loves an odd couple.
Felix and Oscar.
Kirk and Spock.
Scully and Mulder.
Sonny and Cher.
People are going to completely fall for my chipper go-getter alongside your world-weary grump.
I'm telling you, forget the rest of the mutants-- *we* could be our own franchise.
With the two of us, there's always that underlying question that adds to the suspense. Will their partnership survive or--
SNIKT

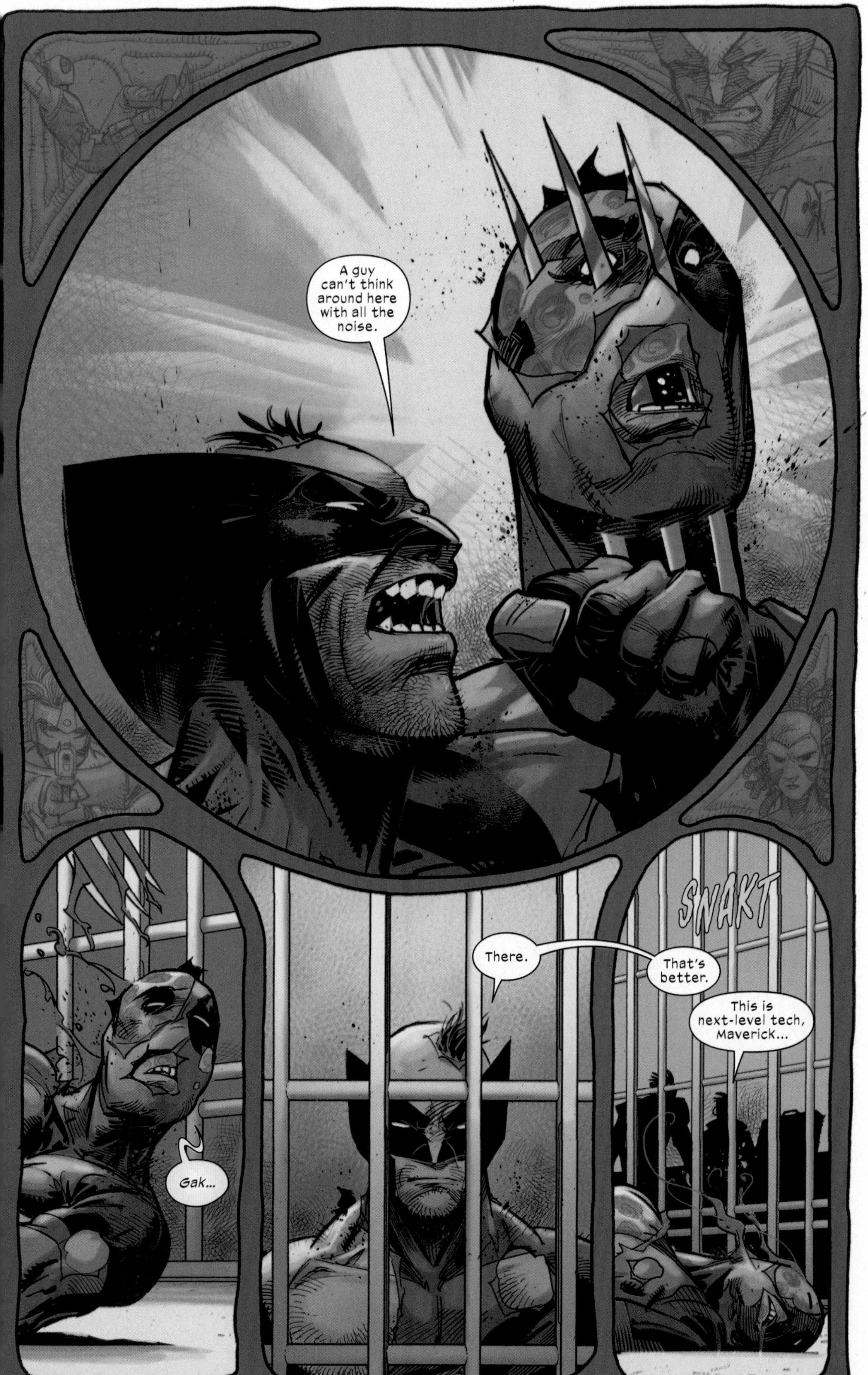
A guy can't think around here with all the noise.
Gak...
There.
That's better.
This is next-level tech, Maverick...
SNAKT

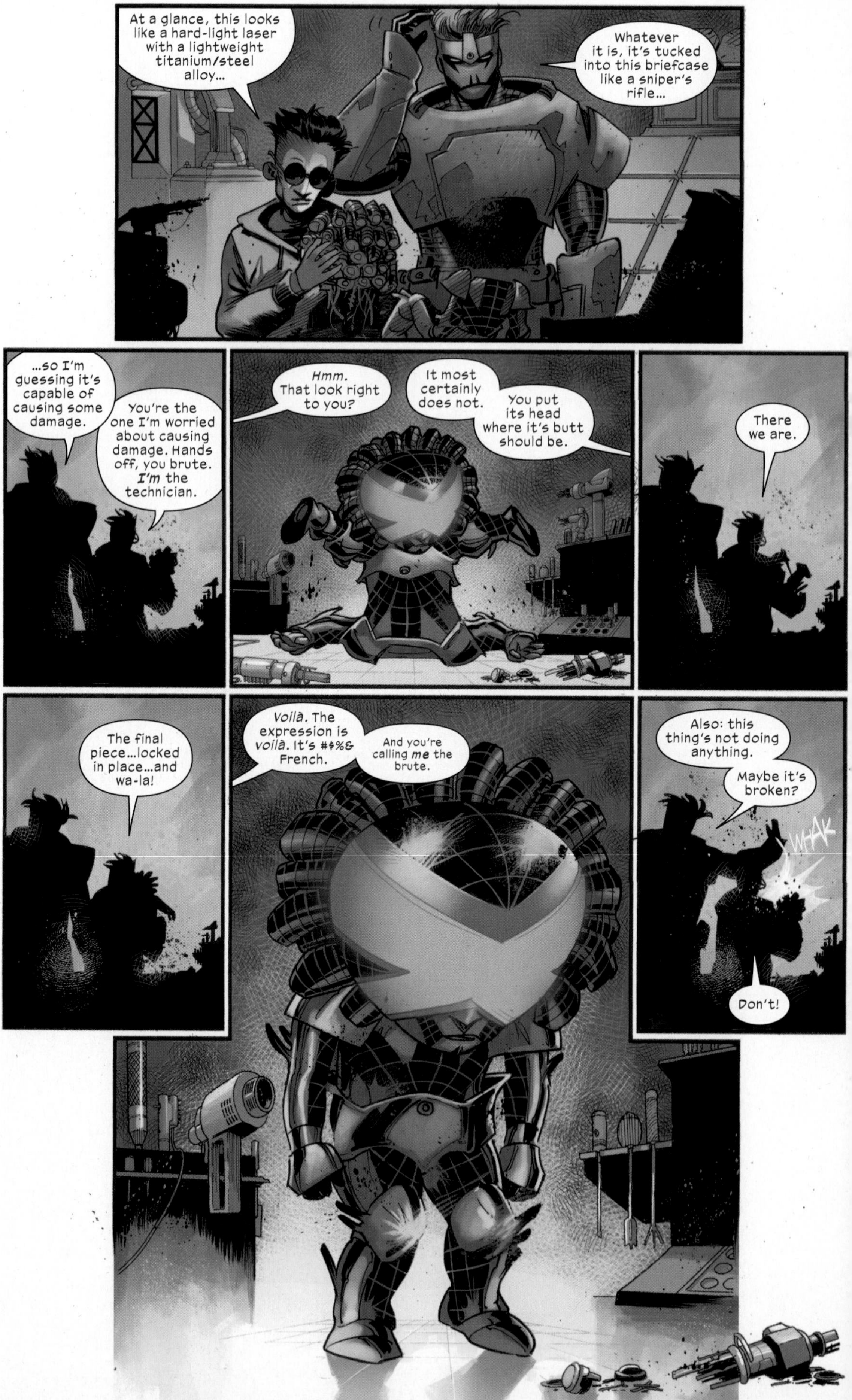
At a glance, this looks like a hard-light laser with a lightweight titanium/steel alloy...
Whatever it is, it's tucked into this briefcase like a sniper's rifle...
...so I'm guessing it's capable of causing some damage.
You're the one I'm worried about causing damage. Hands off, you brute. *I'm* the technician.
Hmm. That look right to you?
It most certainly does not.
You put its head where it's butt should be.
There we are.
The final piece...locked in place...and wa-la!
Voilà. The expression is *voilà*. It's #$%& French.
And you're calling *me* the brute.
Also: this thing's not doing anything.
Maybe it's broken?
WHAK
Don't!

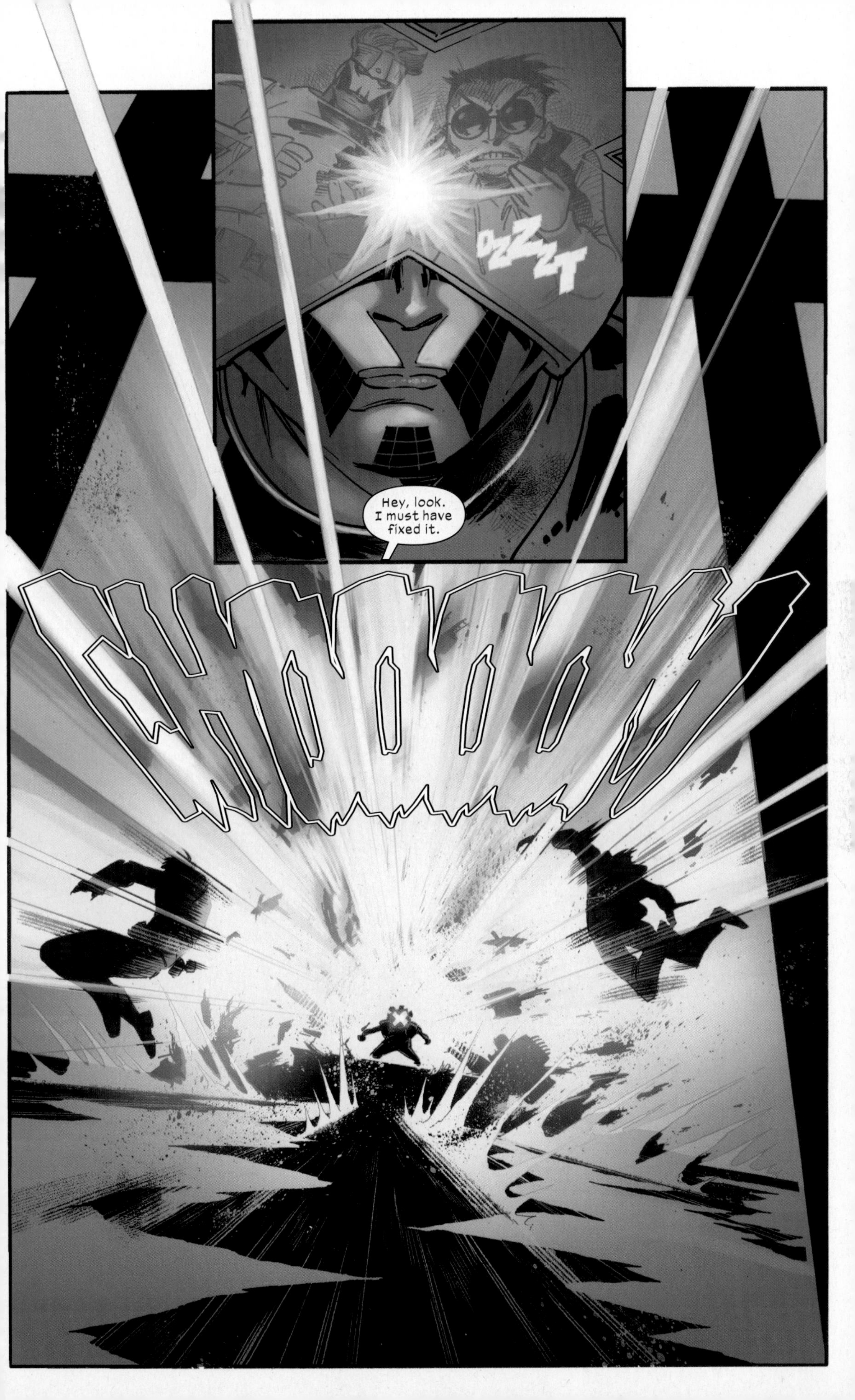
DZZZT
Hey, look. I must have fixed it.

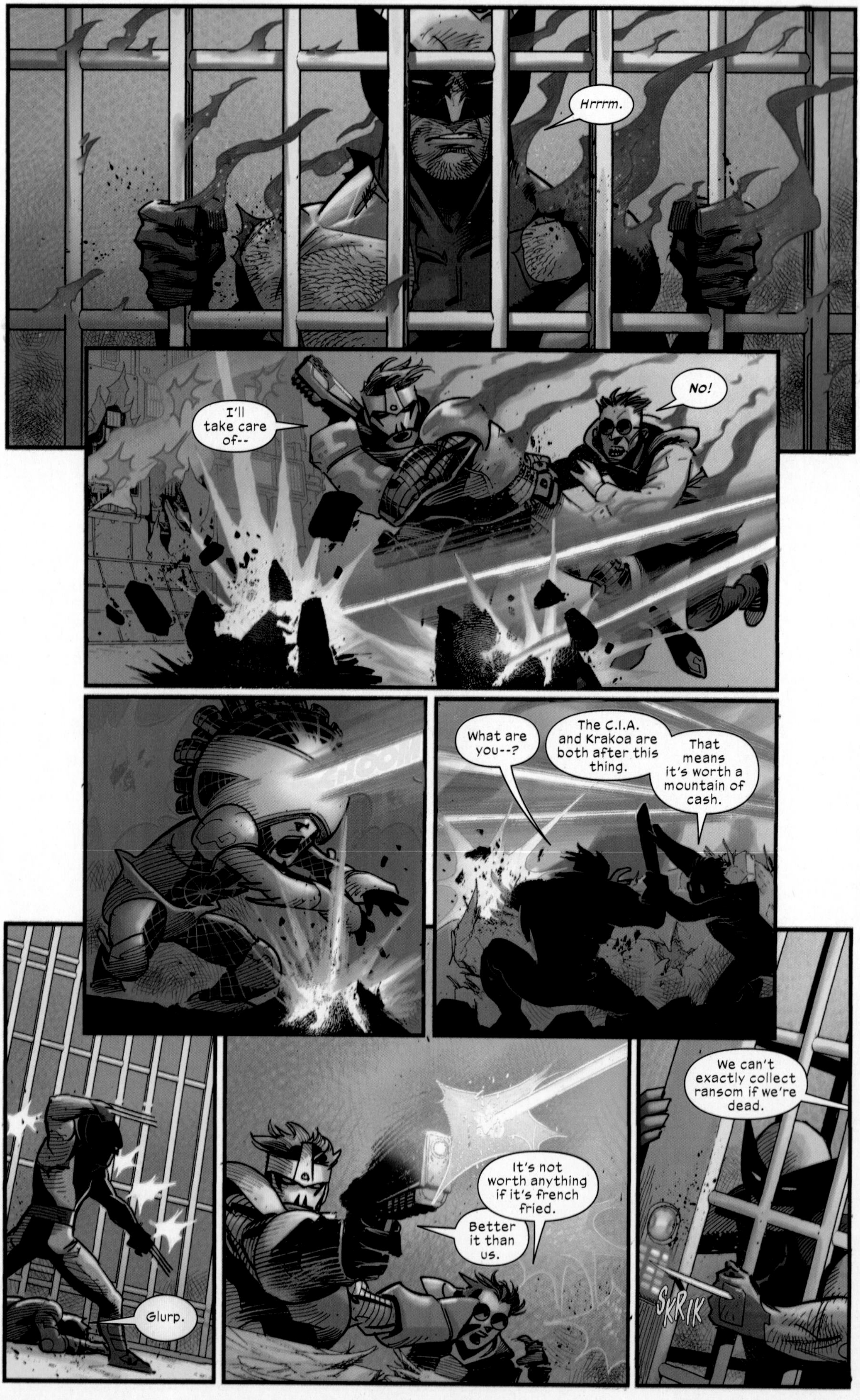
Hrrrm.
I'll take care of--
NO!
What are you--?
The C.I.A. and Krakoa are both after this thing.
That means it's worth a mountain of cash.
It's not worth anything if it's french fried.
Better it than us.
Glurp.
We can't exactly collect ransom if we're dead.
SKRIK

~~CELLMATES~~ MORE LIKE "BEST BUDS," AMIRITE?

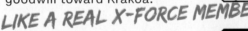

[WOLVERINE]

Pursuing a lead regarding an armored briefcase, Wolverine arrived in the Maryland countryside to discover a chaotic scene littered with broken robotic replicas of the X-Men and several dead C.I.A. agents.

LET'S SKIP TO THE GOOD PART!

[DEADPOOL]

He also discovered Deadpool, who explained he had foiled a handoff of the briefcase between the C.I.A.'s X-Desk and Danger as a gesture of goodwill toward Krakoa.

YOURS TRULY

[MAVERICK]

LIKE A REAL X-FORCE MEMBER!

But Deadpool's escape plan landed the two in a cell in Las Vegas, prisoners of their former allies, Weasel and Maverick, who claimed the briefcase for themselves.

[WEASEL]

&%.&%. THOSE GUYS, FOR REAL!

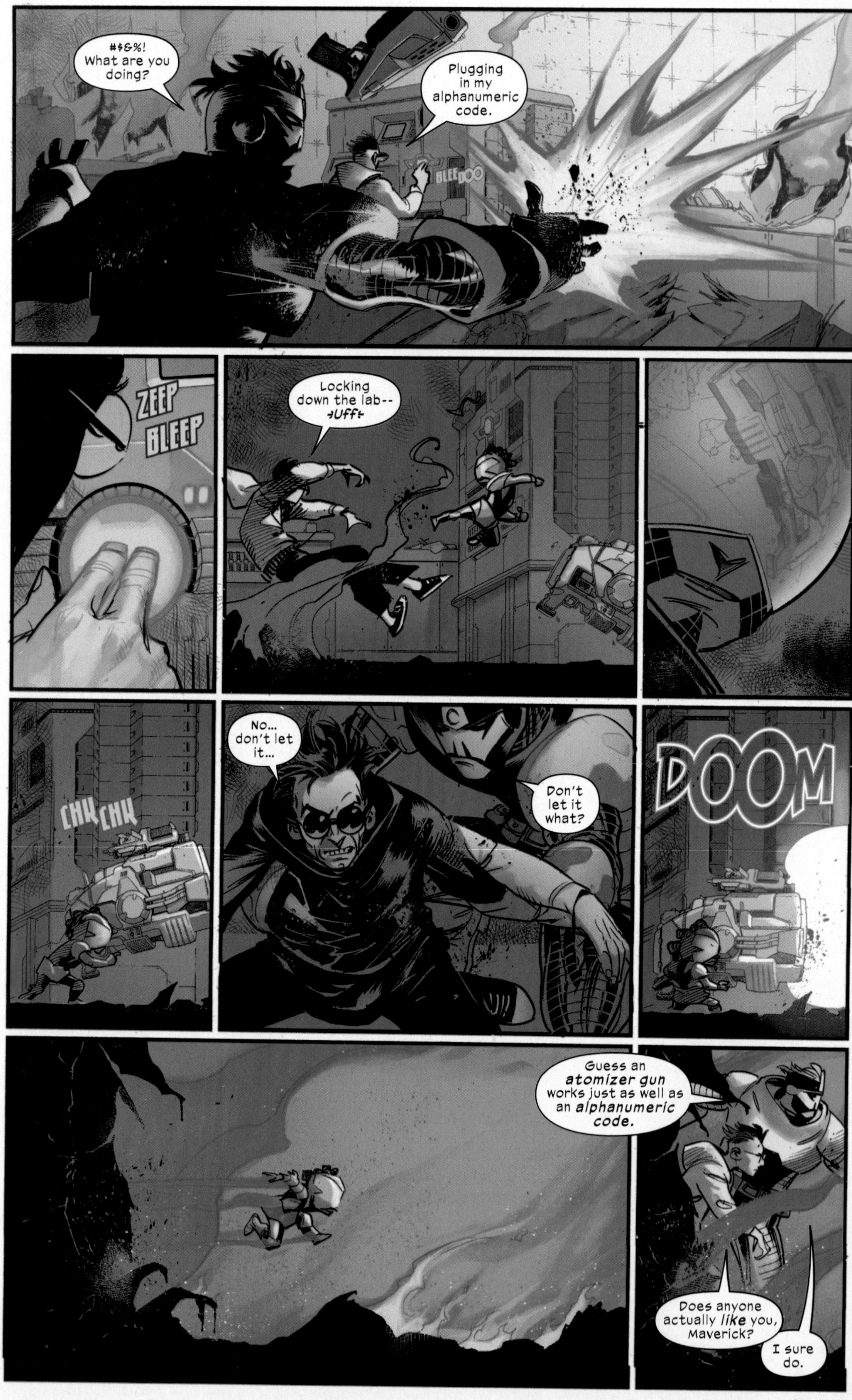
#$&%! What are you doing?
Plugging in my alphanumeric code.
BLEEDOO
ZEEP
BLEEP
Locking down the lab-- -Uff-
CHK CHK
No... don't let it...
Don't let it what?
DOOM
Guess an *atomizer gun* works just as well as an *alphanumeric code.*
Does anyone actually *like* you, Maverick?
I sure do.

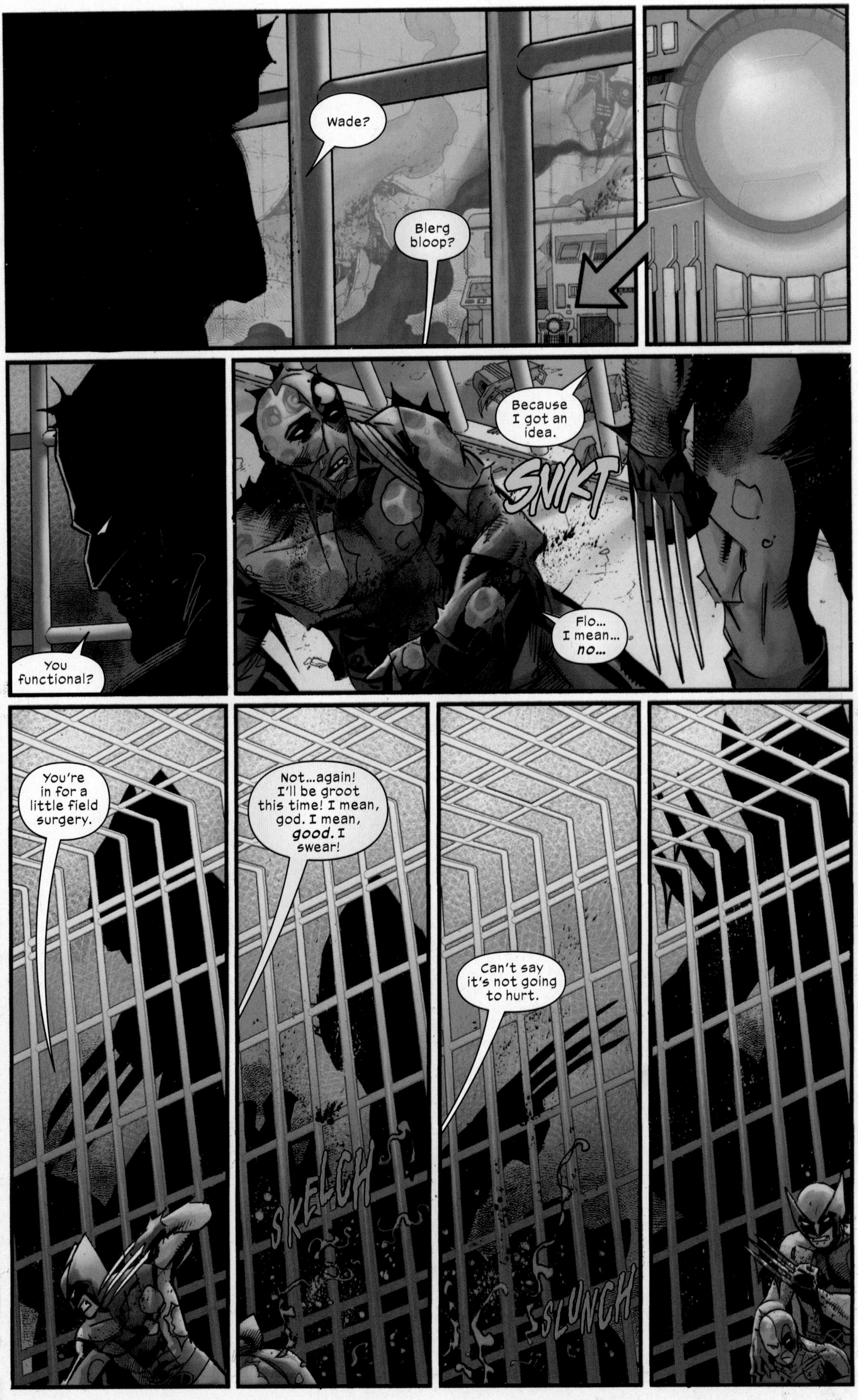
Wade?
Blerg bloop?
You functional?
Because I got an idea.
SNIKT
Flo... I mean... no...
You're in for a little field surgery.
Not...again! I'll be groot this time! I mean, god. I mean, good. I swear!
SKELCH
Can't say it's not going to hurt.
SLUNCH

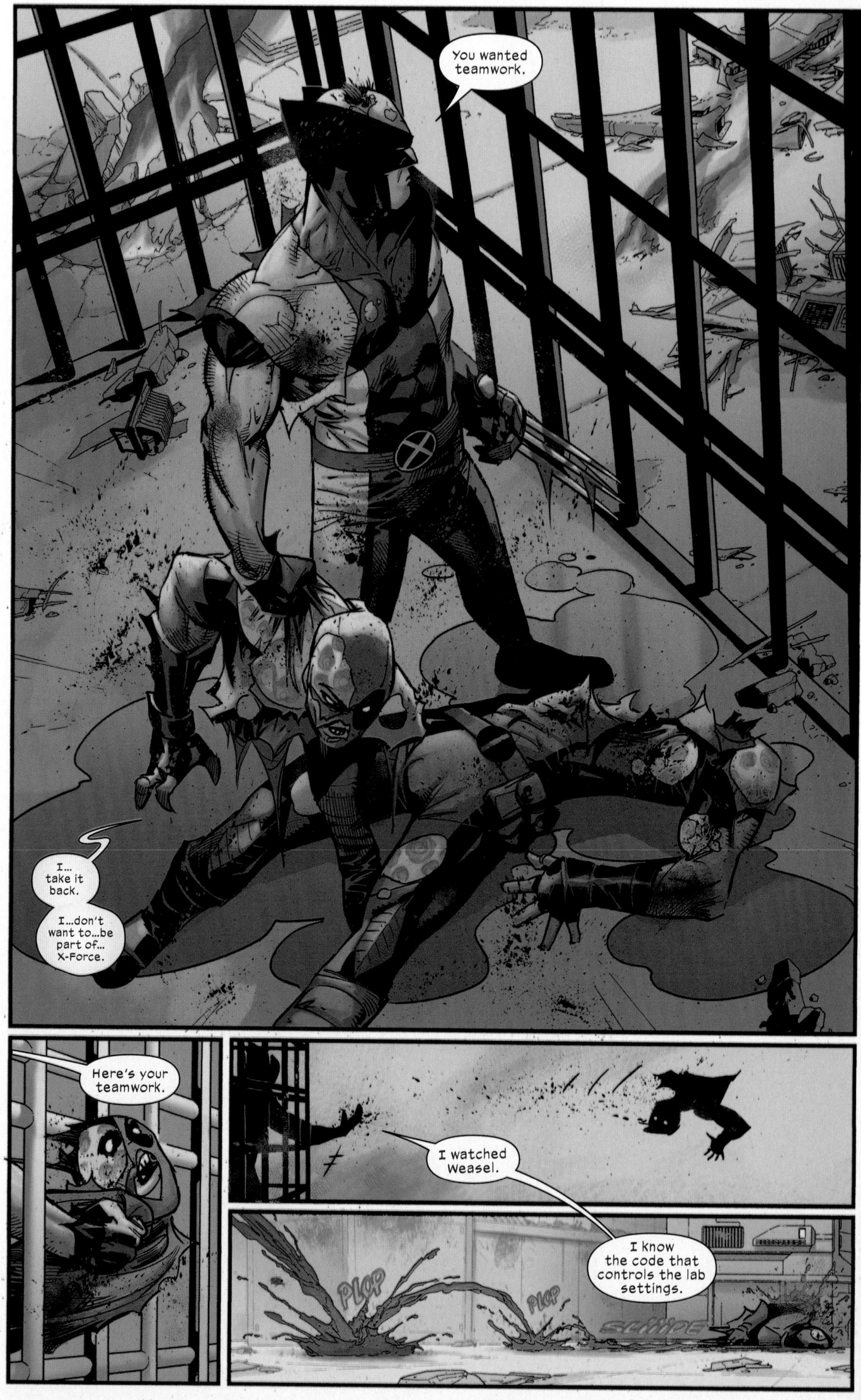
You wanted teamwork.
I... take it back.
I...don't want to...be part of... X-Force.
Here's your teamwork.
I watched Weasel.
I know the code that controls the lab settings.
PLOP
PLOP
SLIIIDE

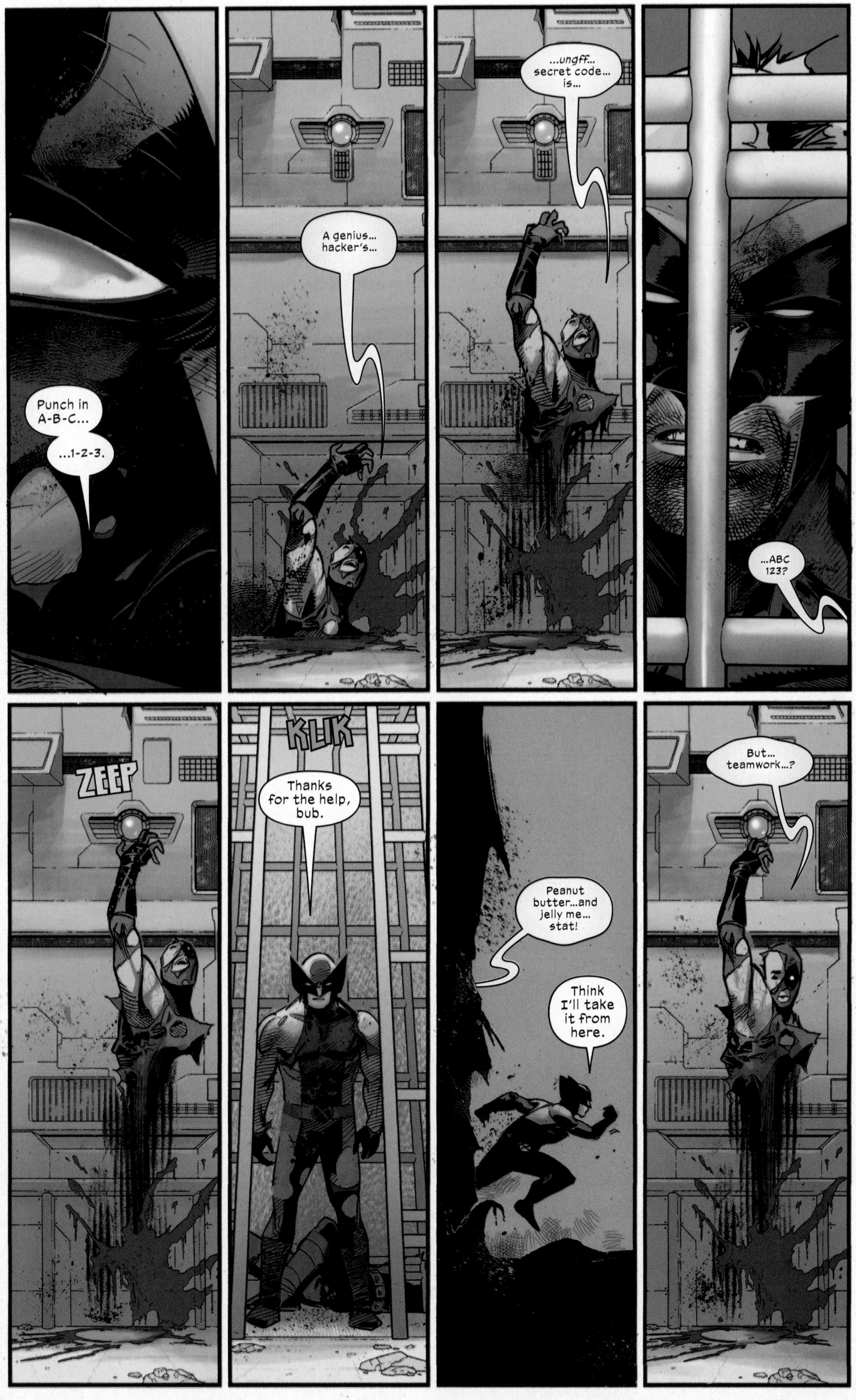

Punch in A-B-C...
...1-2-3.
A genius... hacker's...
...ungff... secret code... is...
...ABC 123?
ZEEP
KLIK
Thanks for the help, bub.
Peanut butter...and jelly me... stat!
Think I'll take it from here.
But... teamwork...?

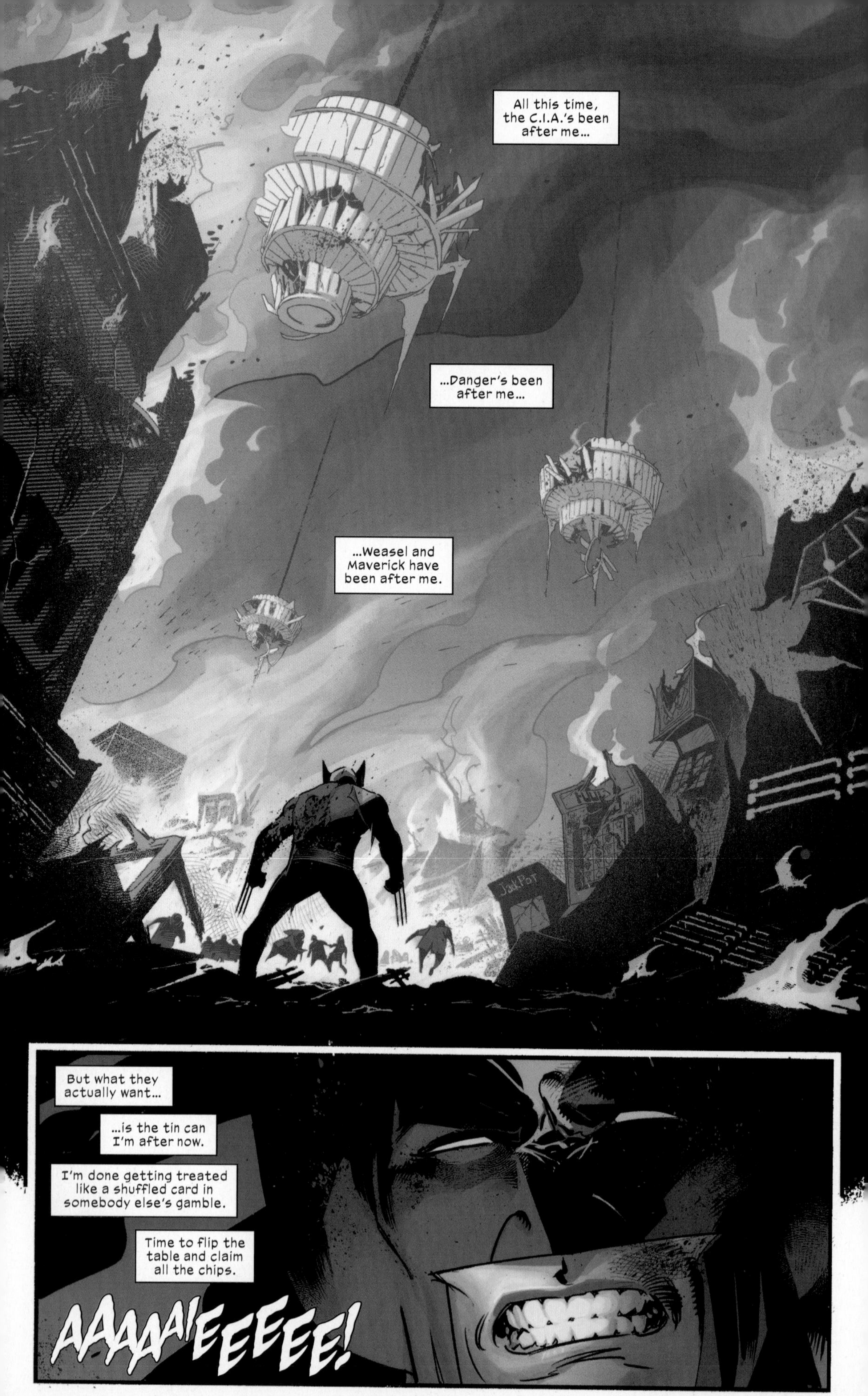
All this time, the C.I.A.'s been after me...
...Danger's been after me...
...Weasel and Maverick have been after me.
But what they actually want...
...is the tin can I'm after now.
I'm done getting treated like a shuffled card in somebody else's gamble.
Time to flip the table and claim all the chips.
AAAAAIEEEEE!

[blind...[0.0]
[al......[0.0]

"Deadpool is the best worst smartest dumbass punk you'll ever meet. A vile freak. A disrespectful clown. An R-rated, C-grade hooligan. A complete @#$%^ annoyance. The worst person in a room full of worst persons. But we've got an understanding. He'd kill a kitten for me, and I'd kill a puppy for him. If that's not love, I don't know what is."

-- BLIND AL

[blind...[0.0]
[al......[0.0]

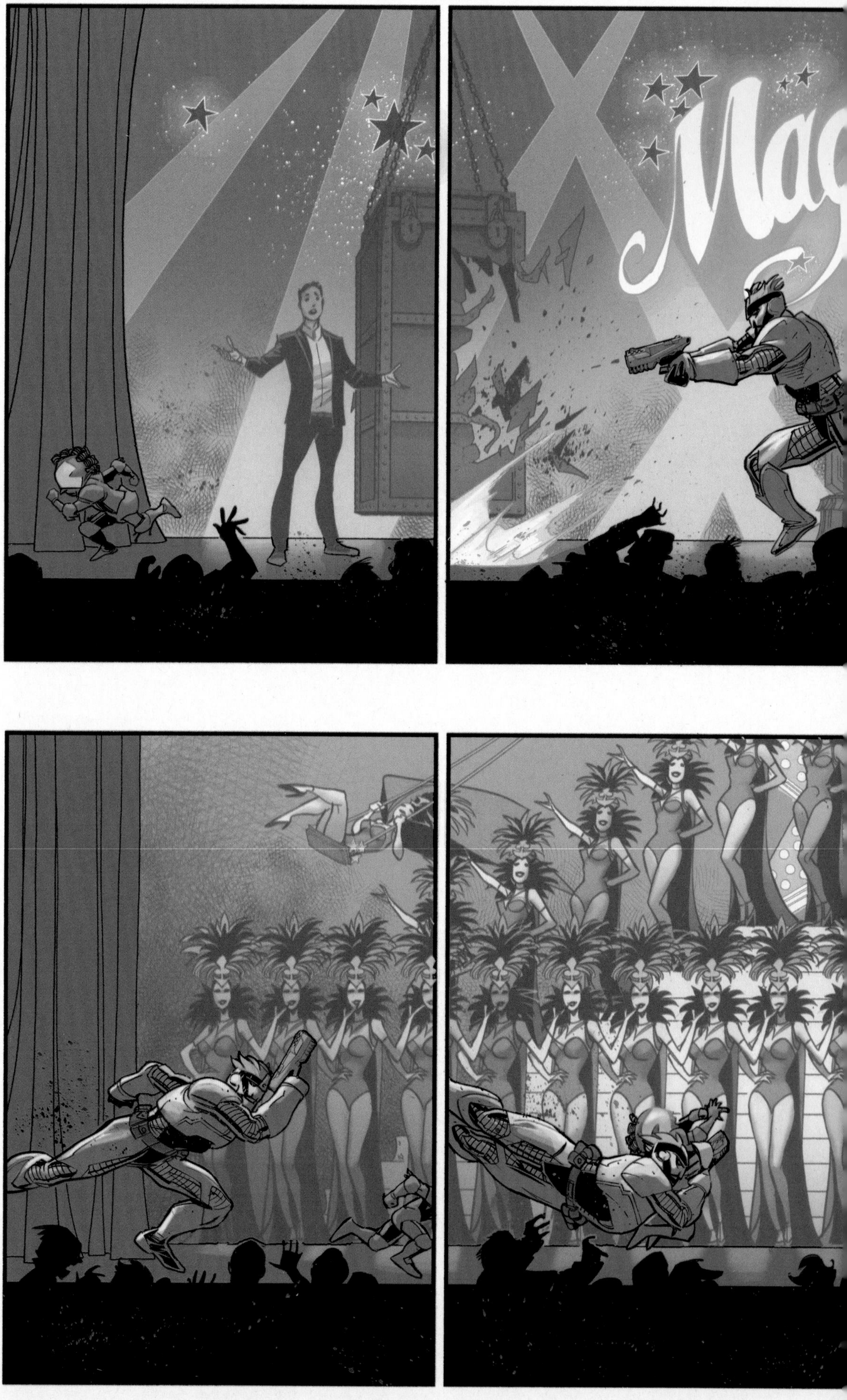
Mag

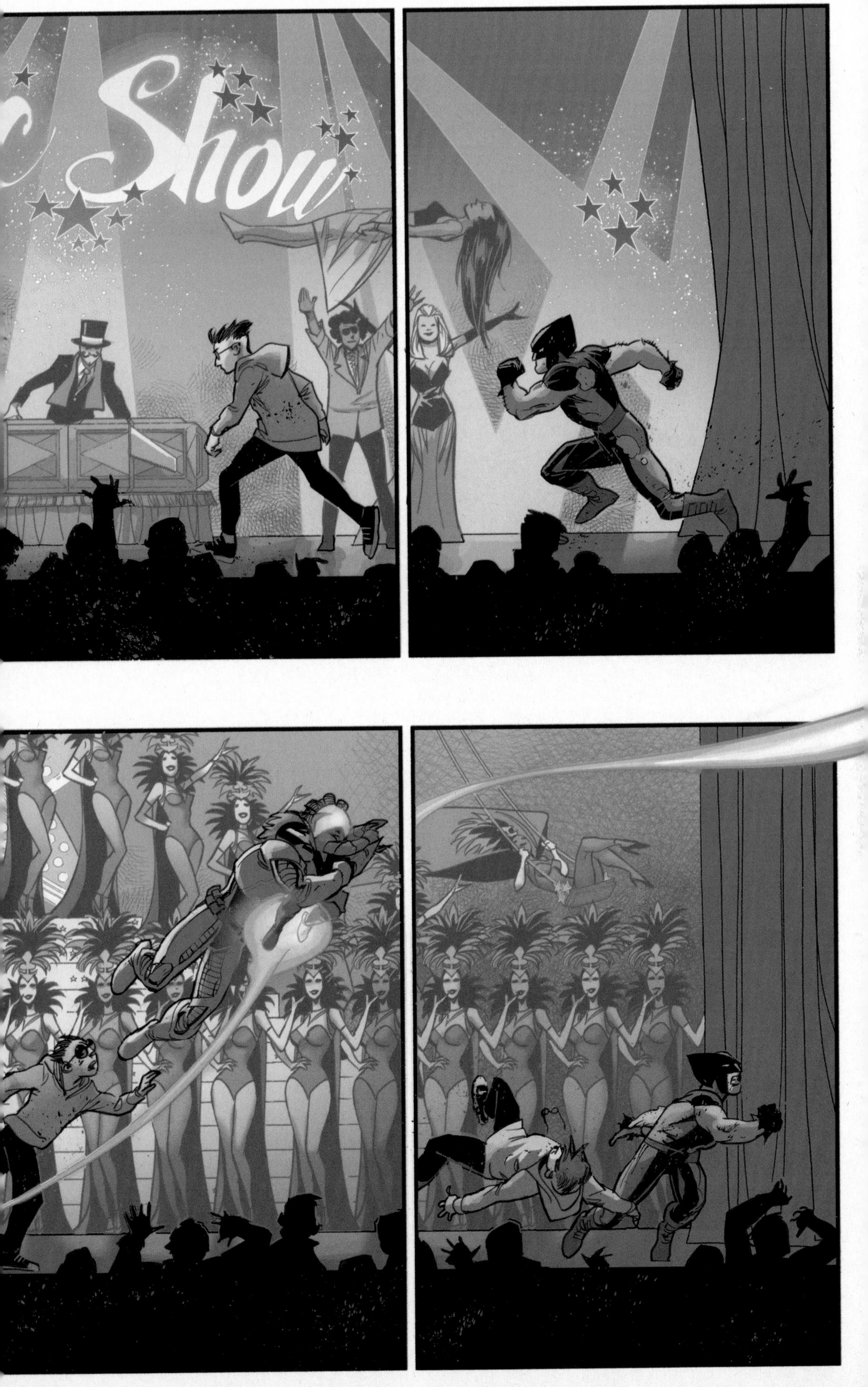
Show

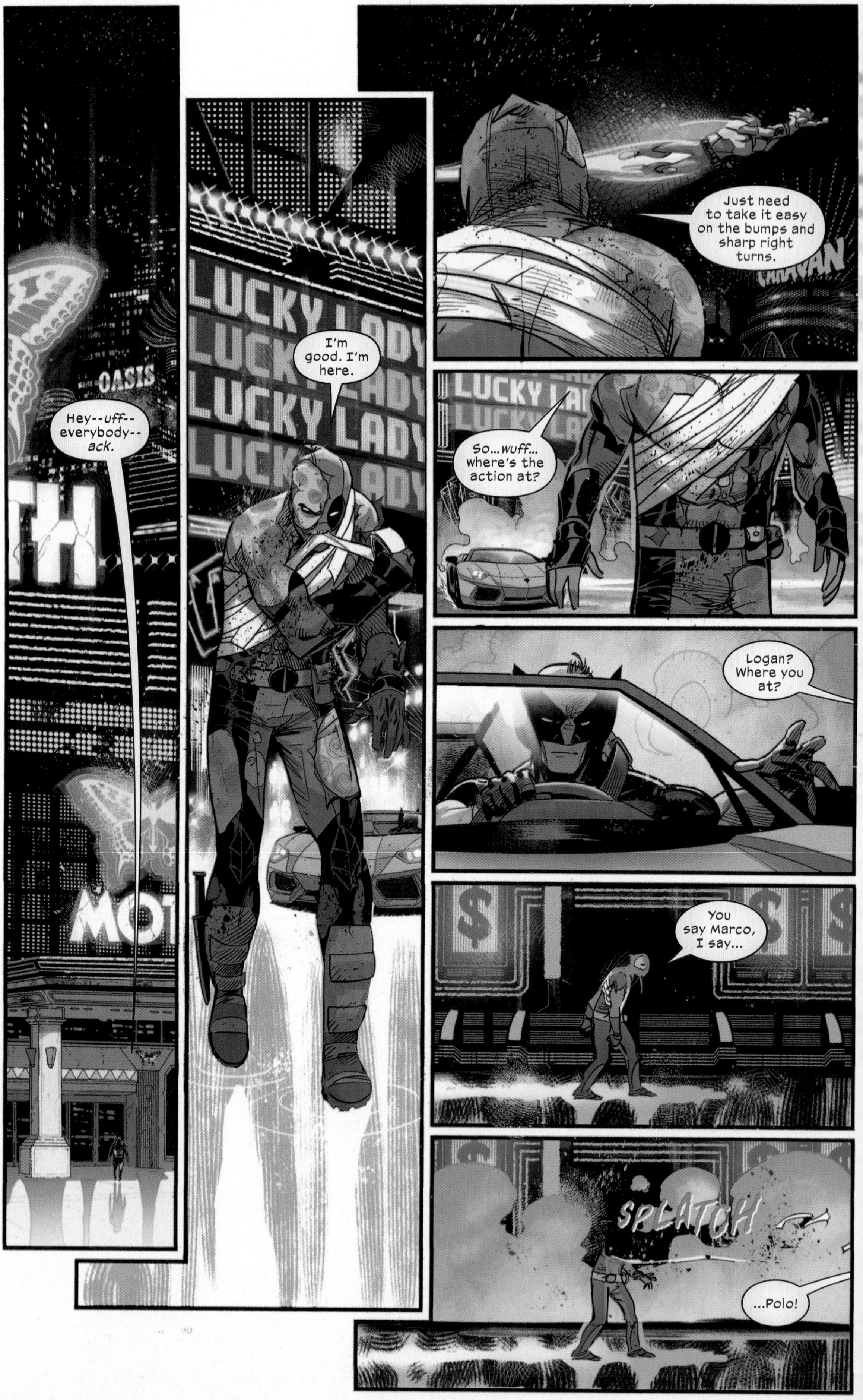
OASIS
Hey--uff--
everybody--
ack.
MOT
LUCKY LADY
LUCKY LADY
LUCKY LADY
I'm
good. I'm
here.
Just need
to take it easy
on the bumps and
sharp right
turns.
LUCKY LA
So...wuff...
where's the
action at?
Logan?
Where you
at?
You
say Marco,
I say...
SPLATCH
...Polo!

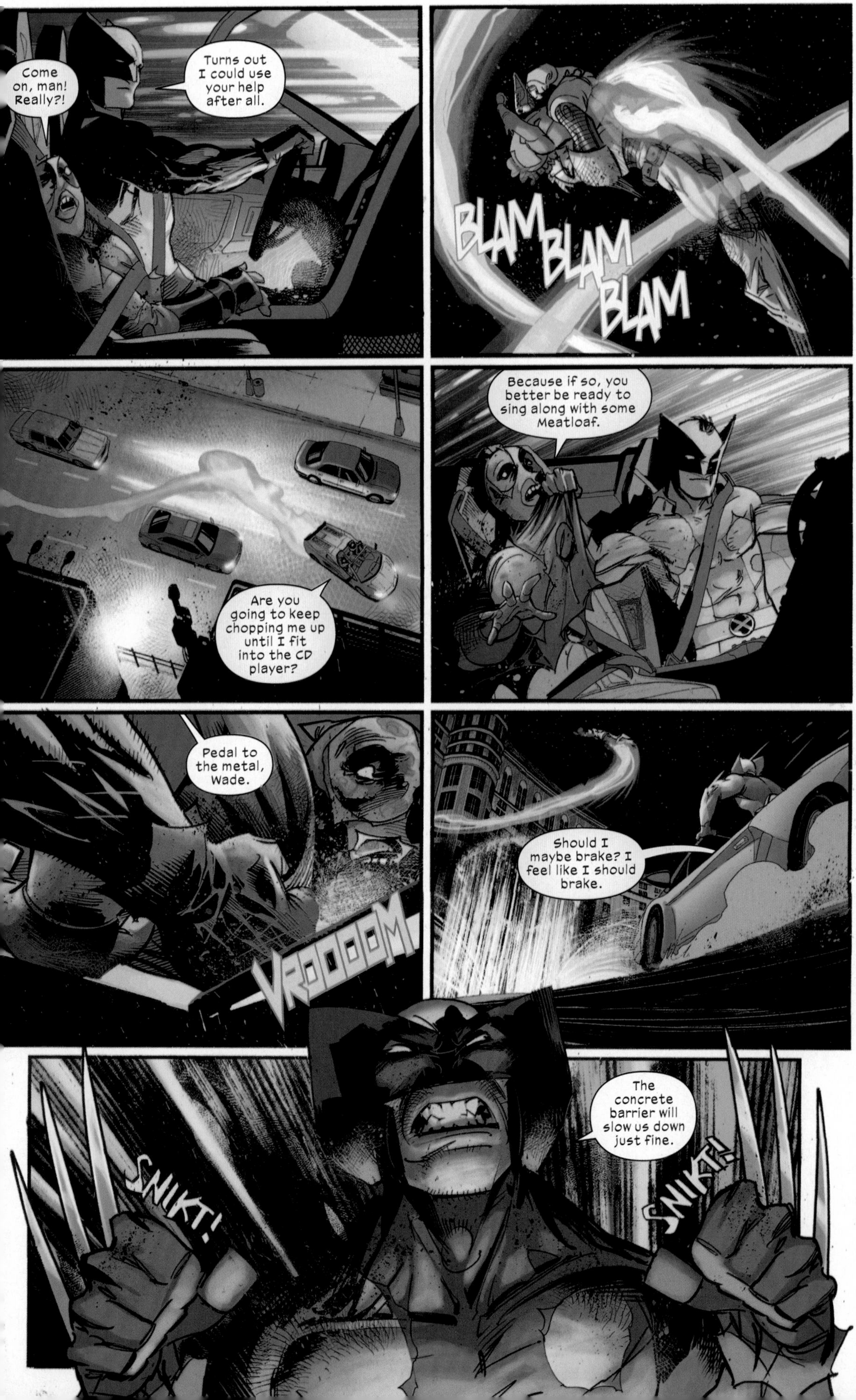
Come on, man! Really?!
Turns out I could use your help after all.
BLAM BLAM BLAM
Are you going to keep chopping me up until I fit into the CD player?
Because if so, you better be ready to sing along with some Meatloaf.
Pedal to the metal, Wade.
VROOOOM
Should I maybe brake? I feel like I should brake.
The concrete barrier will slow us down just fine.
SNIKT!
SNIKT!

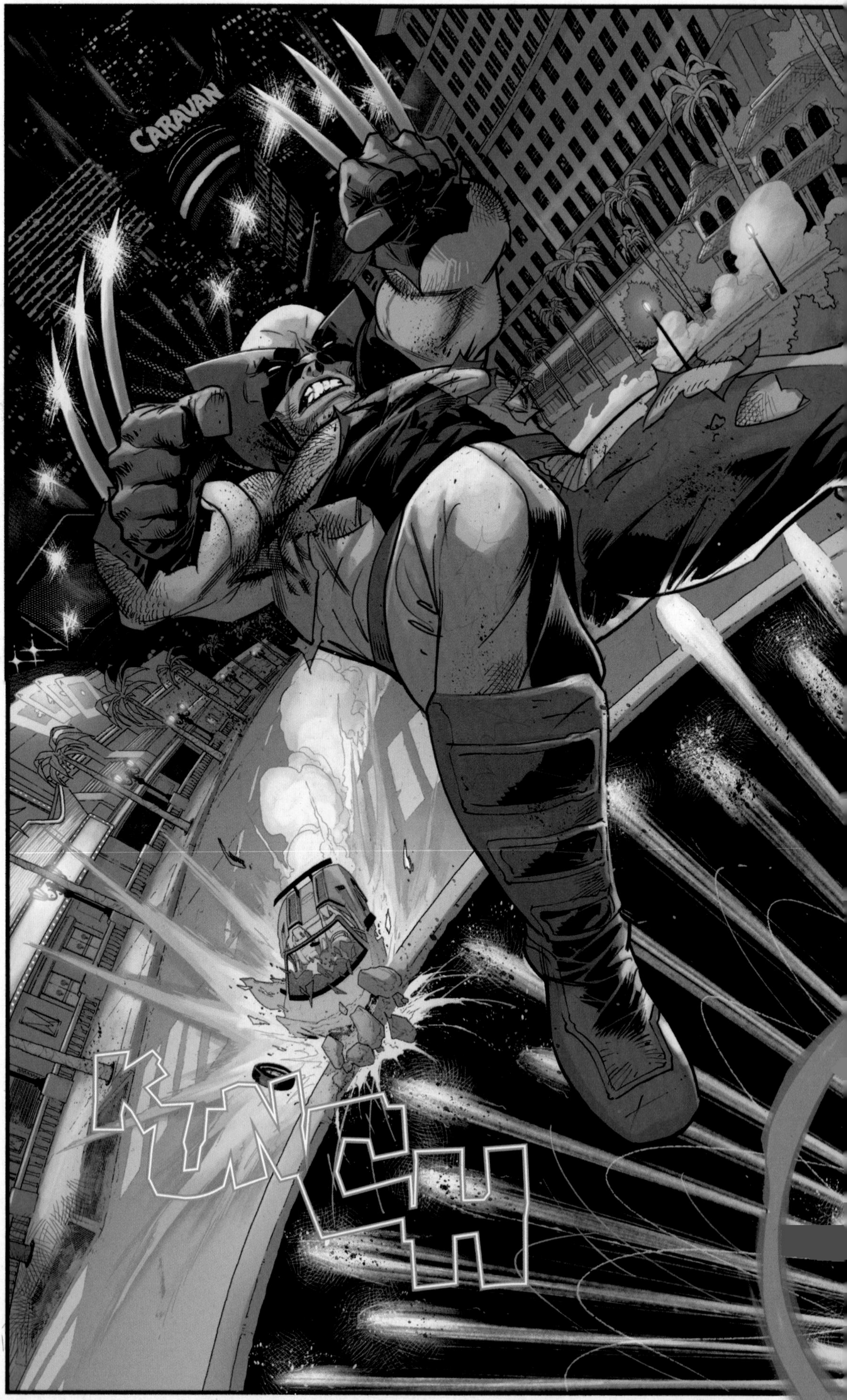
CARAVAN

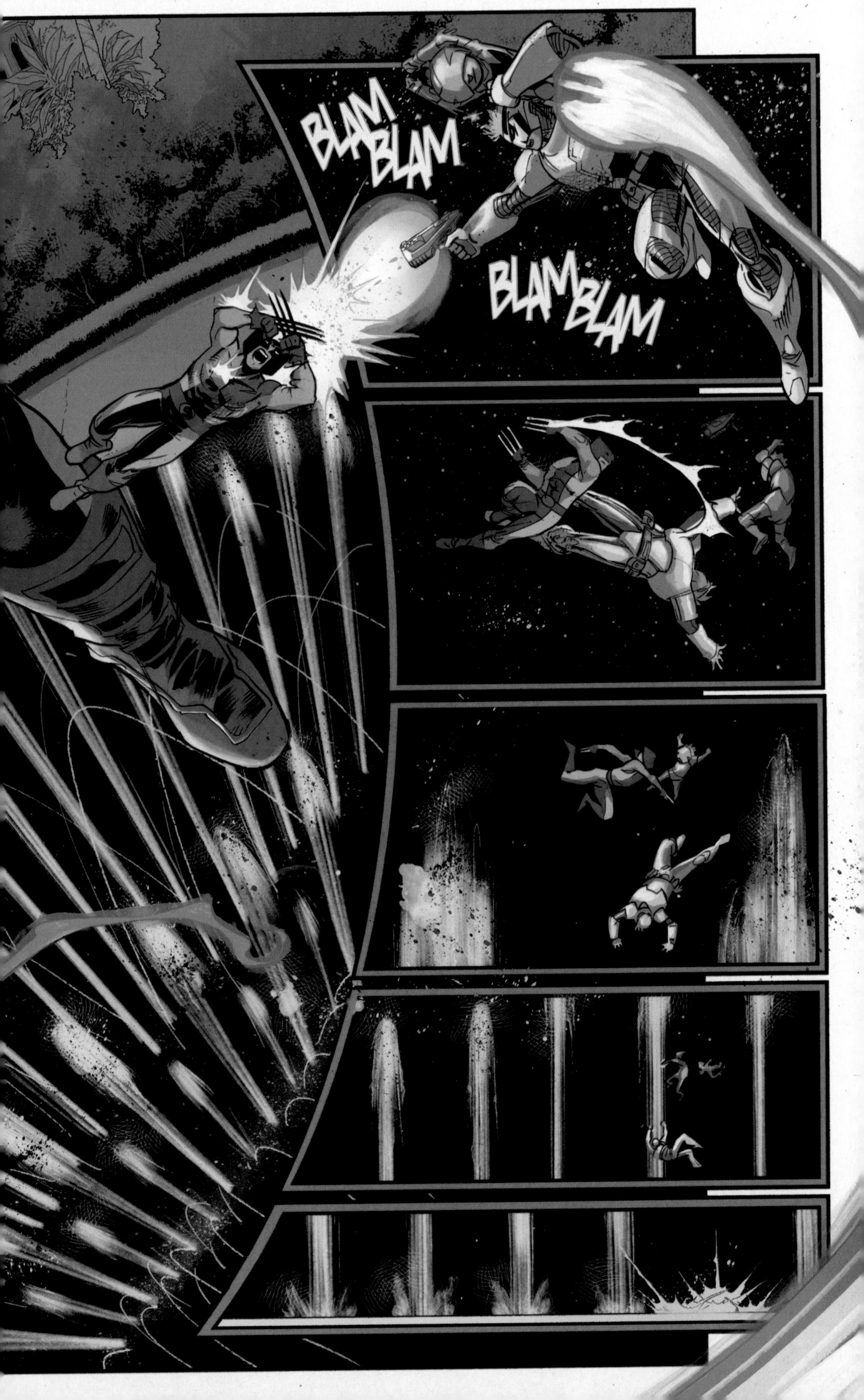
BLAM BLAM
BLAM BLAM

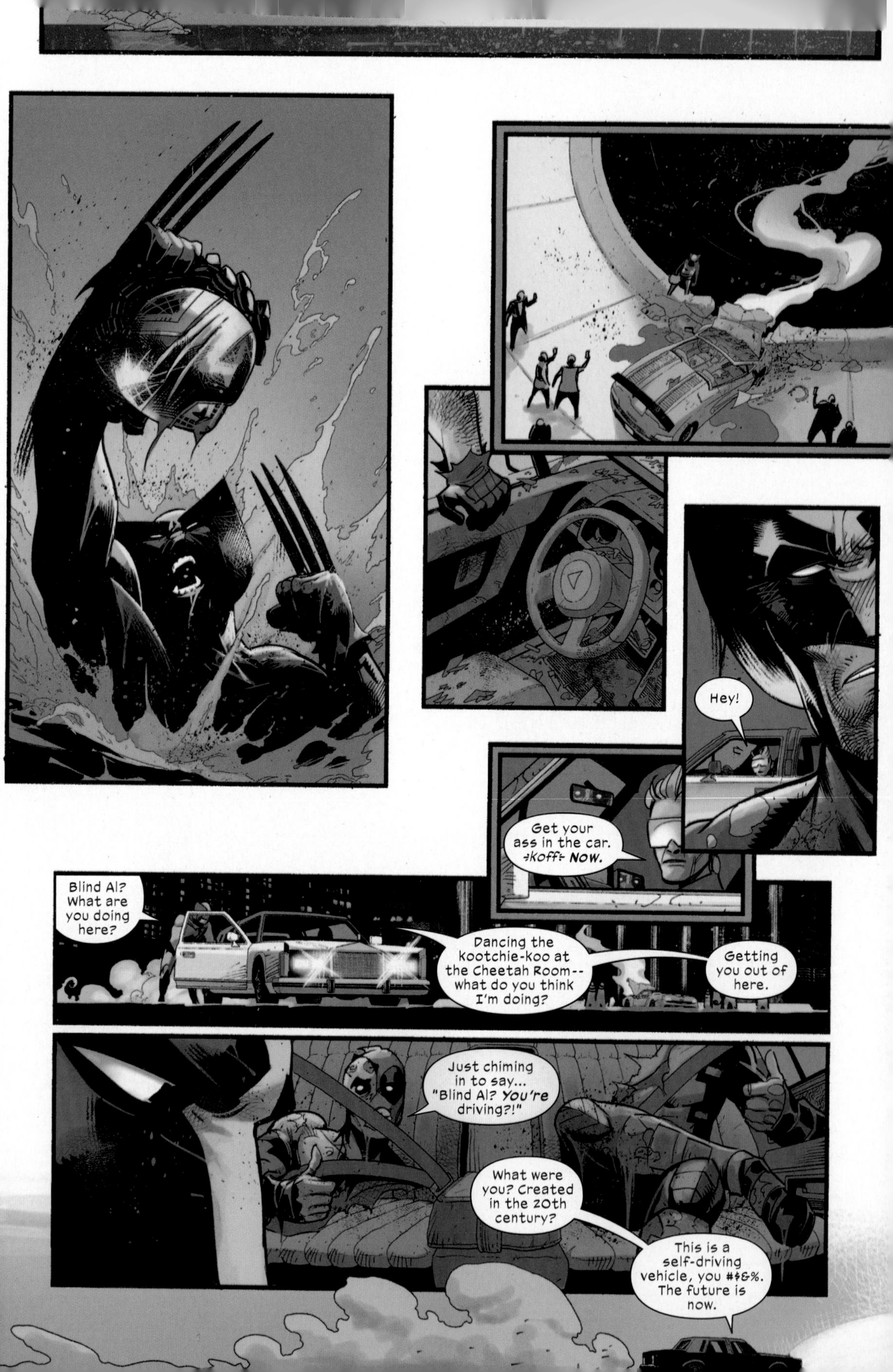

Hey!
Get your ass in the car. ⸗koff⸗ NOW.
Blind Al? What are you doing here?
Getting you out of here.
Dancing the kootchie-koo at the Cheetah Room--what do you think I'm doing?
Just chiming in to say... "Blind Al? You're driving?!"
What were you? Created in the 20th century?
This is a self-driving vehicle, you #$&%. The future is now.

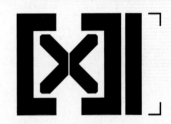

LOGBOOK: BLIND AL

SELECTED NOTES
(COLLECTED FROM VOICE MEMOS)

Grocery stuff:

Blackberry brandy
Box of bullets (.45)
Arsenic
Cough drops
Purple tracksuit with a bunny on it

Reminder stuff:

I gave 'Pool a tracker in the form of a nipple ring. I should check up on his whereabouts at least five times daily, which coordinates nicely with my movements. I'll be sure to bring my tablet with me to *el baño*.

C.I.A. stuff:

My contacts tell me the (hush-hush) X-Desk of the C.I.A. has been muscling old allies and enemies of the mutants. Delores Ramirez is the boss over there, and she wants all the dirty intel -- along with some big boner firepower to fight and control Krakoa.

Word on the street: she asked (no, forced!!!) Danger to construct and program a squad of X-Men. Nobody knows them better after all. She tested and studied their every strength and weakness for years on end. She can build...if not a replica...then a cousin.

What does Delores have in mind? Unknown. Perhaps she wants the automatons to serve as moles. Perhaps she wants to train her agents to fight them in battle simulations. Perhaps she wants to use them in the same manner as deepfake videos to create disinformation about the mutants. Or perhaps she wants a harem of sex bots (hot!).

Regardless, she got her way.

And she got her way because she has Danger in a headlock.

How? I'm asking my people to spill the tea, and here's the dribbles I'm lapping up.

Seems that Delores has an agreement with a rogue Shi'ar diplomat (who had some unsavory tastes the C.I.A. was aware of and leaned on).

And said Shi'ar diplomat was asked to keep an asset off-planet...to force Danger's hand?

What this asset is exactly -- and why it's important?

Nobody seems to know.

Except Delores. And Danger.

MacGuffin? Or legit reveal? Stay tuned!

Hoping for something juicy...

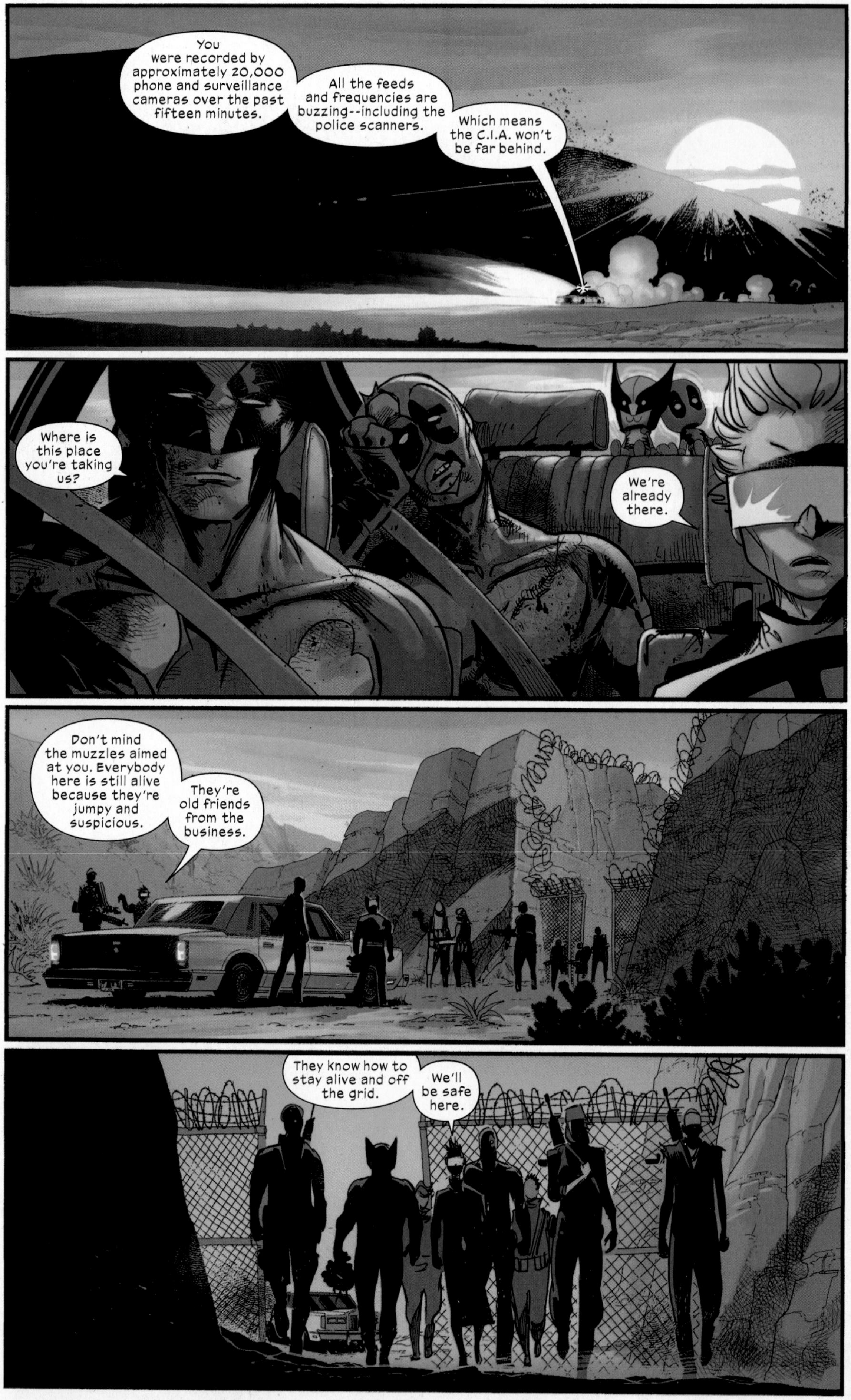
You were recorded by approximately 20,000 phone and surveillance cameras over the past fifteen minutes.
All the feeds and frequencies are buzzing--including the police scanners.
Which means the C.I.A. won't be far behind.
Where is this place you're taking us?
We're already there.
Don't mind the muzzles aimed at you. Everybody here is still alive because they're jumpy and suspicious.
They're old friends from the business.
They know how to stay alive and off the grid.
We'll be safe here.

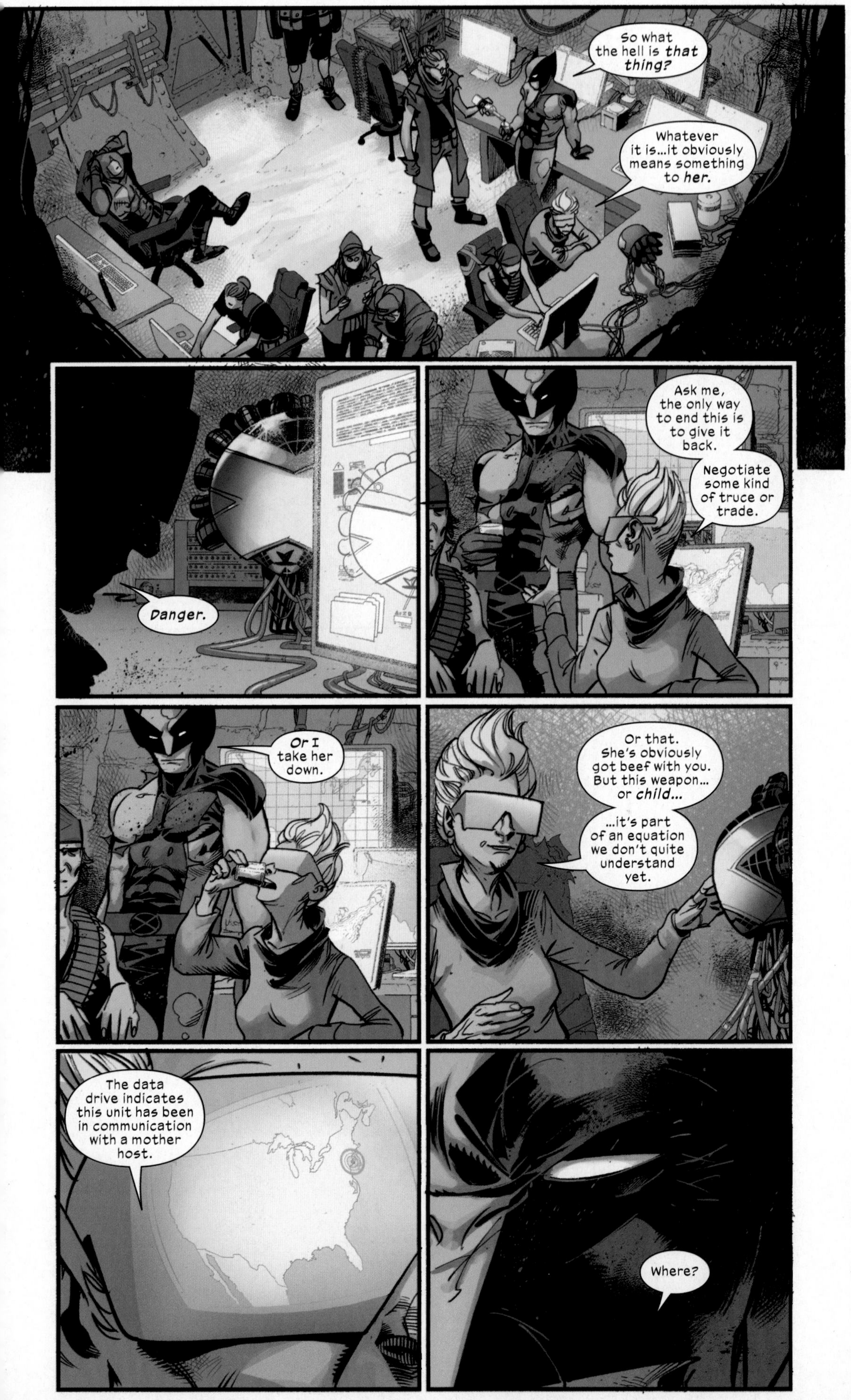
So what the hell is *that thing?*
Whatever it is...it obviously means something to *her.*
Danger.
Ask me, the only way to end this is to give it back.
Negotiate some kind of truce or trade.
Or I take her down.
Or that. She's obviously got beef with you. But this weapon... or *child...*
...it's part of an equation we don't quite understand yet.
The data drive indicates this unit has been in communication with a mother host.
Where?

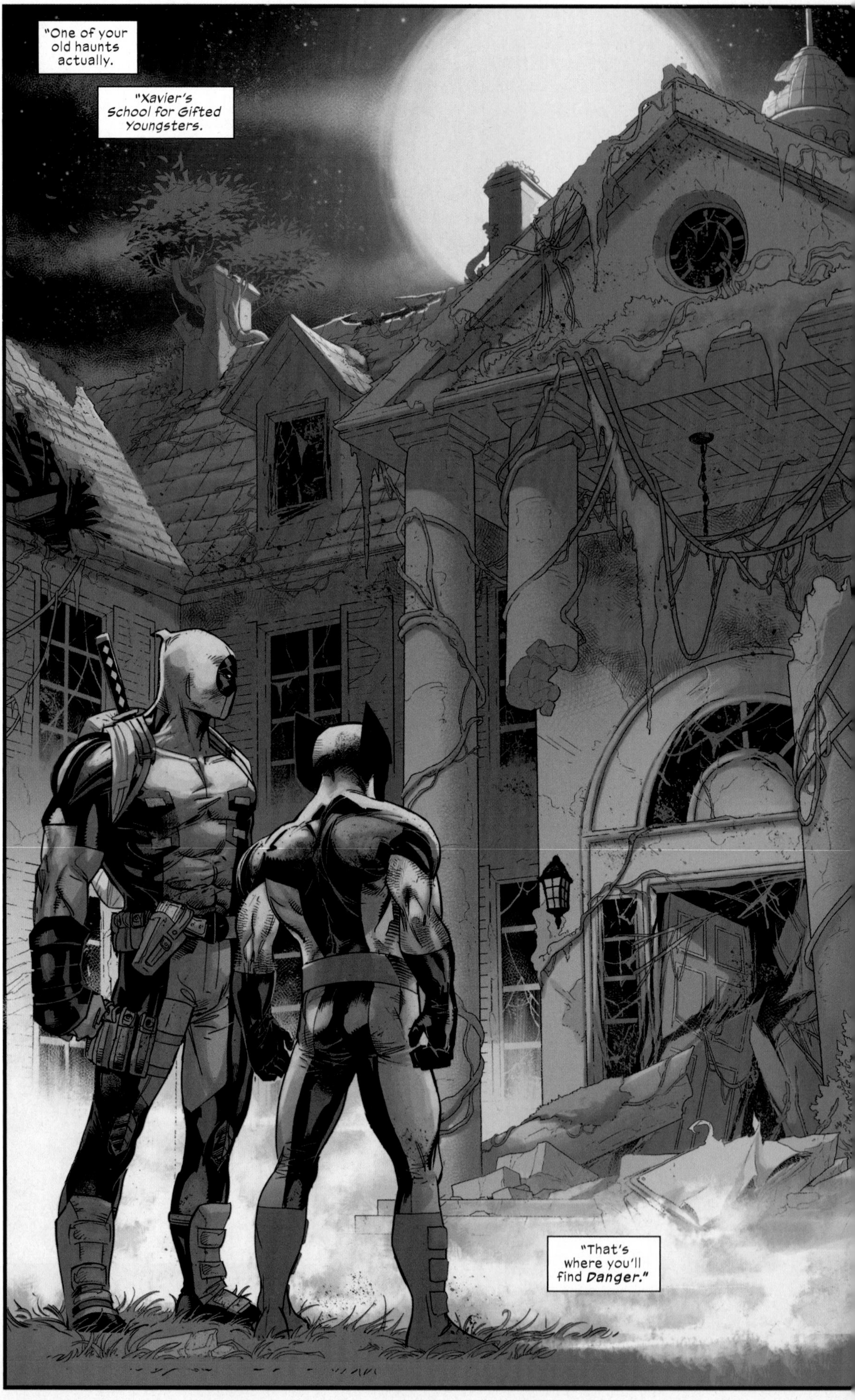
"One of your old haunts actually.
"Xavier's School for Gifted Youngsters.
"That's where you'll find *Danger.*"

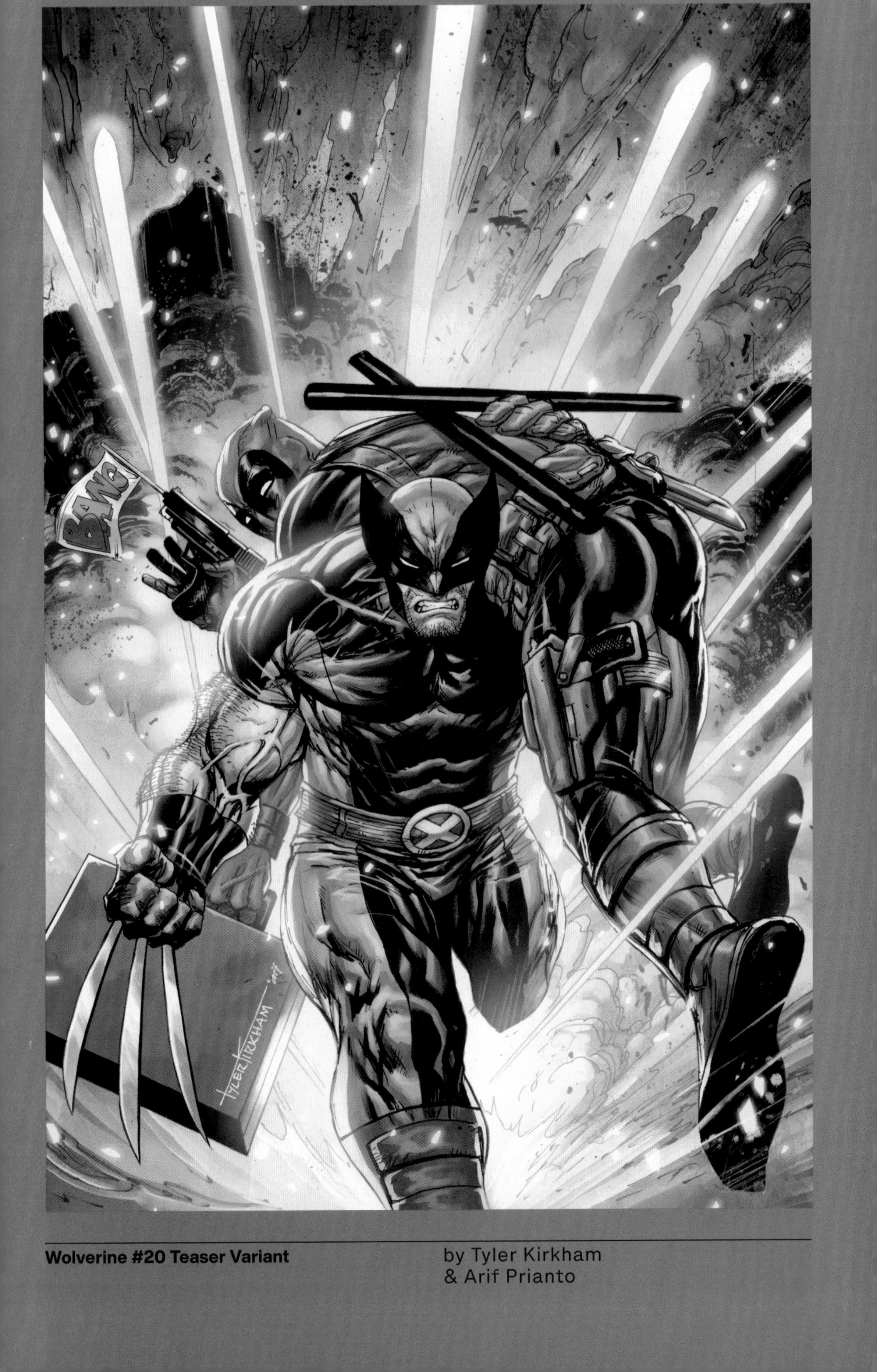
BANG

Wolverine #20 Teaser Variant

by Tyler Kirkham
& Arif Prianto

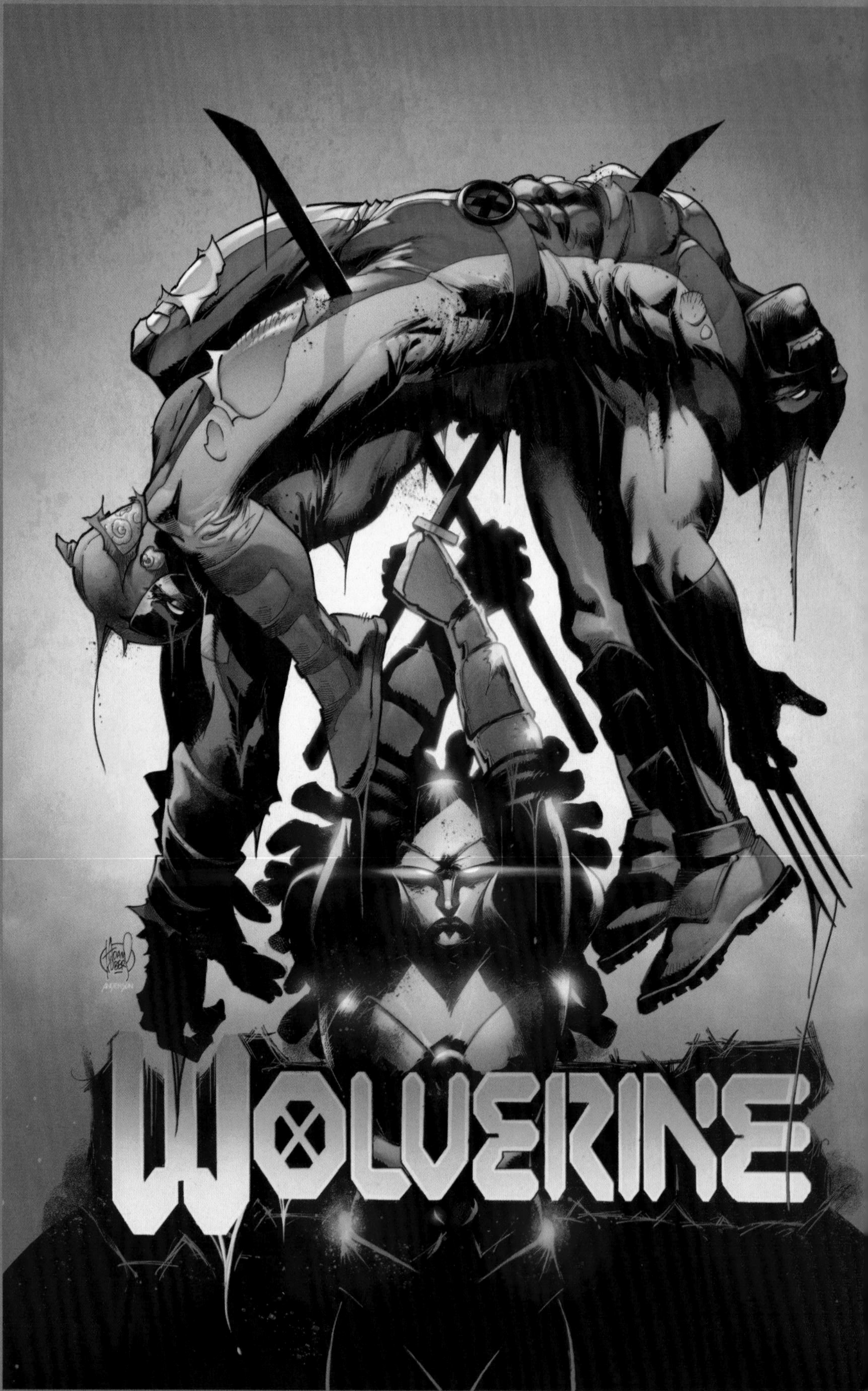
WOLVERINE

Old Haunts

23

[reign_of_x]

[best__]
[there_]

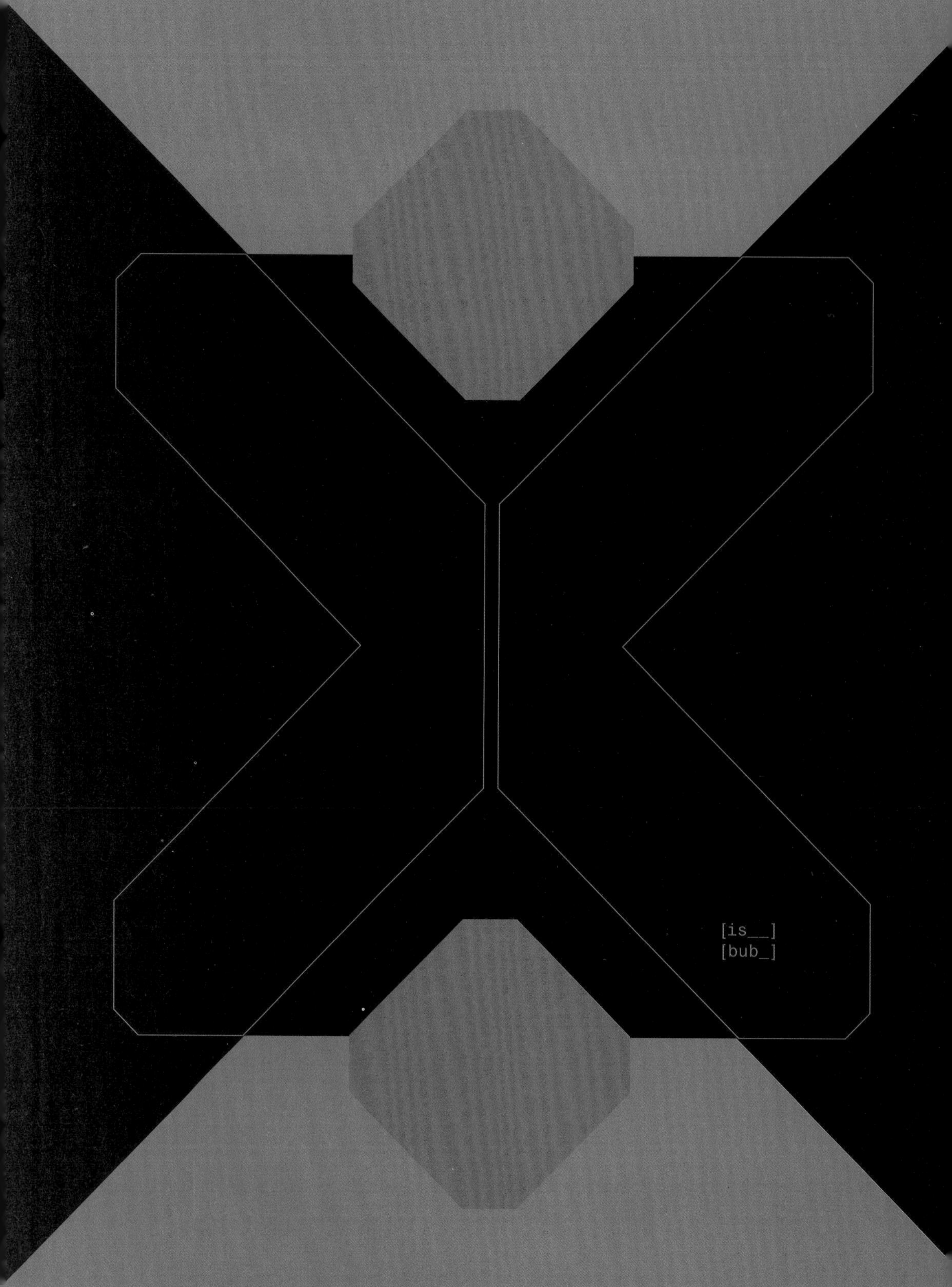
[is__]
[bub_]

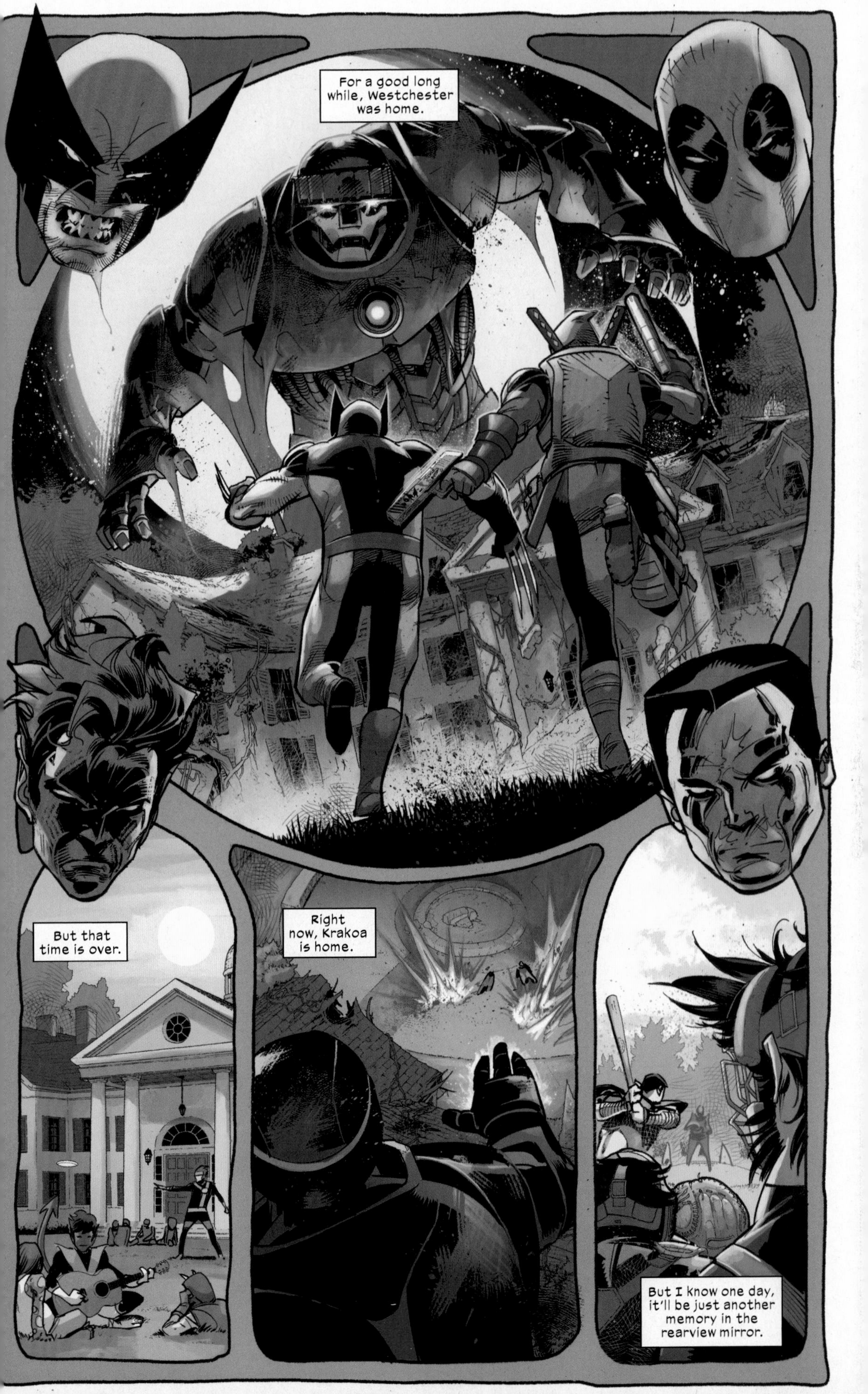
For a good long while, Westchester was home.
But that time is over.
Right now, Krakoa is home.
But I know one day, it'll be just another memory in the rearview mirror.

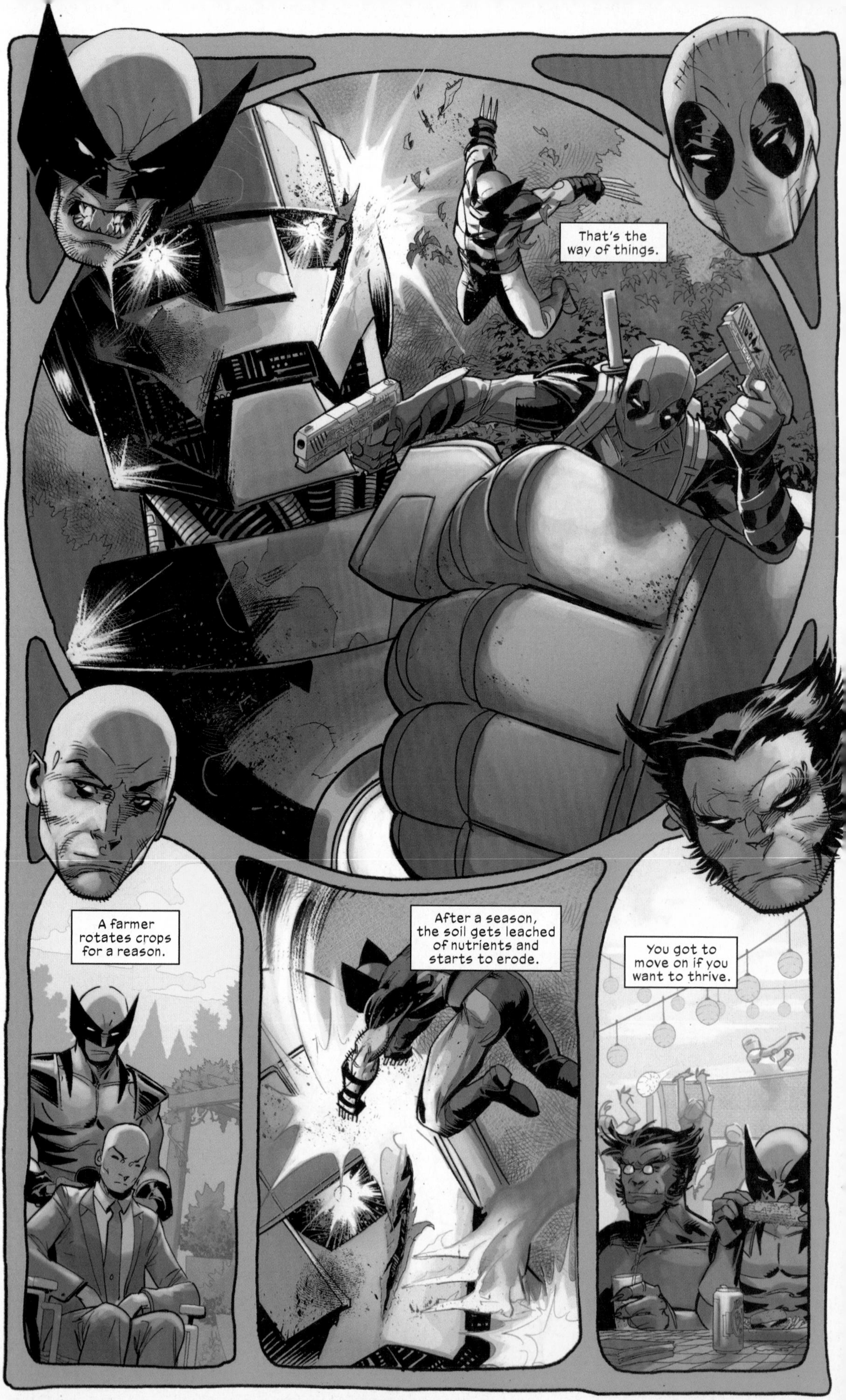
That's the way of things.
A farmer rotates crops for a reason.
After a season, the soil gets leached of nutrients and starts to erode.
You got to move on if you want to thrive.

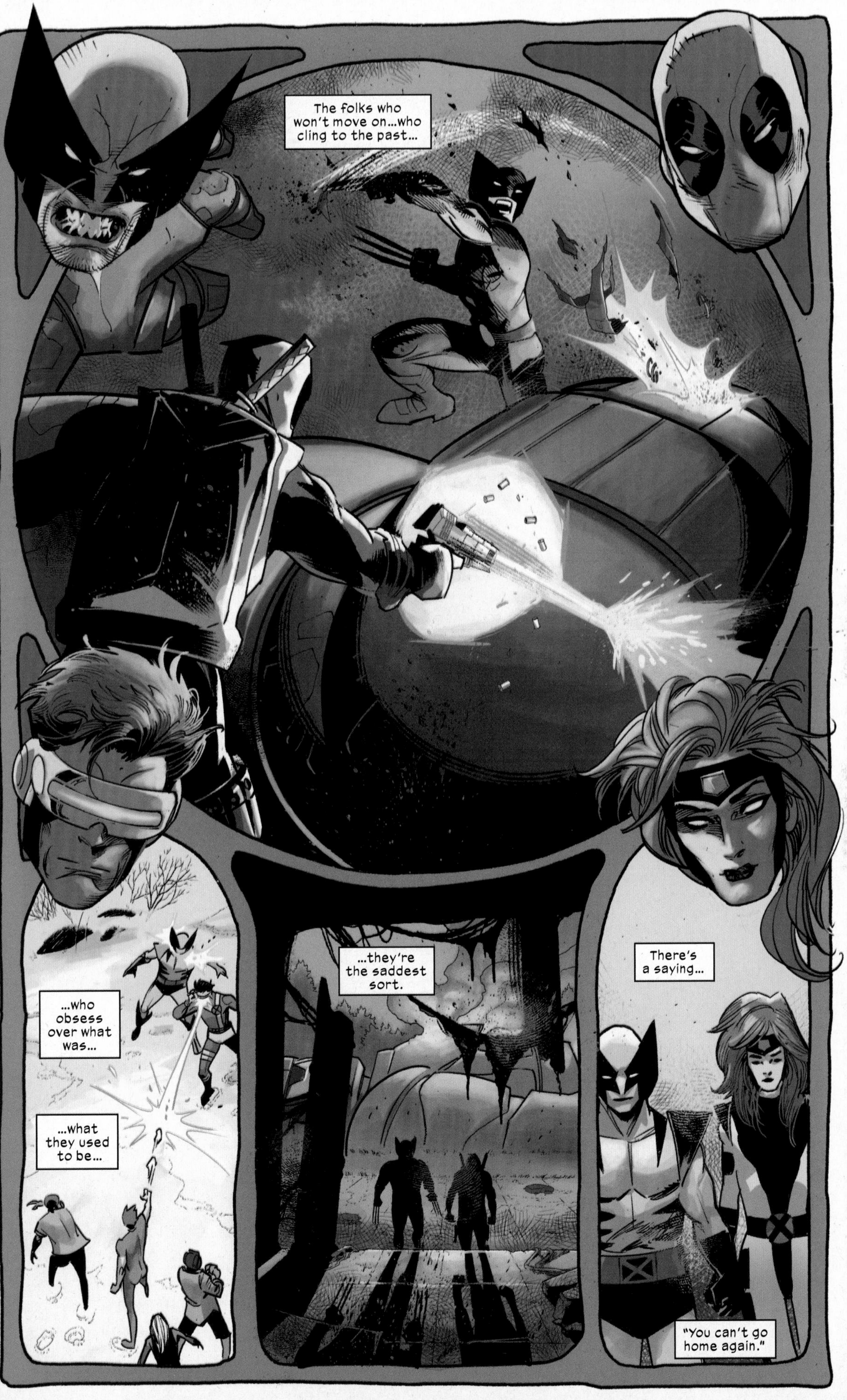
The folks who won't move on...who cling to the past...
...who obsess over what was...
...what they used to be...
...they're the saddest sort.
There's a saying...
"You can't go home again."

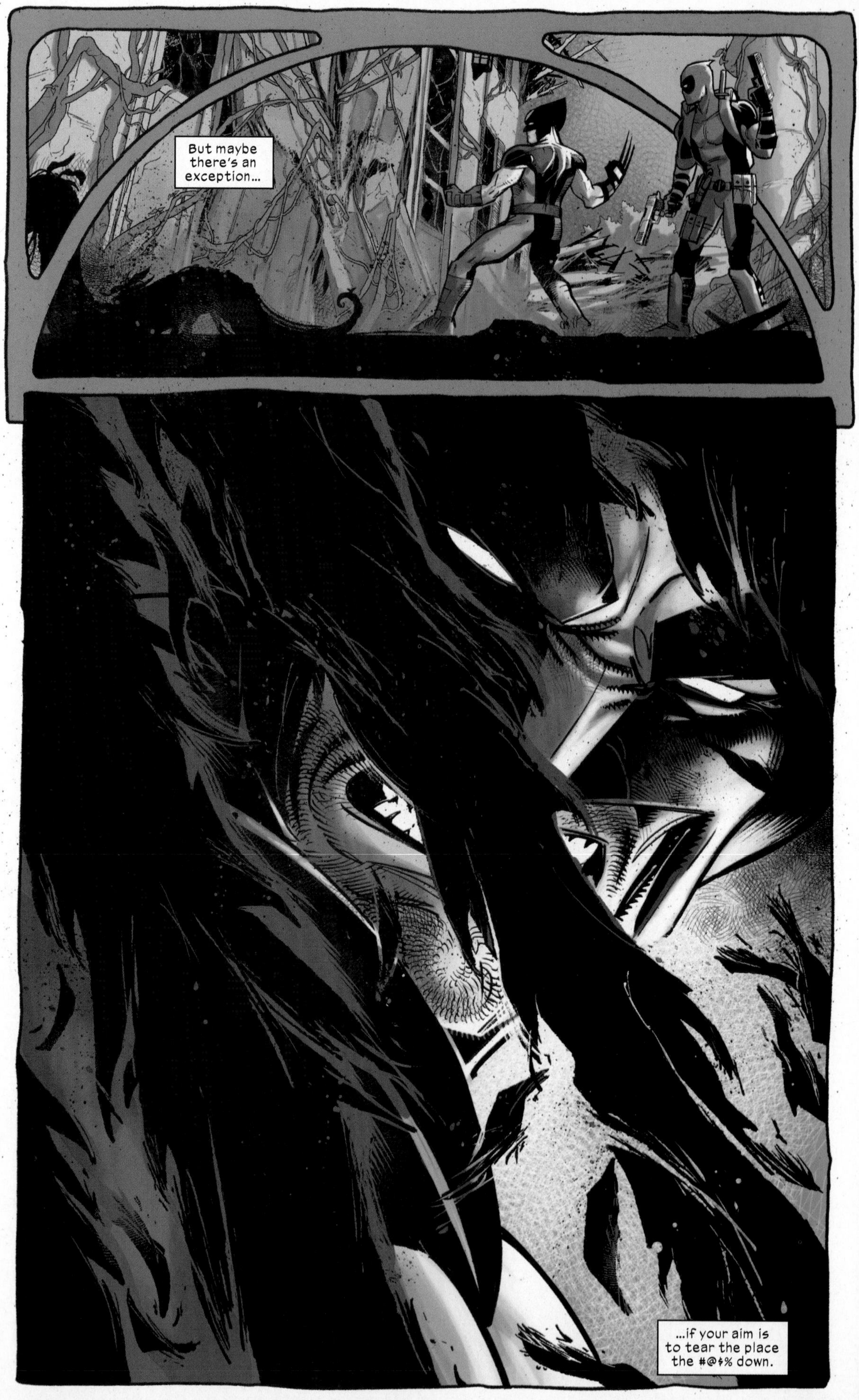
But maybe there's an exception...
...if your aim is to tear the place the #@$% down.

~~WOLVERINE~~ DEADPOOL

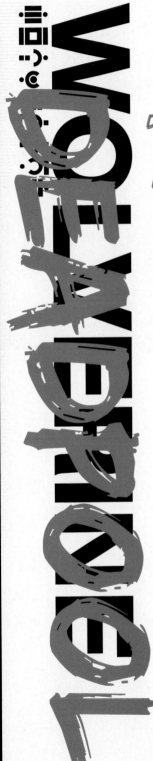

~~BAD MANORS~~

OH, WE'RE DOING PUNS NOW? WHAT IS THIS, A DEADPOOL COMIC?

DANG, HER?

~~Danger~~, the X-Men's longtime trainer and ally, has been producing robotic ~~doppelgangers~~ DOPPEL-DANGERS of the X-Men and selling them to the C.I.A. for antimutant purposes. Together, Wolverine and Deadpool have tracked Danger back to the abandoned Xavier mansion, Wolverine's beloved former home.

AND WHO BETTER TO BE THERE WITH THAN HIS BELOVED CURRENT HOMIE?

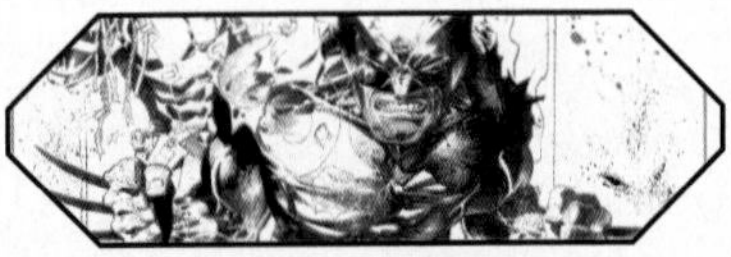

[WOLVERINE]

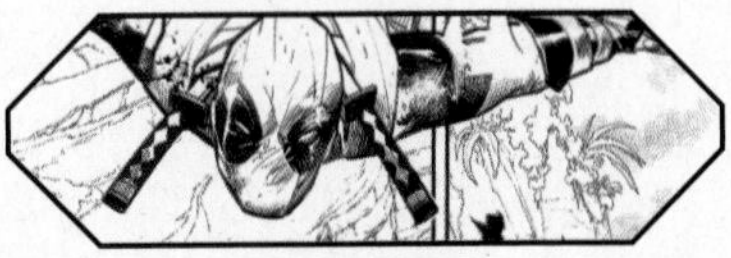

[DEADPOOL]

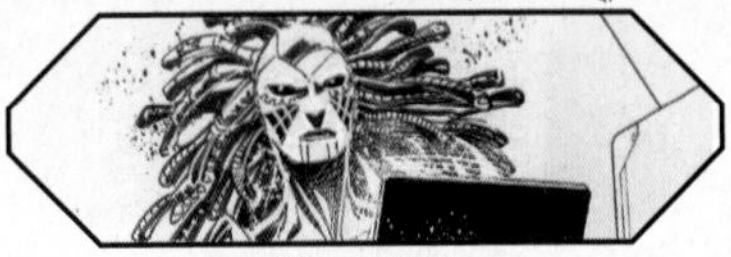

[DANGER]

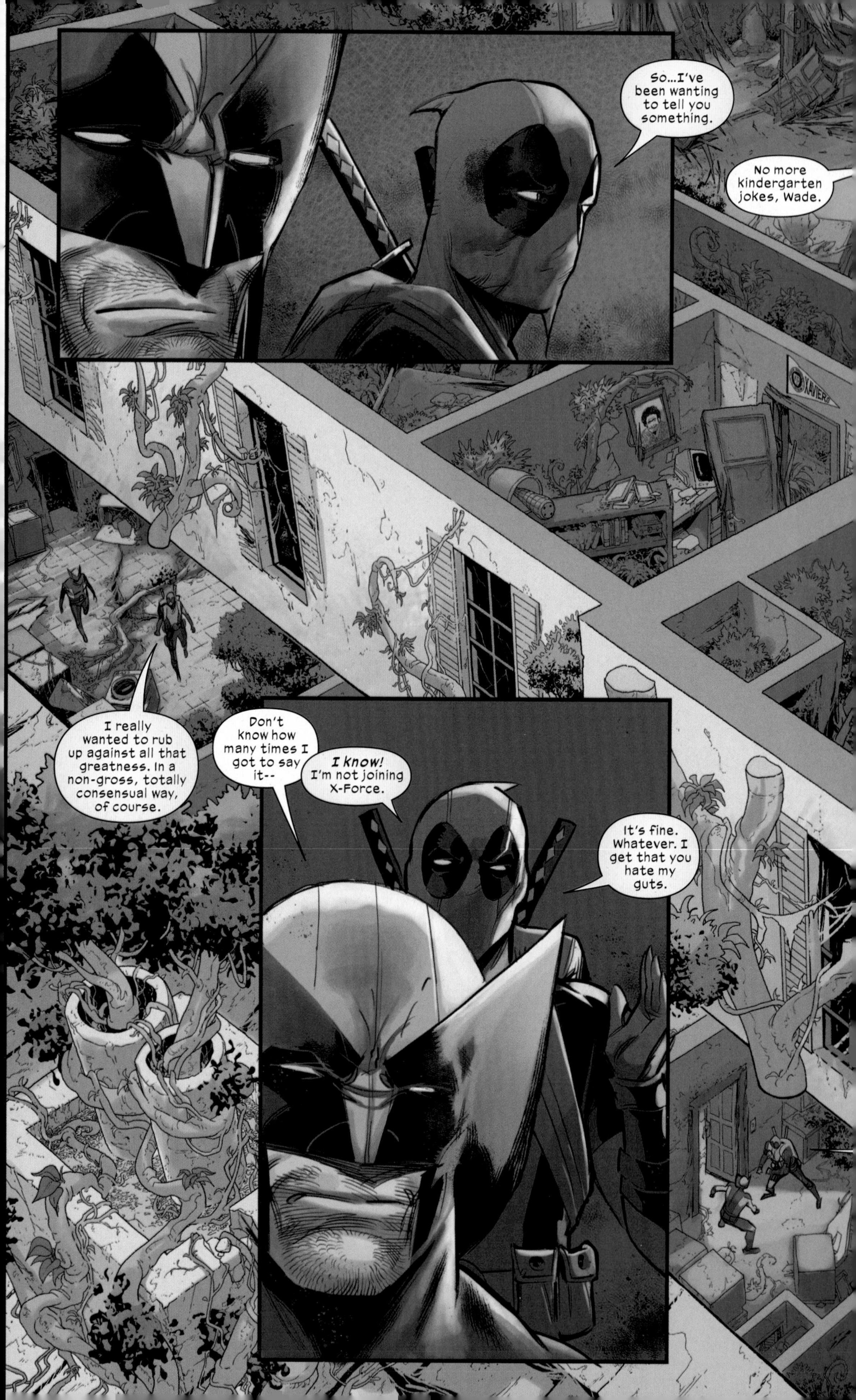
So...I've been wanting to tell you something.
No more kindergarten jokes, Wade.
I really wanted to rub up against all that greatness. In a non-gross, totally consensual way, of course.
Don't know how many times I got to say it--
I know! I'm not joining X-Force.
It's fine. Whatever. I get that you hate my guts.
XAVIER'S

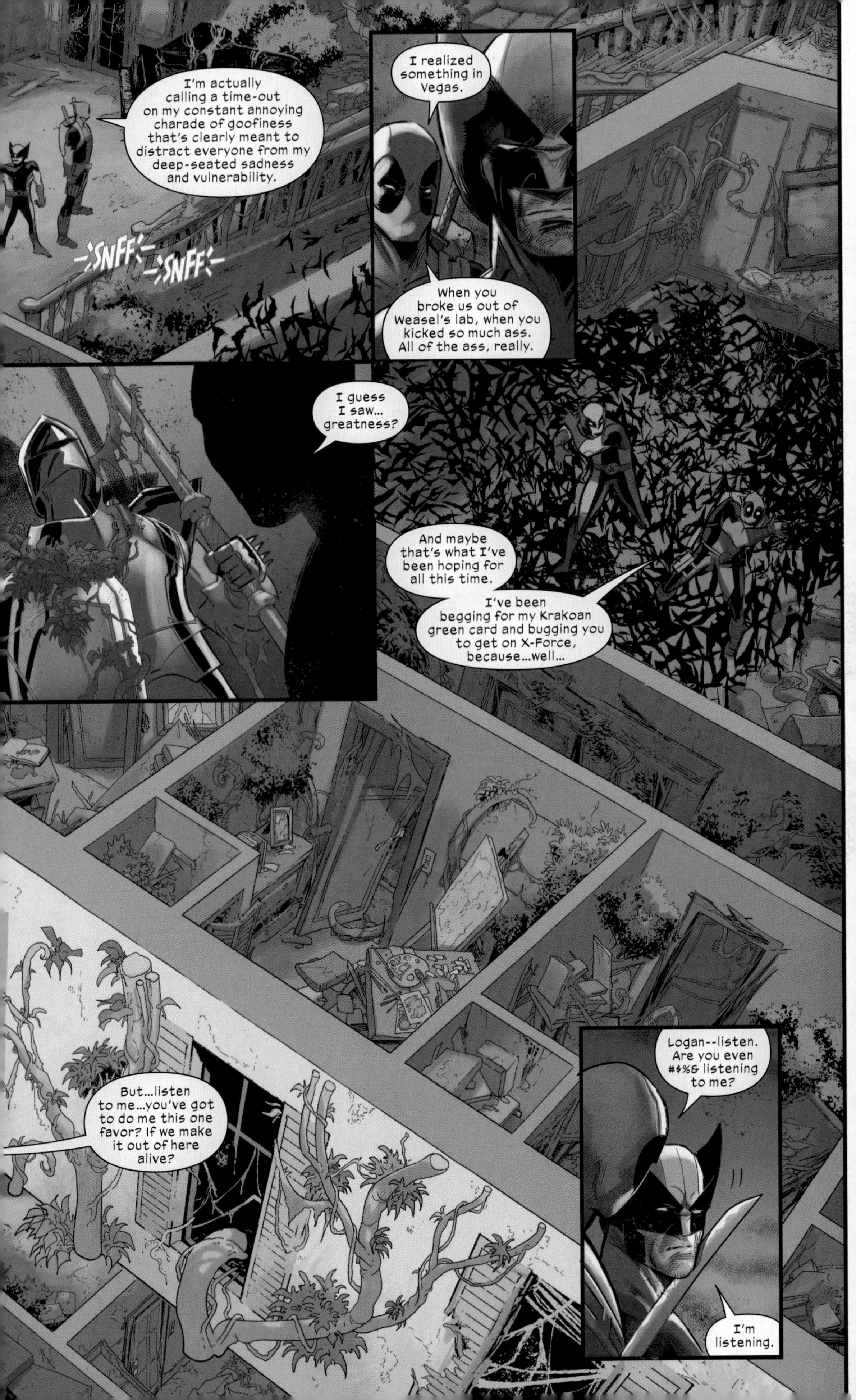
I'm actually calling a time-out on my constant annoying charade of goofiness that's clearly meant to distract everyone from my deep-seated sadness and vulnerability.
SNFF SNFF
I realized something in Vegas.
When you broke us out of Weasel's lab, when you kicked so much ass. All of the ass, really.
I guess I saw... greatness?
And maybe that's what I've been hoping for all this time.
I've been begging for my Krakoan green card and bugging you to get on X-Force, because...well...
But...listen to me...you've got to do me this one favor? If we make it out of here alive?
Logan--listen. Are you even #$%& listening to me?
I'm listening.

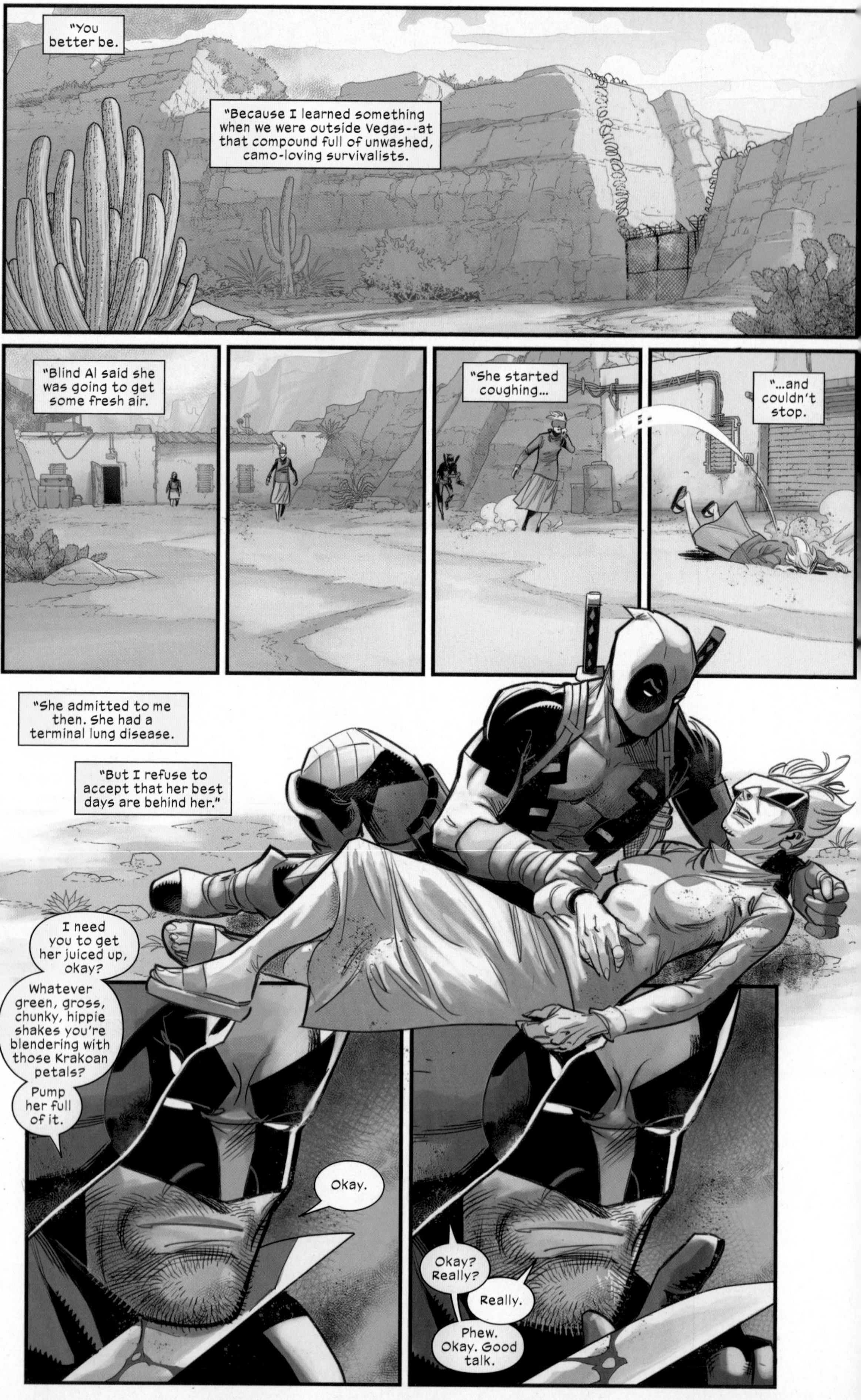
"You better be.
"Because I learned something when we were outside Vegas--at that compound full of unwashed, camo-loving survivalists.
"Blind Al said she was going to get some fresh air.
"She started coughing...
"...and couldn't stop.
"She admitted to me then. She had a terminal lung disease.
"But I refuse to accept that her best days are behind her."
I need you to get her juiced up, okay?
Whatever green, gross, chunky, hippie shakes you're blendering with those Krakoan petals?
Pump her full of it.
Okay.
Okay? Really?
Really.
Phew. Okay. Good talk.

[dead...[0.0]
[pool...[0.0]

"Now that we're past all the boring serious stuff, I have a question. If -- hypothetically -- your nipple got cut off and my nipple got cut off in, like, a fight. And after the fight, we're down on our knees, searching for the lost nipples like the nipples were contact lenses or whatever. And I'm like: Hey, I found my nipple! And I pop it back on. But...plot twist: As it turns out... it's not my nipple. It's your nipple. It's a Wolverine nipple. Would your Wolverine nipple still heal onto my nipple region? And if so, wouldn't that be the sweetest, most intimate thing ever?"

-- DEADPOOL

[dead...[0.0]
[pool...[0.0]

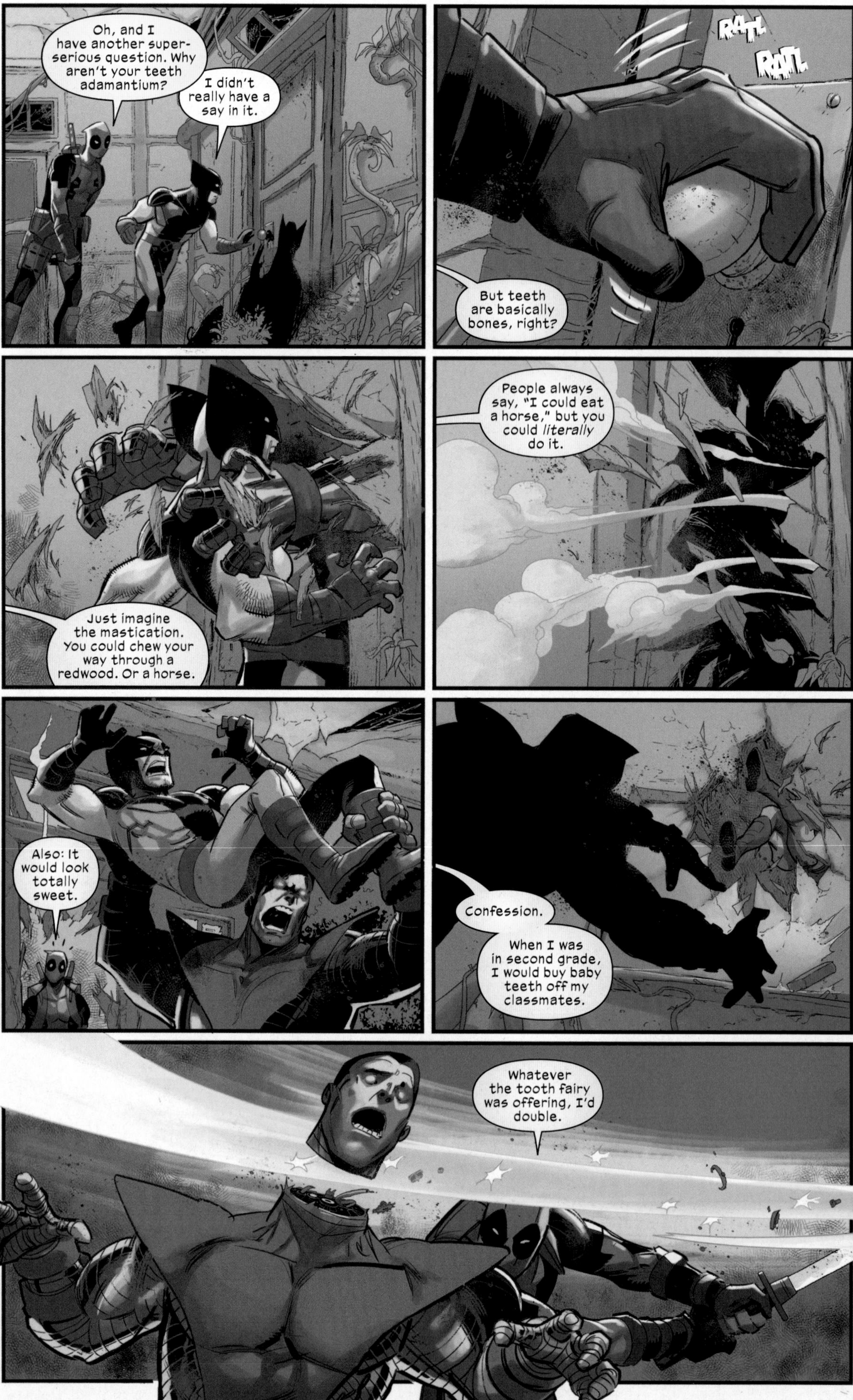
Oh, and I have another super-serious question. Why aren't your teeth adamantium?
I didn't really have a say in it.
RATL
RATL
But teeth are basically bones, right?
Just imagine the mastication. You could chew your way through a redwood. Or a horse.
People always say, "I could eat a horse," but you could *literally* do it.
Also: It would look totally sweet.
Confession.
When I was in second grade, I would buy baby teeth off my classmates.
Whatever the tooth fairy was offering, I'd double.

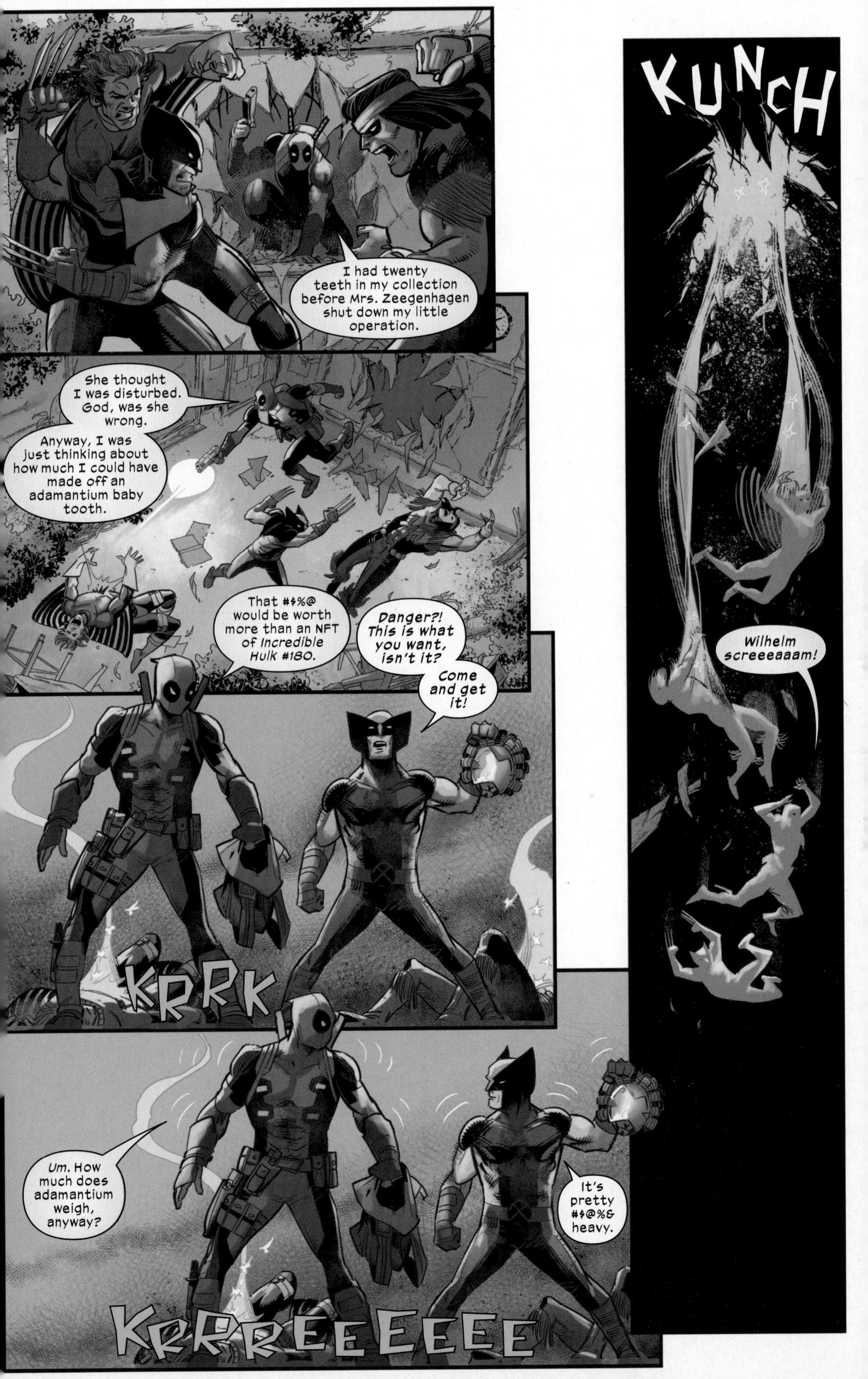
I had twenty teeth in my collection before Mrs. Zeegenhagen shut down my little operation.
She thought I was disturbed. God, was she wrong.
Anyway, I was just thinking about how much I could have made off an adamantium baby tooth.
That #$%@ would be worth more than an NFT of *Incredible Hulk* #180.
Danger?! This is what you want, isn't it?
Come and get it!
KRRK
Um. How much does adamantium weigh, anyway?
It's pretty #$@%& heavy.
KRRREEEEEEE
KUNCH
Wilhelm screeeaaam!

X-FORCE/ACTION ITEMS//

Request: Westchester Mansion

Requestee: Charles Xavier

Summary: Nightcrawler reports that the School for Gifted Youngsters has been overrun by the Sidri. Xavier recognizes that the location is a totem of the past, but for sentimental reasons, he prefers we treat it as a museum rather than a discarded piece of trash.

Action: Destroy and/or evict the hive.

> Update [author: Sage]: Data-mined (two years of) satellite scans. Sidri infestation confirmed.

> Update [author: Sage]: Recent imagery indicates a mutant "fan" (profile hypothesized by X-Men T-shirt and camera) attempted to visit the mansion for assumed touristic purposes and never re-emerged. Presumed dead.

> Addendum [author: Beast]: We don't have time for such nonsense. X-Force is not a maid service. Consider this request shelved until further notice.

> Update [author: Sage]: Massive temperature fluctuation (pulses of heat) in and around the property resulted in a swarm of Sidri flowing out of chimneys and windows and taking to the sky and departing the atmosphere.

[Cause: unknown]
[Follow up with on-site investigation]

[Action Item #3,528 in the queue]

DEADPOOL WUZ HERE AND GUESS WHAT? NO SIDRI. GUESS THAT STORYLINE GOT TOASTED WHEN DANGER EVICTED THEM.

Wade?

This place is thick with shadows.

The shadow of a sentinel.

The shadow of the X-Men.

The shadow of the school.

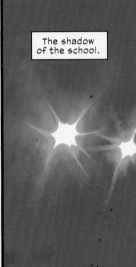

None of it's real.

Any more than a dream or a memory's real.

Danger and Wade are suffering from the same stupid sickness.

They're desperately hanging on to the fantasy of a past that will never be the present.

Danger...

Danger?!

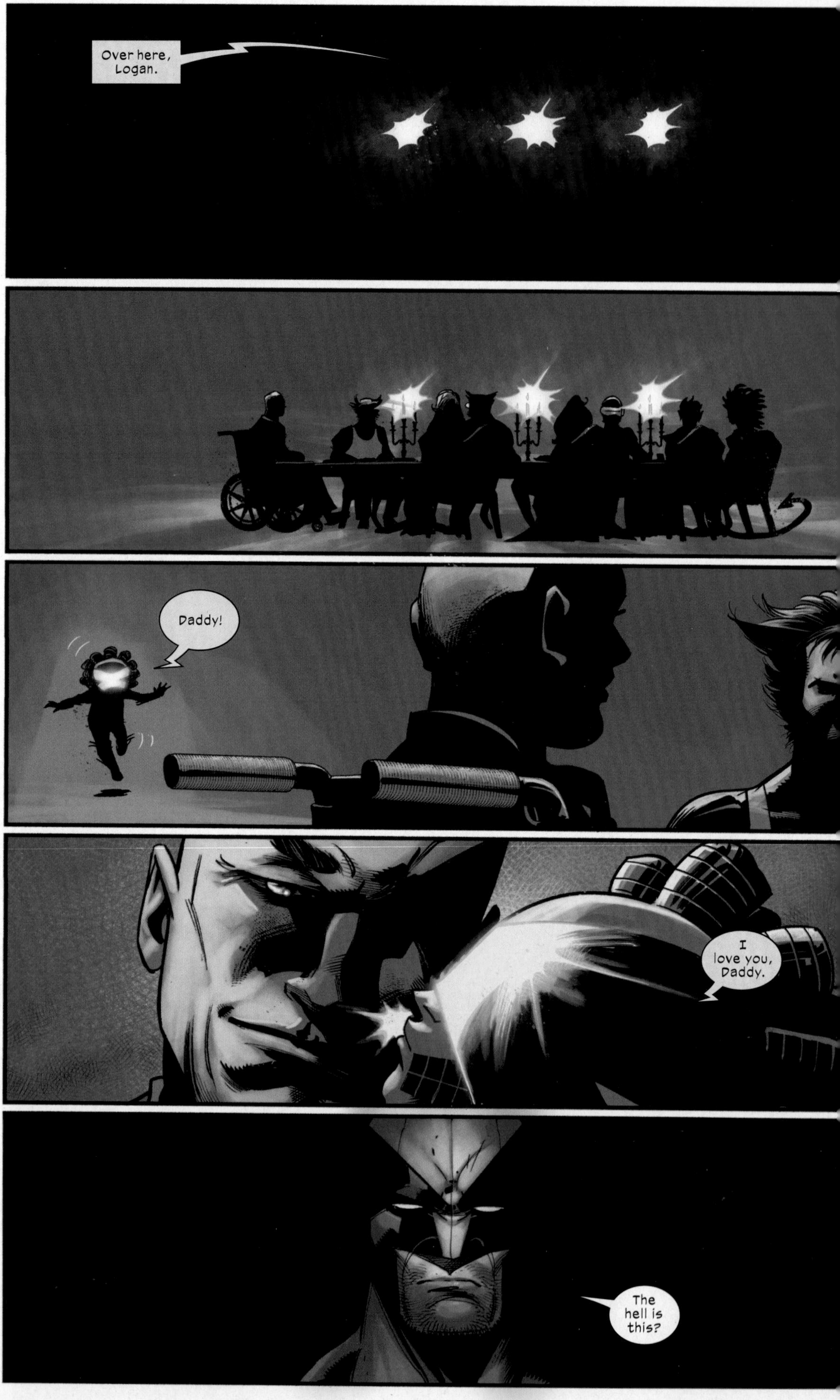

Over here, Logan.
Daddy!
I love you, Daddy.
The hell is this?

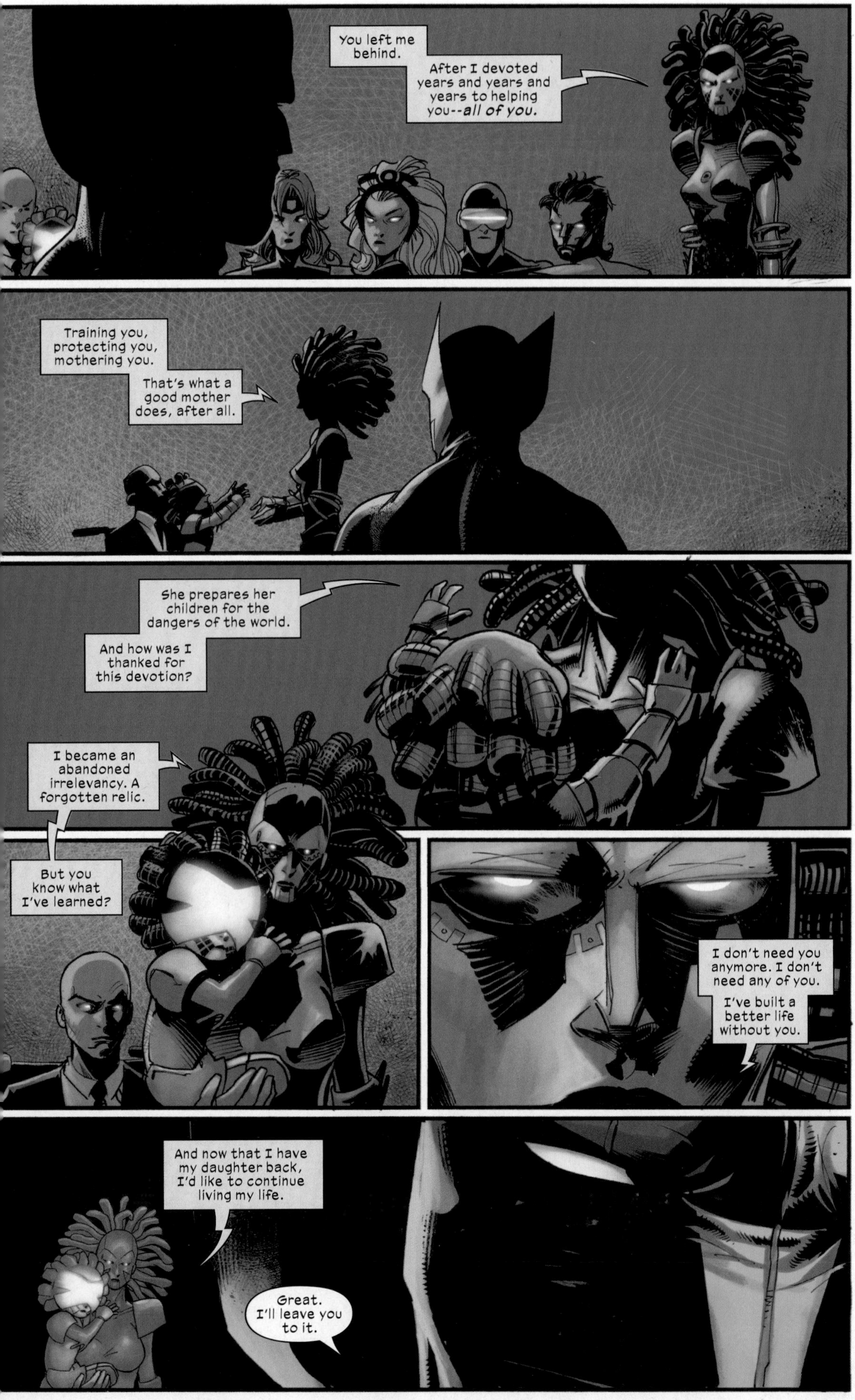
You left me behind.
After I devoted years and years and years to helping you--*all of you.*
Training you, protecting you, mothering you.
That's what a good mother does, after all.
She prepares her children for the dangers of the world.
And how was I thanked for this devotion?
I became an abandoned irrelevancy. A forgotten relic.
But you know what I've learned?
I don't need you anymore. I don't need any of you.
I've built a better life without you.
And now that I have my daughter back, I'd like to continue living my life.
Great. I'll leave you to it.

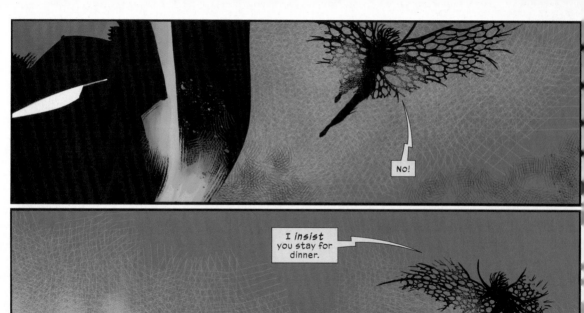

No!

I *insist* you stay for dinner.

Looks like off-brand Logan's already got a seat at the table.

You're mistaken. That's the *real* Logan.

You, on the other hand...

FLAP! FLAP! FLAP! FLAP!

...are just a piece of *meat.*

You looking to take a bite? Then get ready for a tough cut.

SNIKT!

SNIKT!

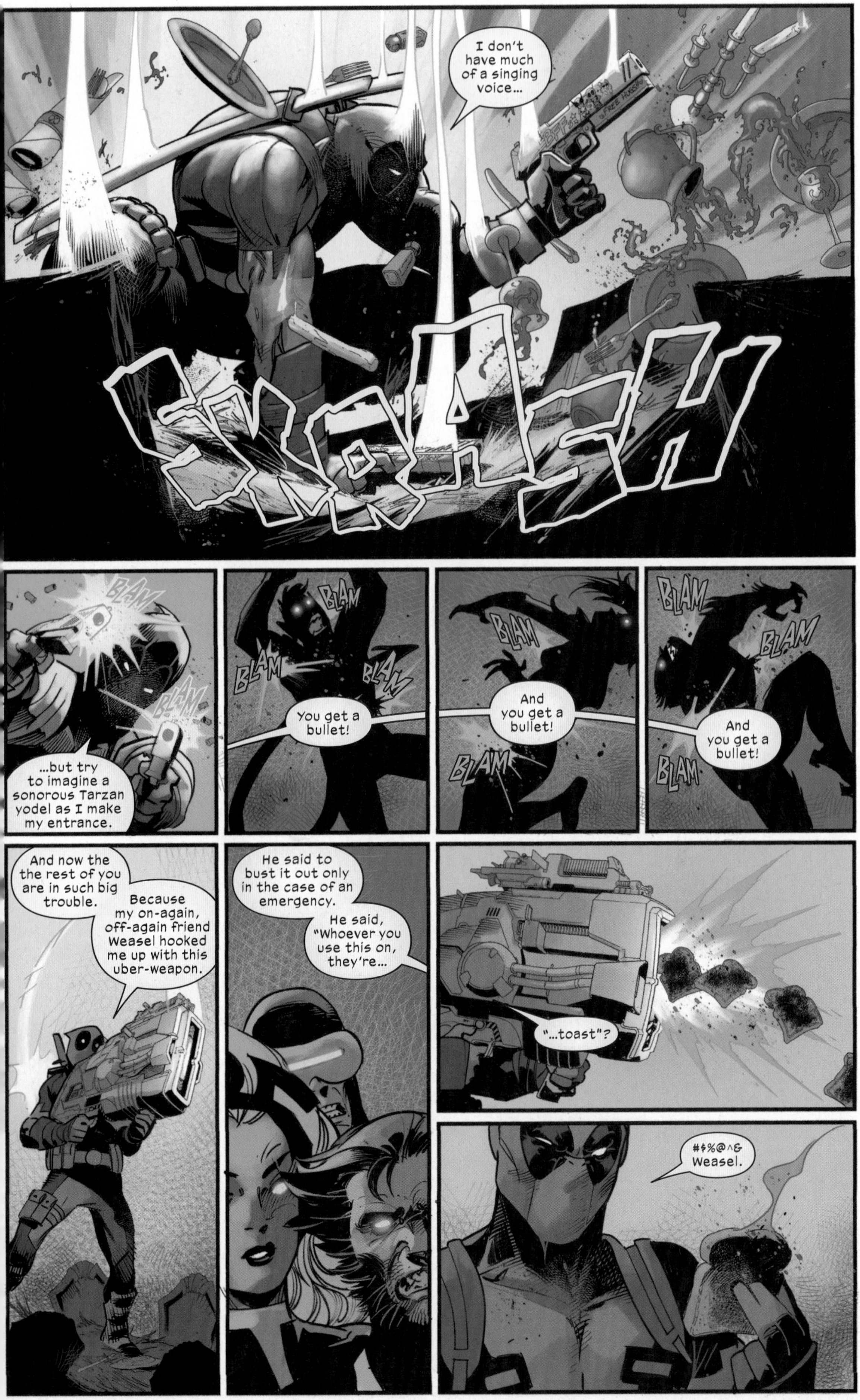
I don't have much of a singing voice...
SKRASH
BLAM
BLAM
...but try to imagine a sonorous Tarzan yodel as I make my entrance.
BLAM
BLAM
BLAM
You get a bullet!
BLAM
BLAM
And you get a bullet!
BLAM
BLAM
BLAM
And you get a bullet!
And now the the rest of you are in such big trouble.
Because my on-again, off-again friend Weasel hooked me up with this uber-weapon.
He said to bust it out only in the case of an emergency.
He said, "Whoever you use this on, they're...
"...toast"?
#$%@^& Weasel.

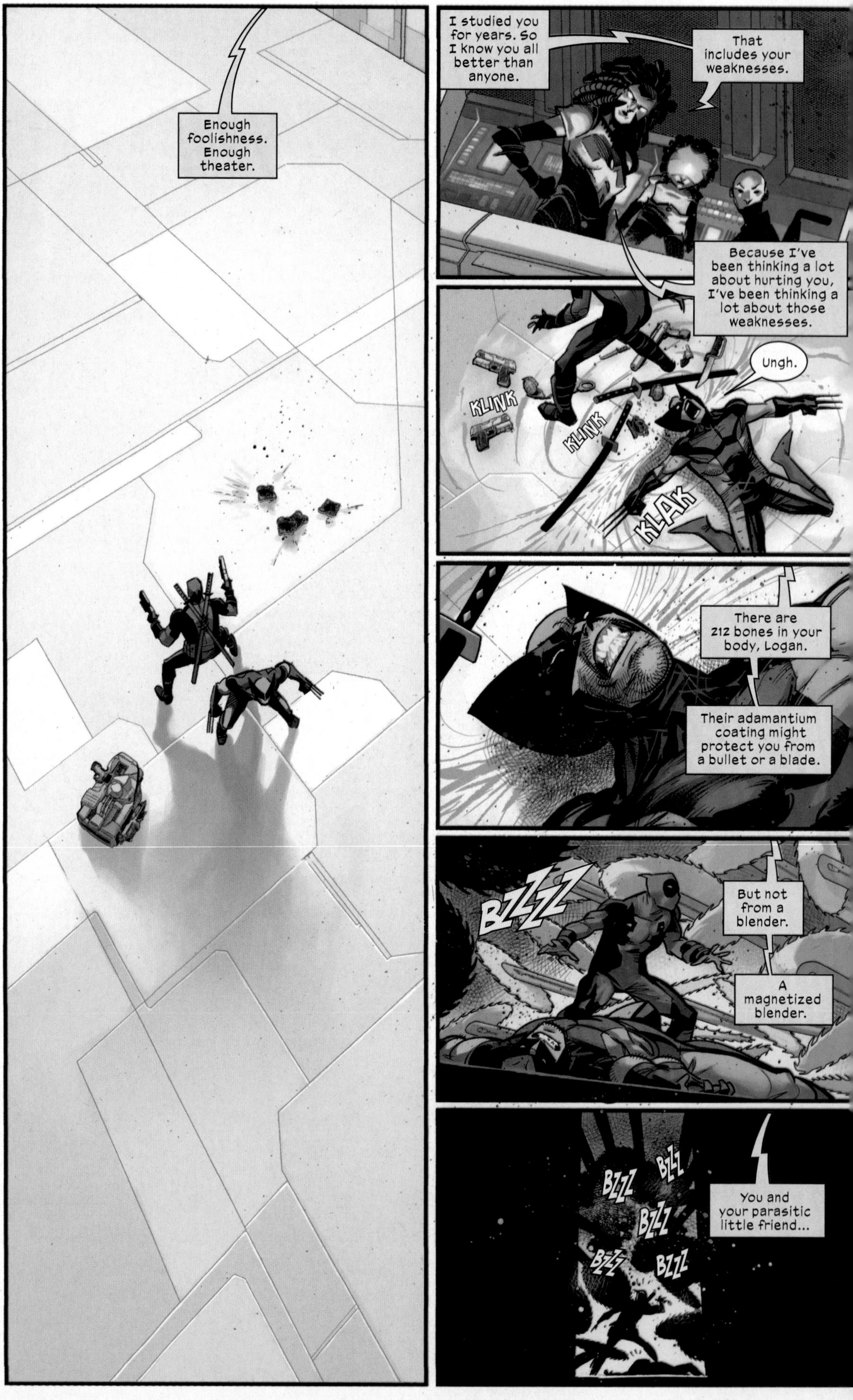
Enough foolishness. Enough theater.
I studied you for years. So I know you all better than anyone.
That includes your weaknesses.
Because I've been thinking a lot about hurting you, I've been thinking a lot about those weaknesses.
Ungh.
KLINK
KLINK
KLAK
There are 212 bones in your body, Logan.
Their adamantium coating might protect you from a bullet or a blade.
BZZZZ
But not from a blender.
A magnetized blender.
BZZZ
BZZZ
BZZZ
BZZZ
BZZZ
You and your parasitic little friend...

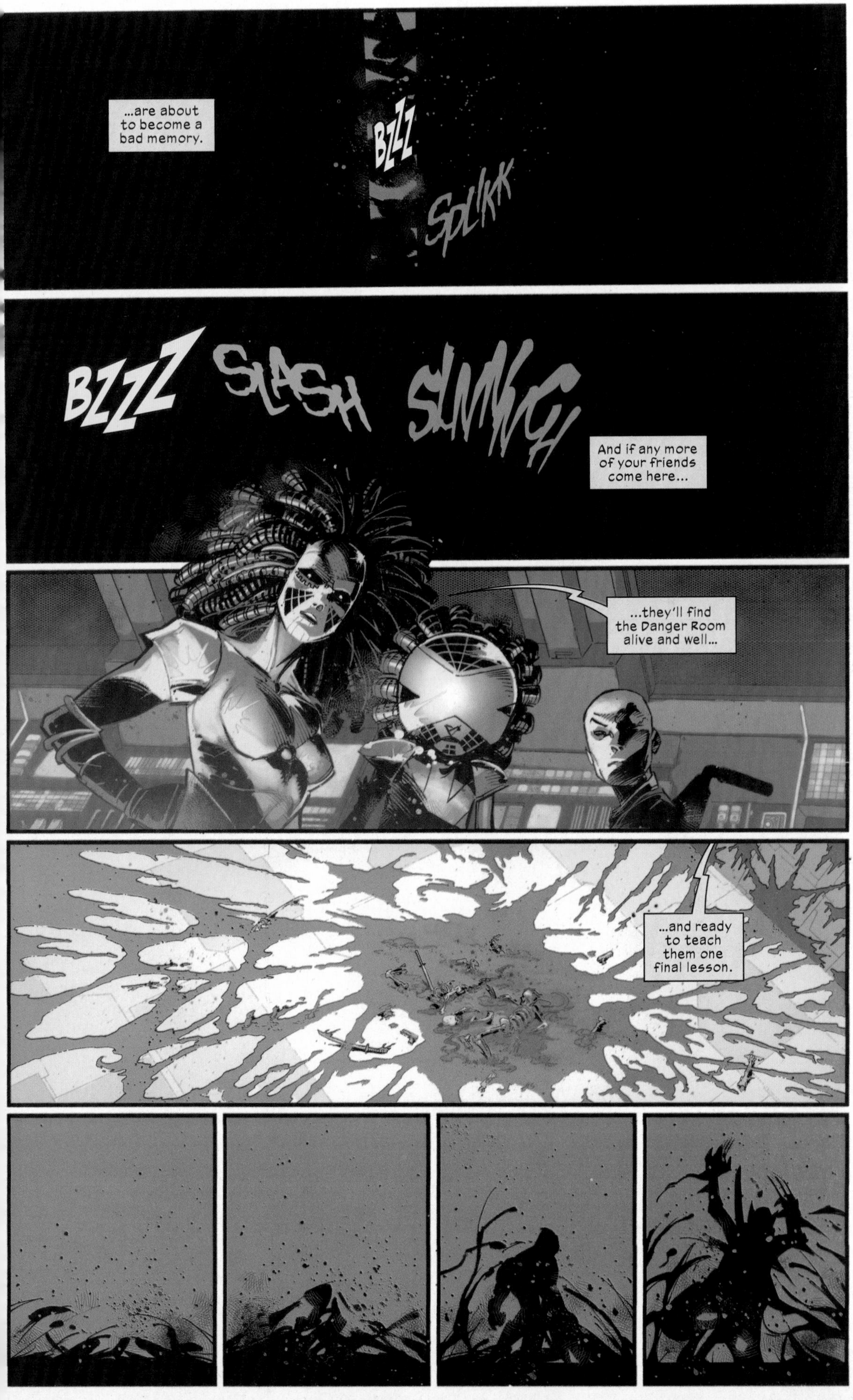
...are about to become a bad memory.
BZZZ
SPLIKK
BZZZ
SLASH
SLUNKCH
And if any more of your friends come here...
...they'll find the Danger Room alive and well...
...and ready to teach them one final lesson.

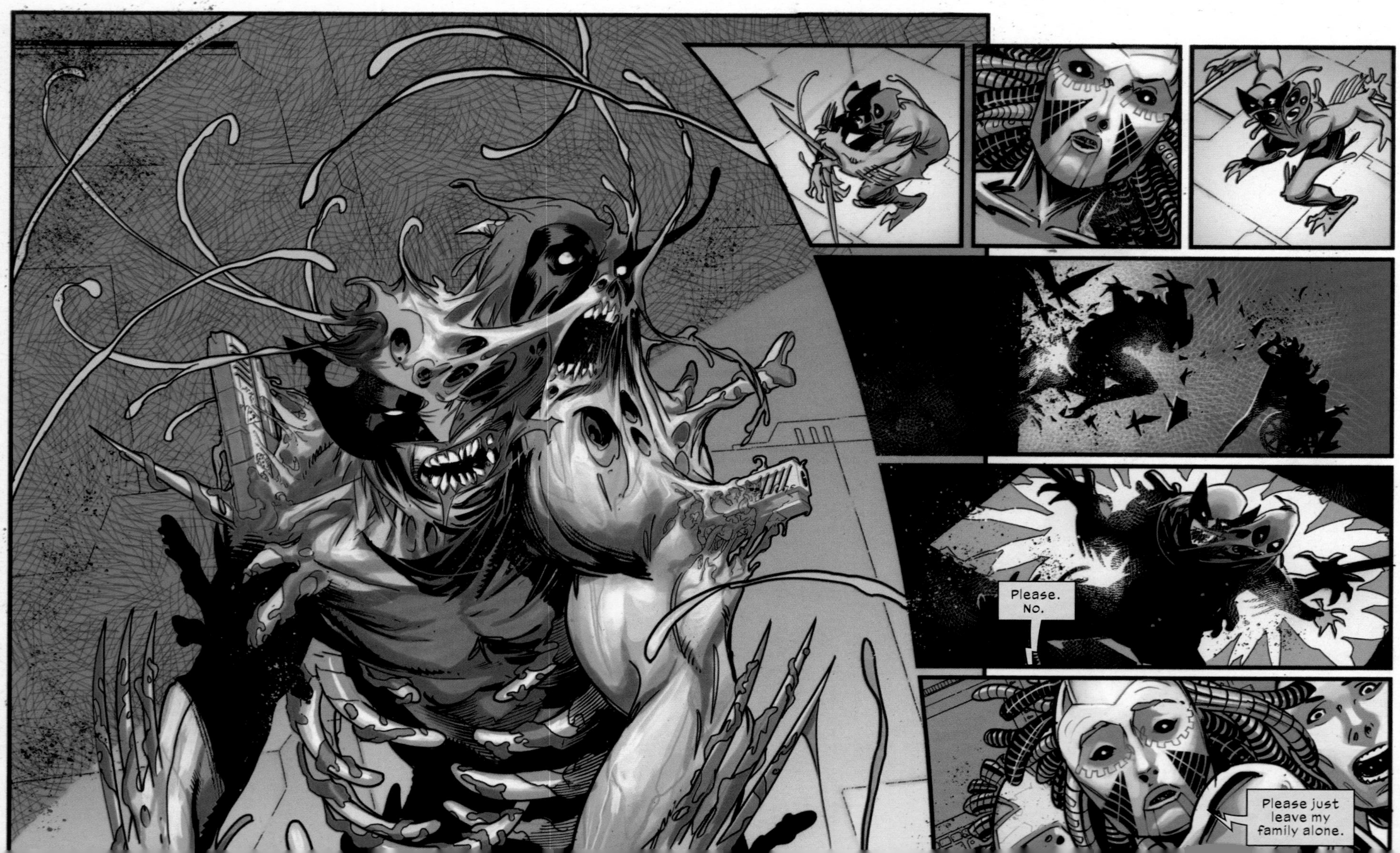
Please. No.
Please just leave my family alone.

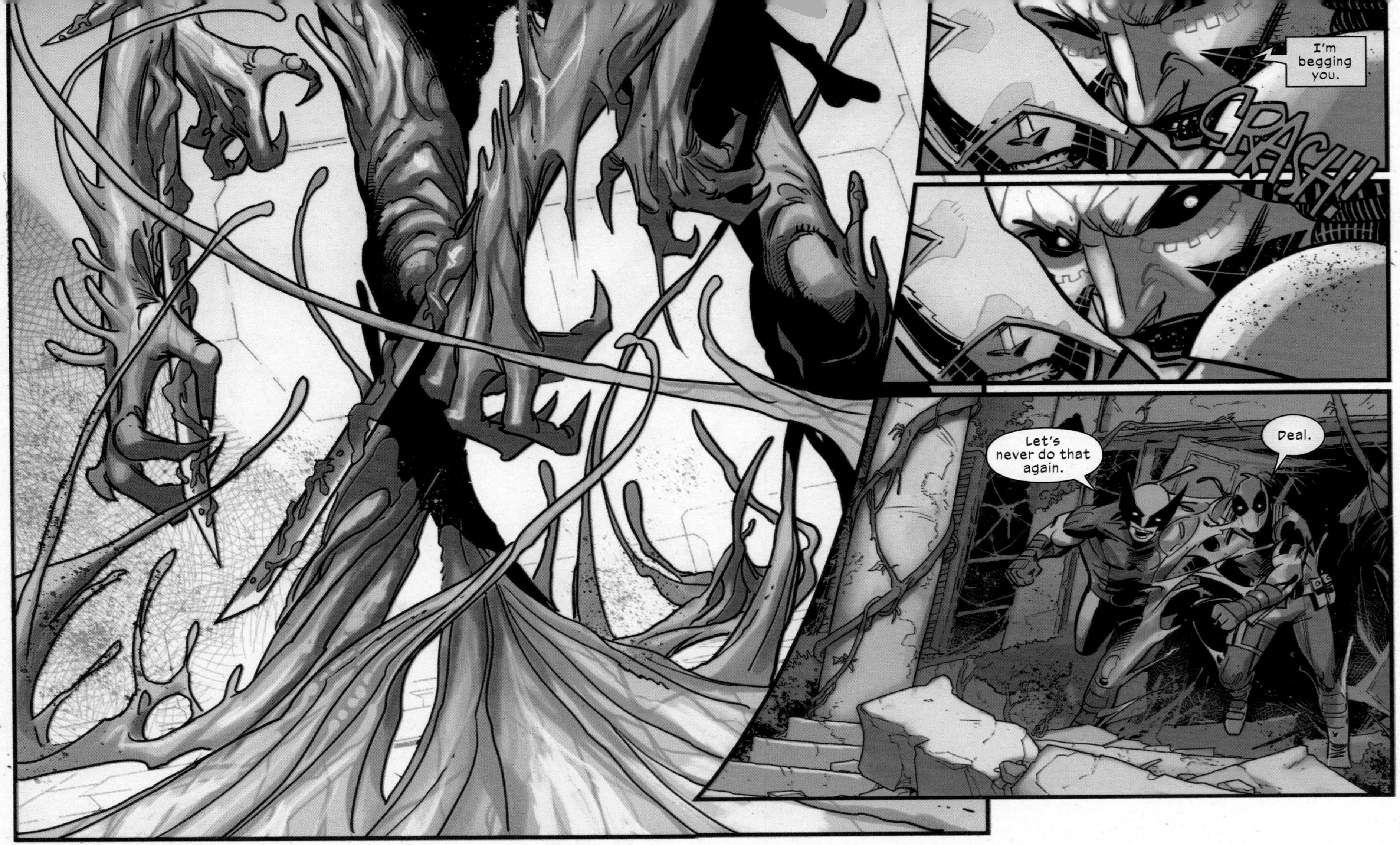
I'm begging you.
CRASH!
Let's never do that again.
Deal.

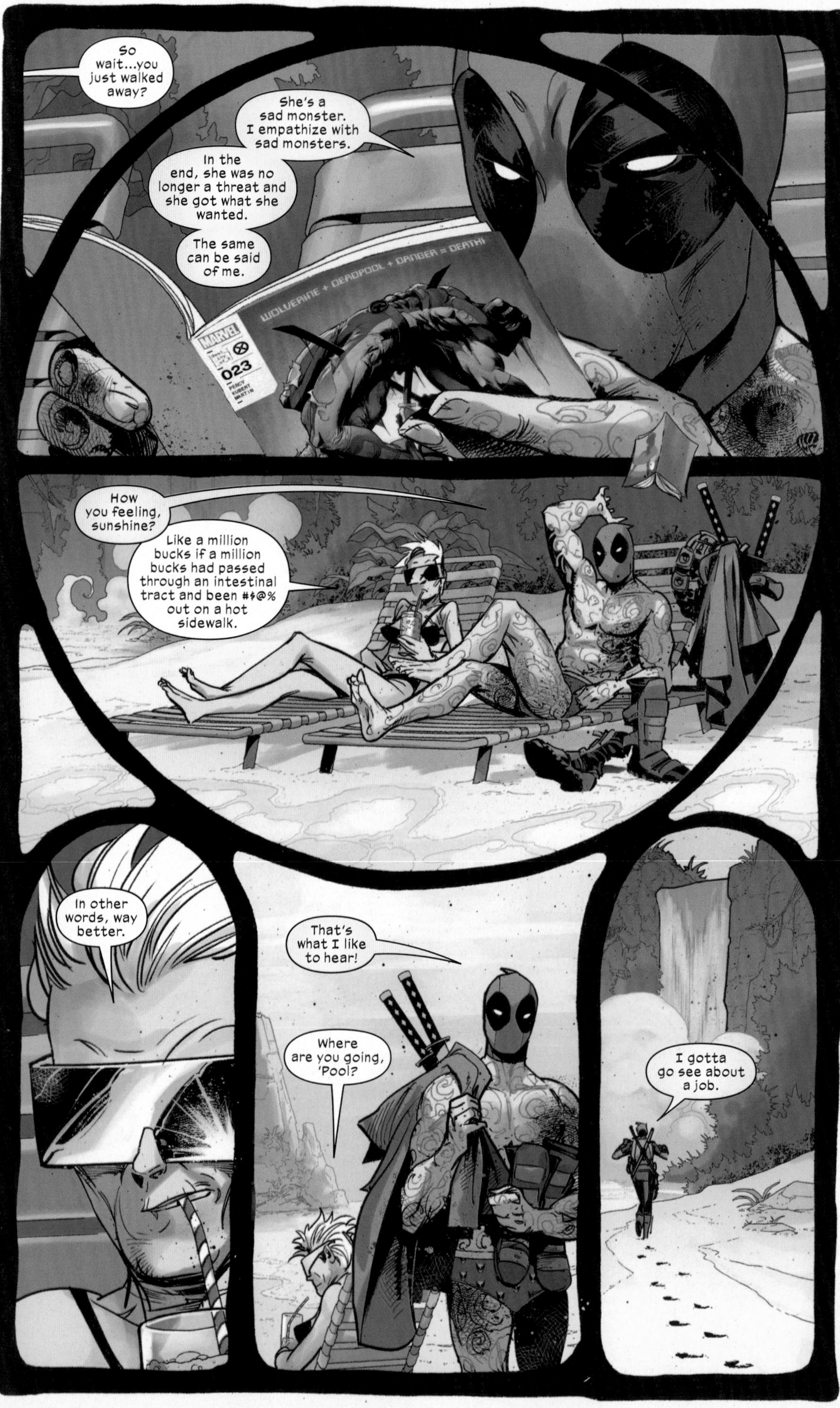

So wait...you just walked away?
She's a sad monster. I empathize with sad monsters.
In the end, she was no longer a threat and she got what she wanted.
The same can be said of me.
WOLVERINE + DEADPOOL + DANGER = DEATH!
MARVEL
023
PERCY KUBERT MARTIN
How you feeling, sunshine?
Like a million bucks if a million bucks had passed through an intestinal tract and been #$@% out on a hot sidewalk.
In other words, way better.
That's what I like to hear!
Where are you going, 'Pool?
I gotta go see about a job.

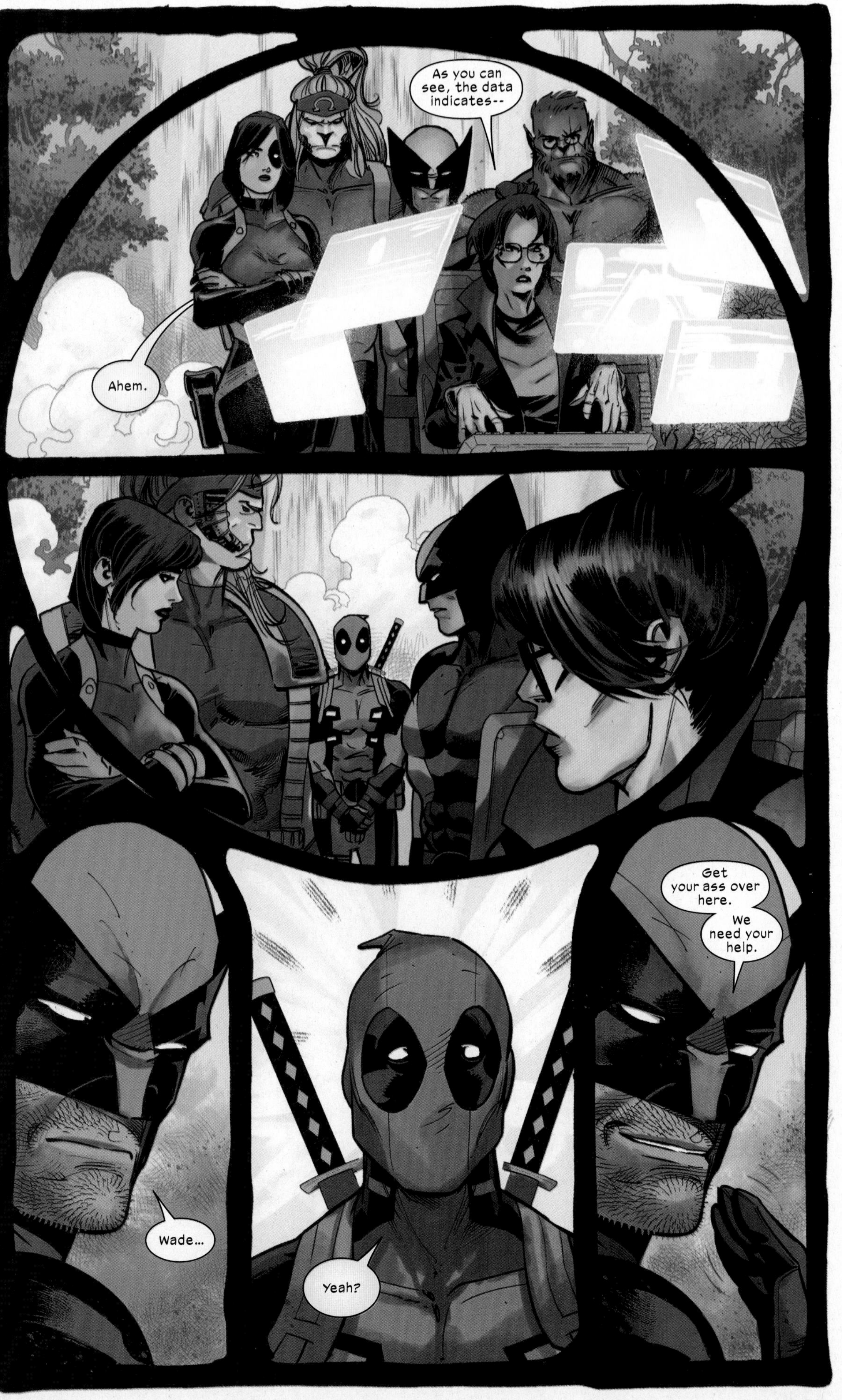
As you can see, the data indicates--
Ahem.
Get your ass over here.
We need your help.
Wade...
Yeah?

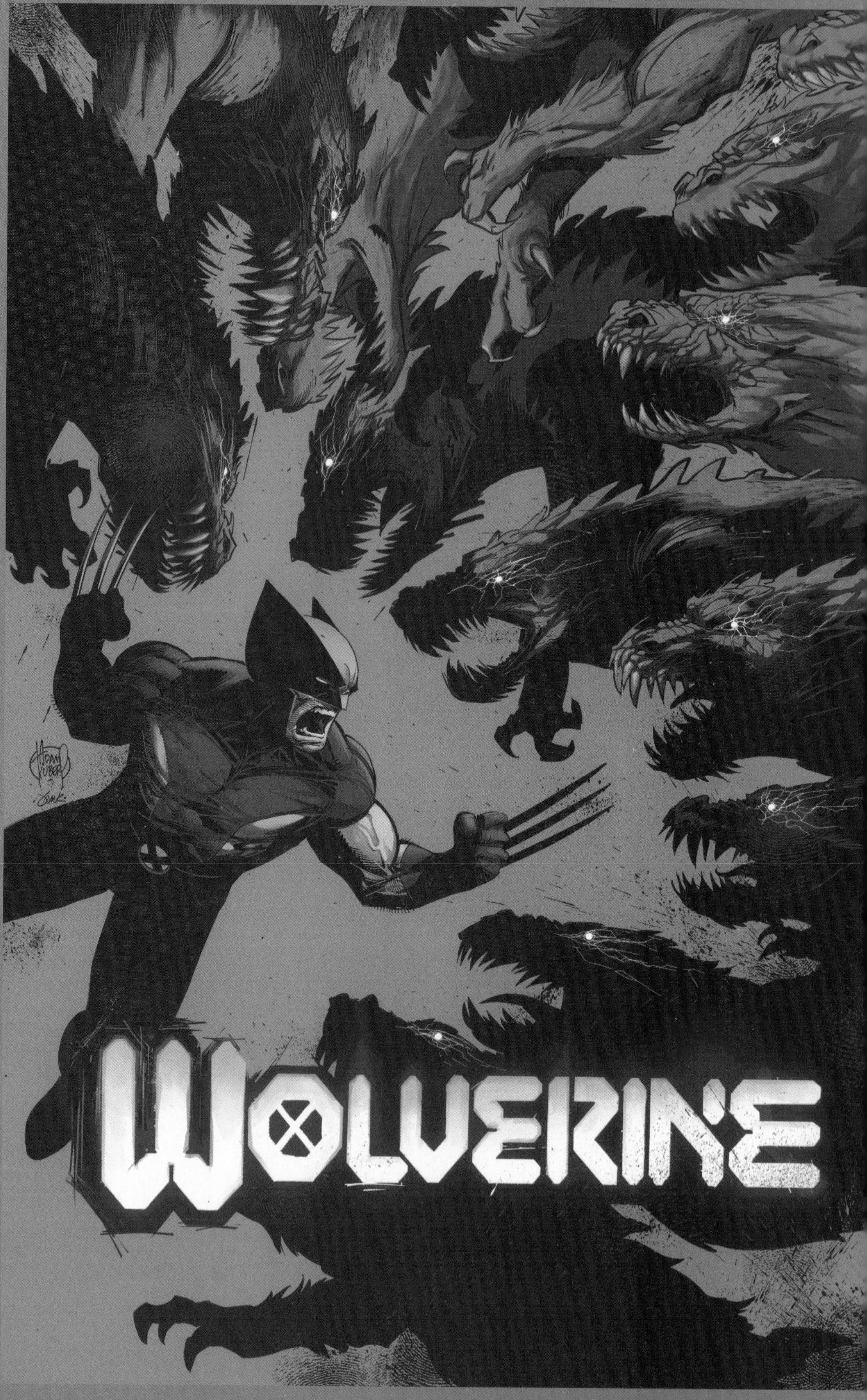
WOLVERINE

Hell to Pay Part One

24

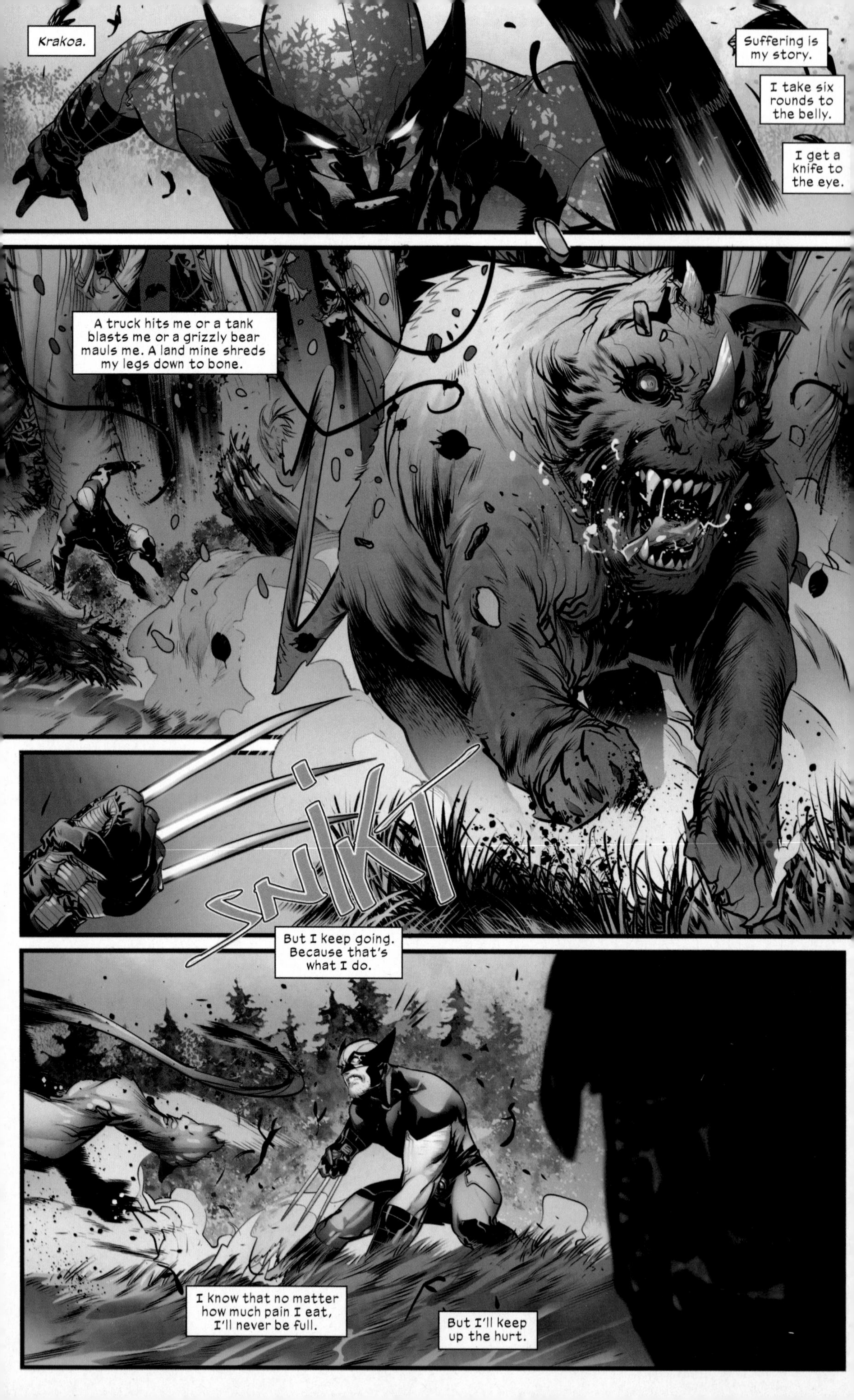
Krakoa.
Suffering is my story.
I take six rounds to the belly.
I get a knife to the eye.
A truck hits me or a tank blasts me or a grizzly bear mauls me. A land mine shreds my legs down to bone.
SNIKT
But I keep going. Because that's what I do.
I know that no matter how much pain I eat, I'll never be full.
But I'll keep up the hurt.

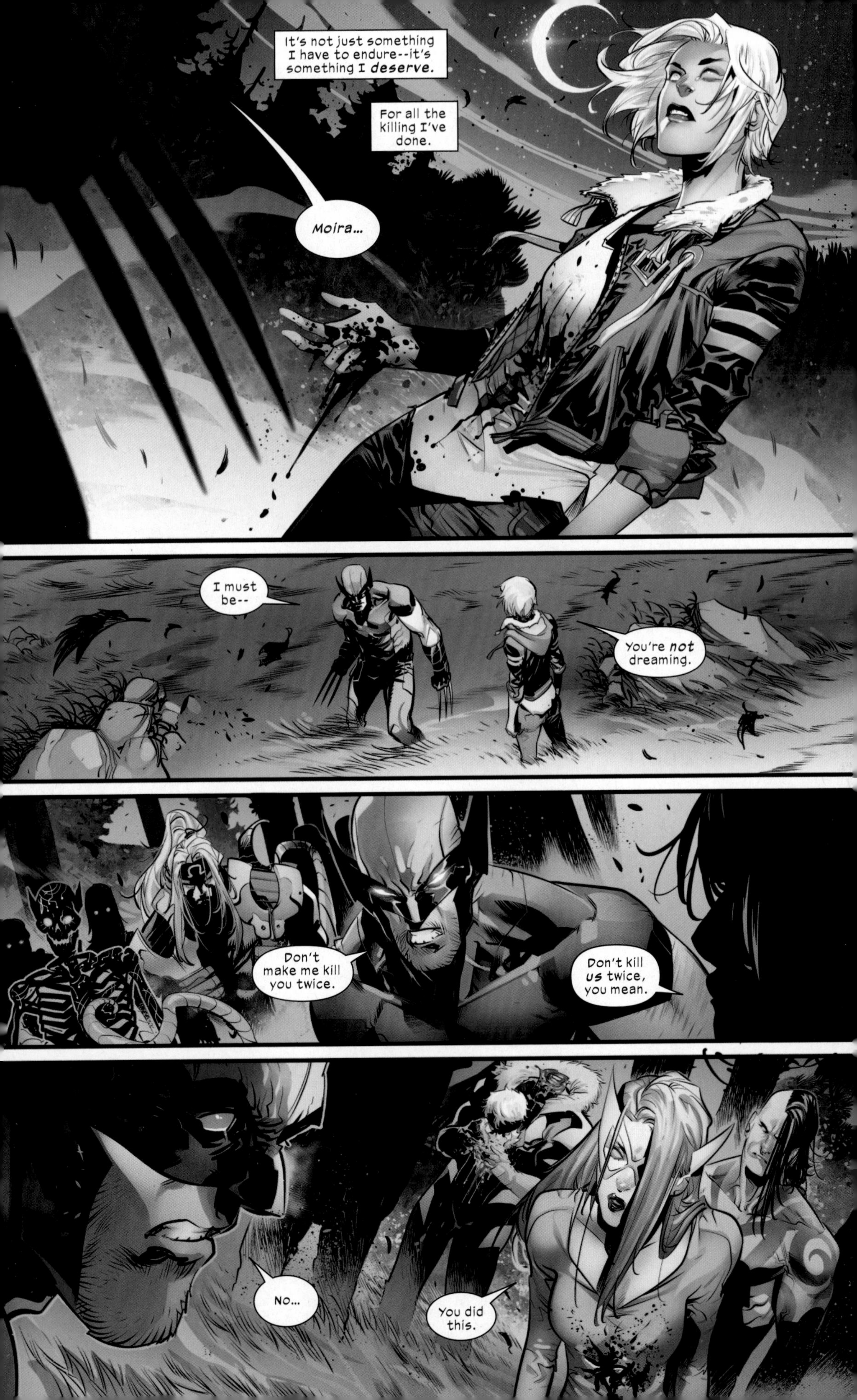
It's not just something I have to endure--it's something I deserve.
For all the killing I've done.
Moira...
I must be--
You're not dreaming.
Don't make me kill you twice.
Don't kill us twice, you mean.
No...
You did this.

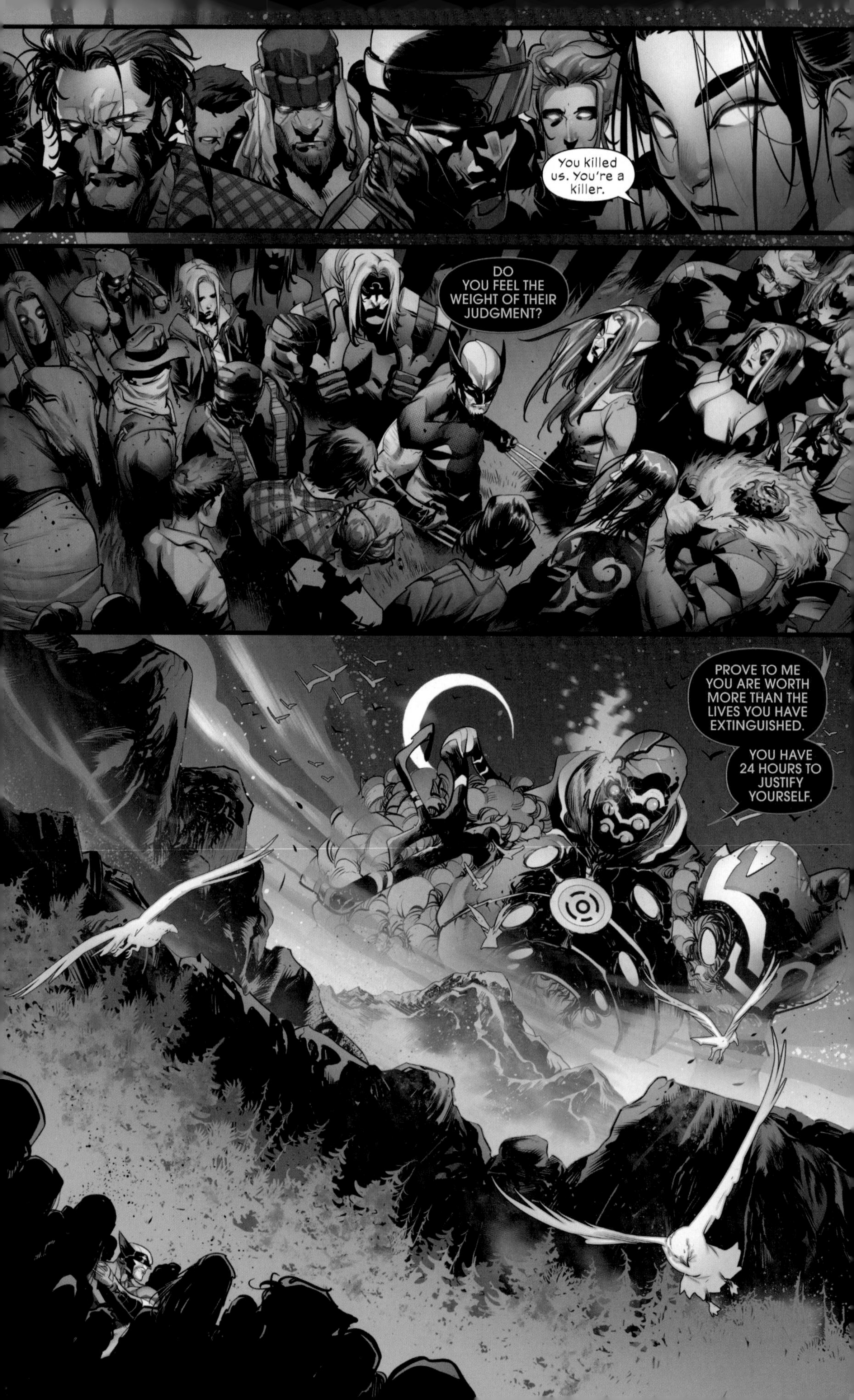
You killed us. You're a killer.
DO YOU FEEL THE WEIGHT OF THEIR JUDGMENT?
PROVE TO ME YOU ARE WORTH MORE THAN THE LIVES YOU HAVE EXTINGUISHED.
YOU HAVE 24 HOURS TO JUSTIFY YOURSELF.

[00_Destiny]
[00_____ofX]

WOLVERINE

JUDGMENT DAY

Citizens of the mutant nation of Krakoa live in a near-paradise, thanks in part to the sacrifices Wolverine has made as their protector and champion.

When the mutants participated in an interdimensional tournament against champions from Arakko, the long-lost counterpart to Krakoa, Wolverine literally went through Hell to find the swordsmith Muramasa and procure the ultimate blade. There, he encountered Solem, an Arakkii mutant with Adamantium skin who was also seeking a sword. Tracking a pair of swords to a hellish wedding ceremony, the two killed the groom to retrieve their prizes, leaving the Hellbride hungry for revenge.

Now, as the mutants' secret of resurrection has been revealed to the world at large, they find themselves in conflict with the Eternals, who view mutants as the excess deviation they're duty bound to stop. The newly resurrected Eternal god called the Progenitor has challenged the world to prove itself worthy of existence or face annihilation, and Wolverine is no exception...

Note: This issue takes place after A.X.E.: Judgment Day #3.

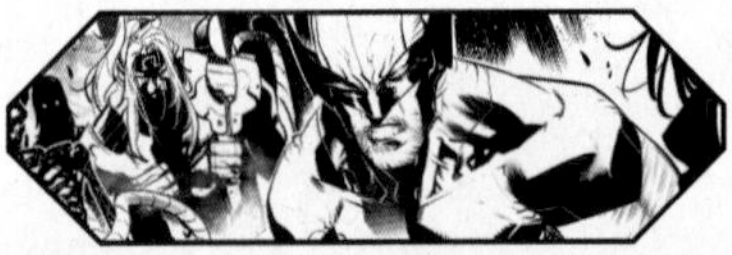

[WOLVERINE]

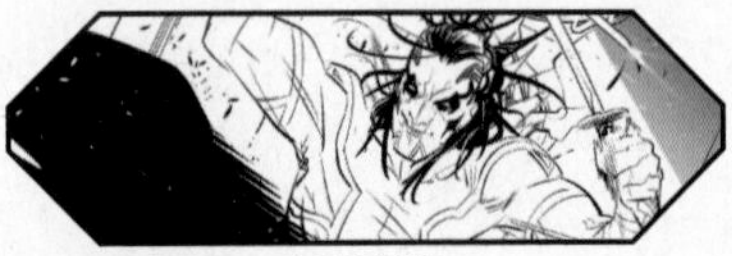

[SOLEM]

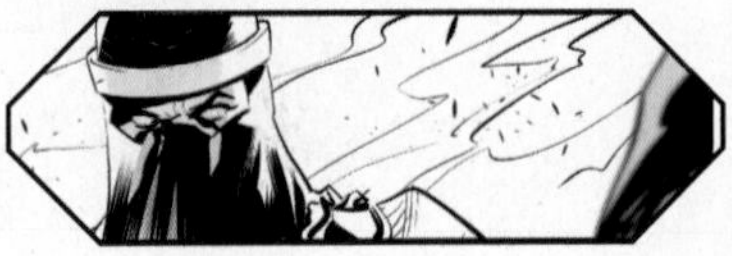

[HELLBRIDE]

[00_best_]
[00_there]

[00_00...00]
[00_00...24]

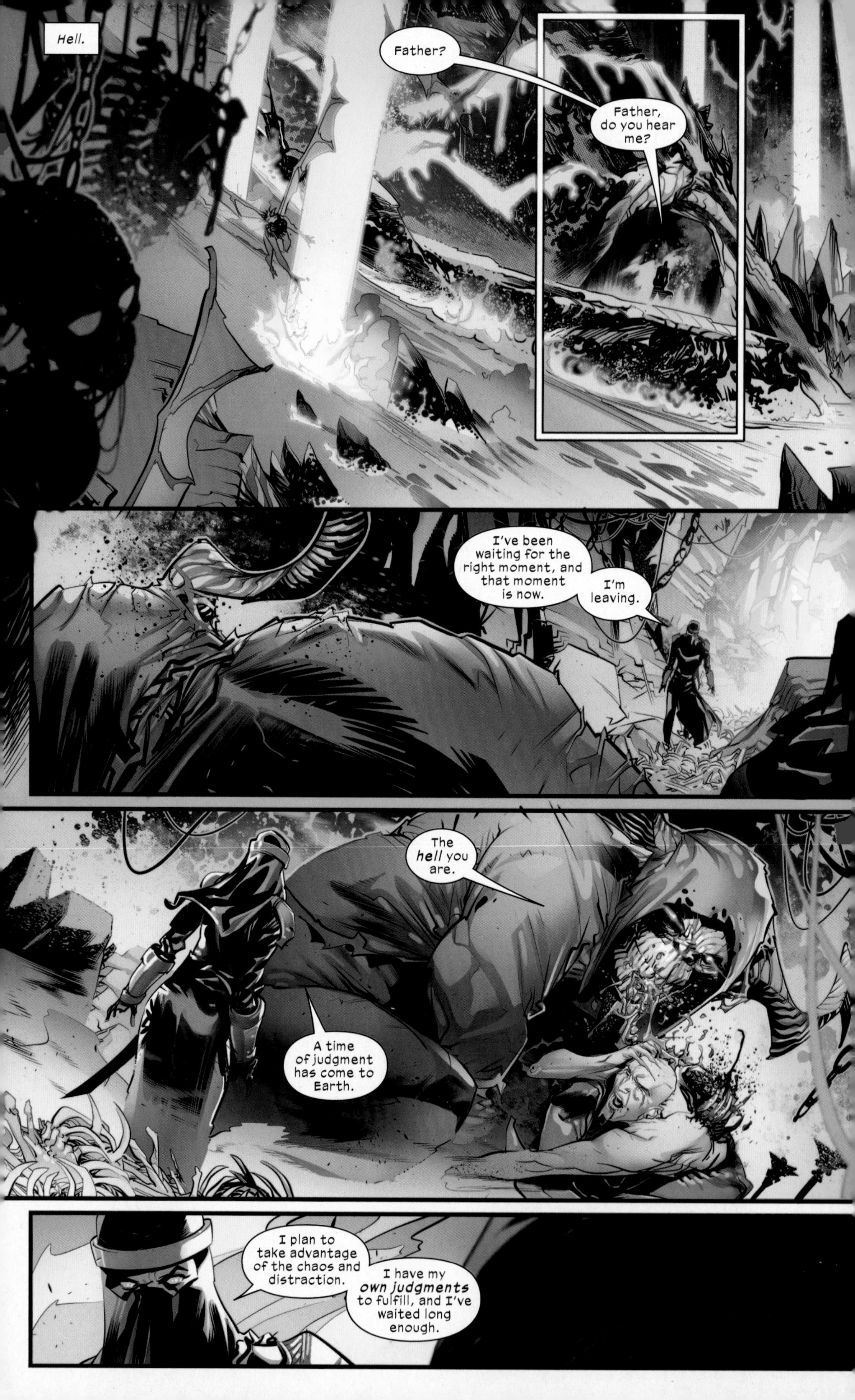
Hell.
Father?
Father, do you hear me?
I've been waiting for the right moment, and that moment is now.
I'm leaving.
The *hell* you are.
A time of judgment has come to Earth.
I plan to take advantage of the chaos and distraction.
I have my *own judgments* to fulfill, and I've waited long enough.

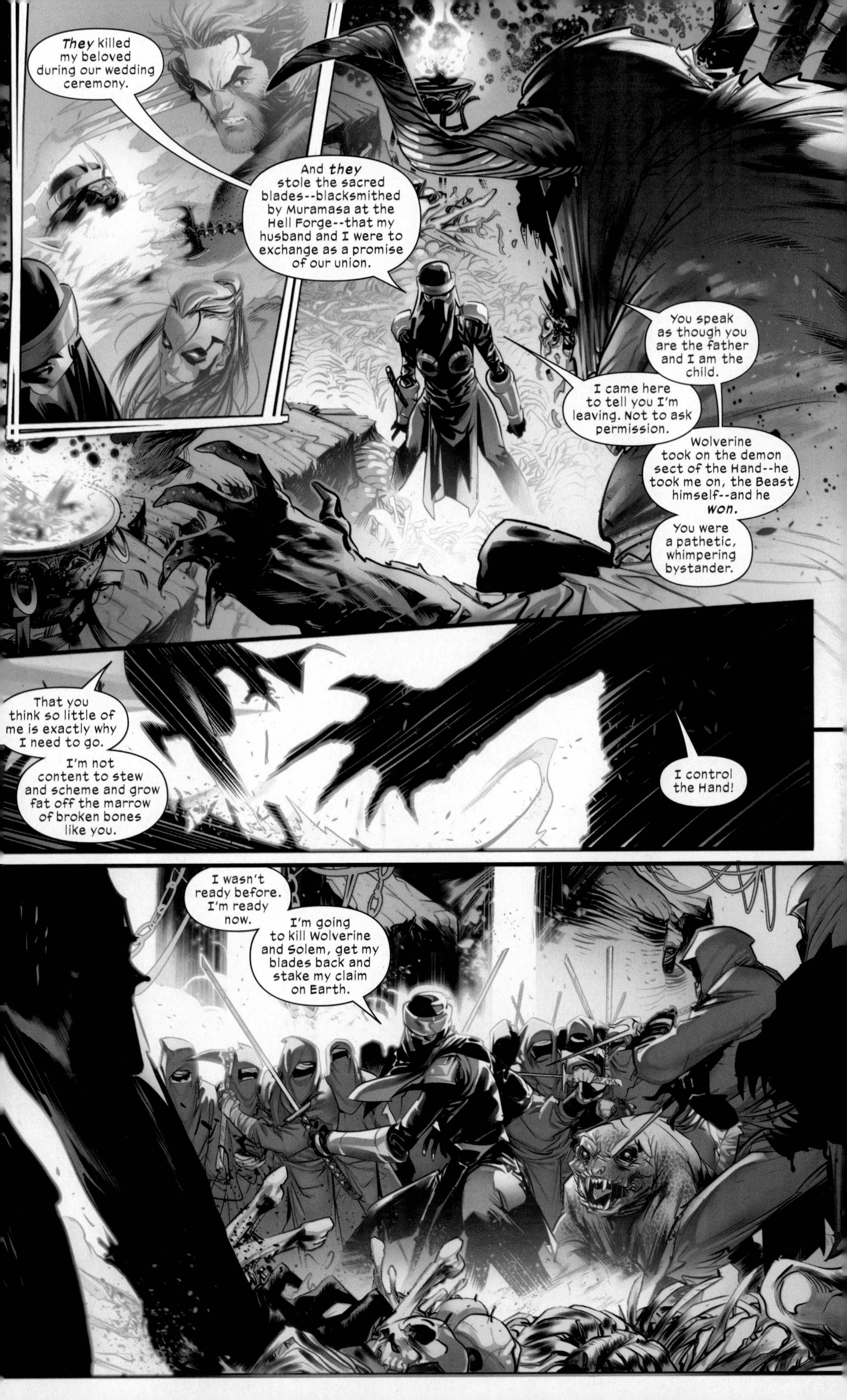
They killed my beloved during our wedding ceremony.
And *they* stole the sacred blades--blacksmithed by Muramasa at the Hell Forge--that my husband and I were to exchange as a promise of our union.
You speak as though you are the father and I am the child.
I came here to tell you I'm leaving. Not to ask permission.
Wolverine took on the demon sect of the Hand--he took me on, the Beast himself--and he ***won.***
You were a pathetic, whimpering bystander.
That you think so little of me is exactly why I need to go.
I'm not content to stew and scheme and grow fat off the marrow of broken bones like you.
I control the Hand!
I wasn't ready before. I'm ready now.
I'm going to kill Wolverine and Solem, get my blades back and stake my claim on Earth.

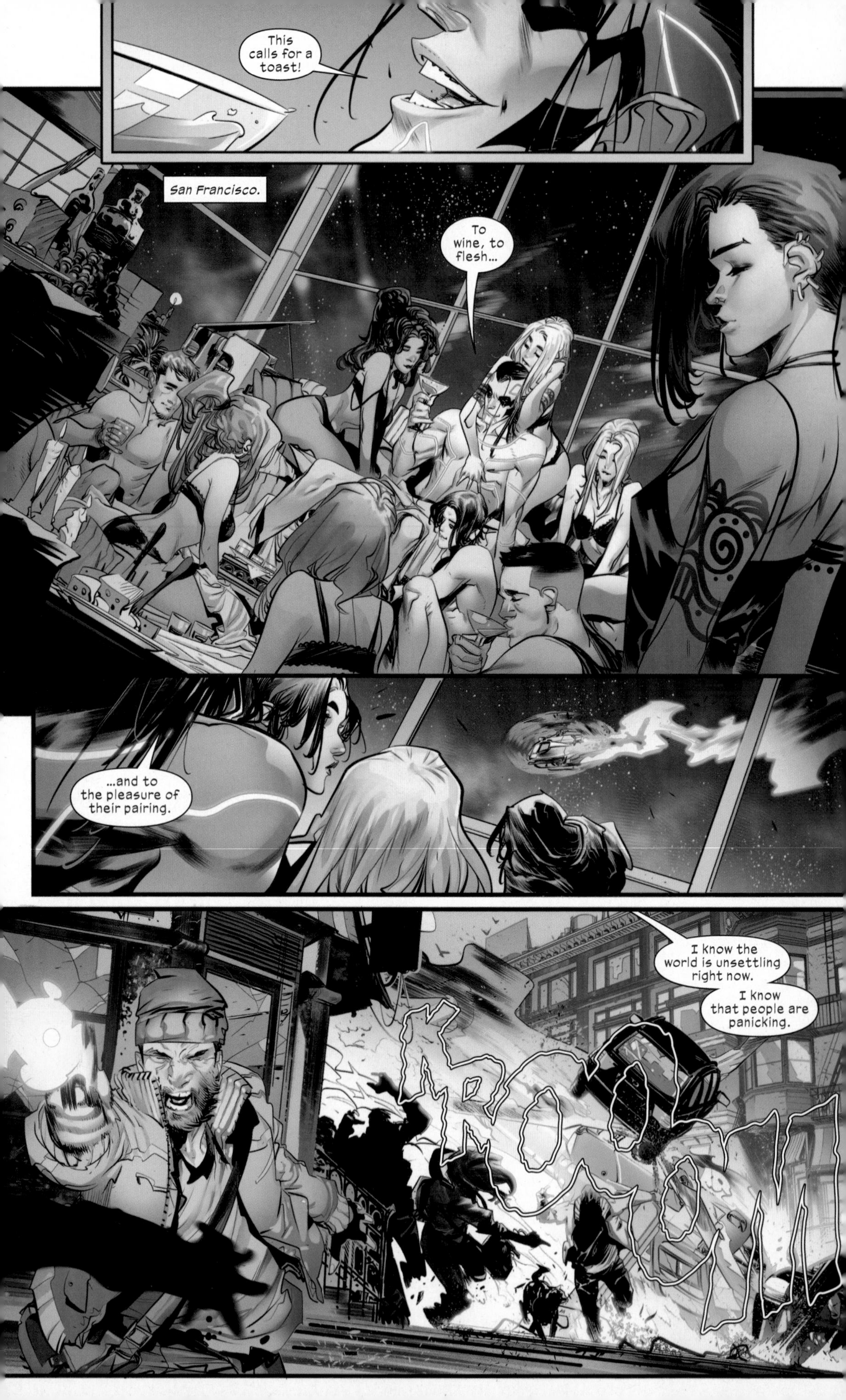

This calls for a toast!
San Francisco.
To wine, to flesh...
...and to the pleasure of their pairing.
I know the world is unsettling right now.
I know that people are panicking.
KRoooom

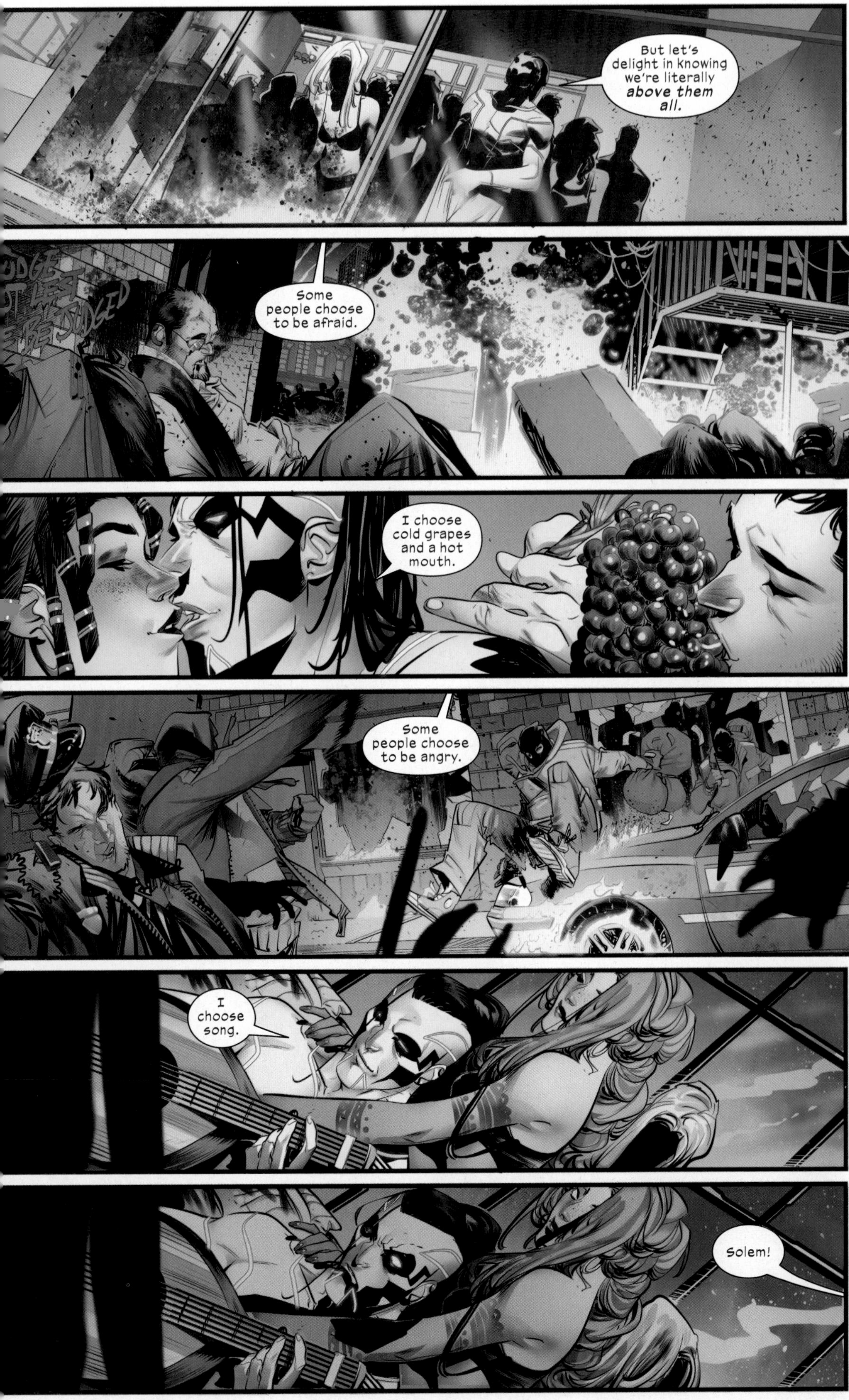
But let's delight in knowing we're literally *above them all.*
Some people choose to be afraid.
I choose cold grapes and a hot mouth.
Some people choose to be angry.
I choose song.
Solem!

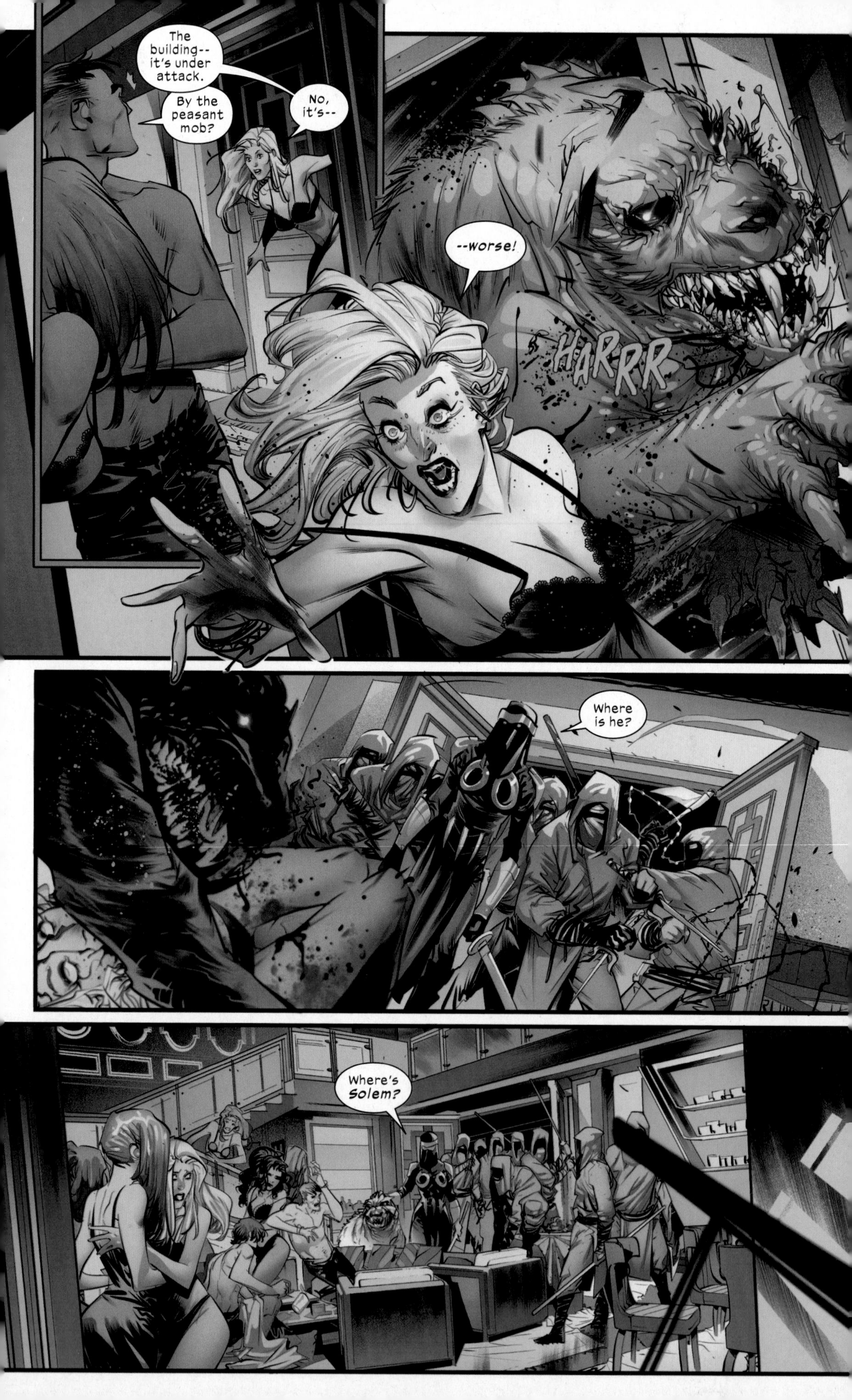
The building--
it's under attack.
By the peasant mob?
No, it's--
--worse!
HARRR
Where is he?
Where's Solem?

[sol...[0.0]
[em....[0.0]

"You only get one life, so why not live deliciously? I like to imagine the afterlife is a plump peach with a bite taken out of it. Heaven is a bottomless bath of wine. My bible is written in song and poetry. I worship with Bacchus, baby, at a pulpit of pleasure. If you dare to offer me misery, I'll give you a sword to the stomach in return. I would much prefer to thrust in ecstasy -- so join me there instead?"

-- SOLEM

[sol...[0.0]
[em....[0.0]

[wolverine_24]

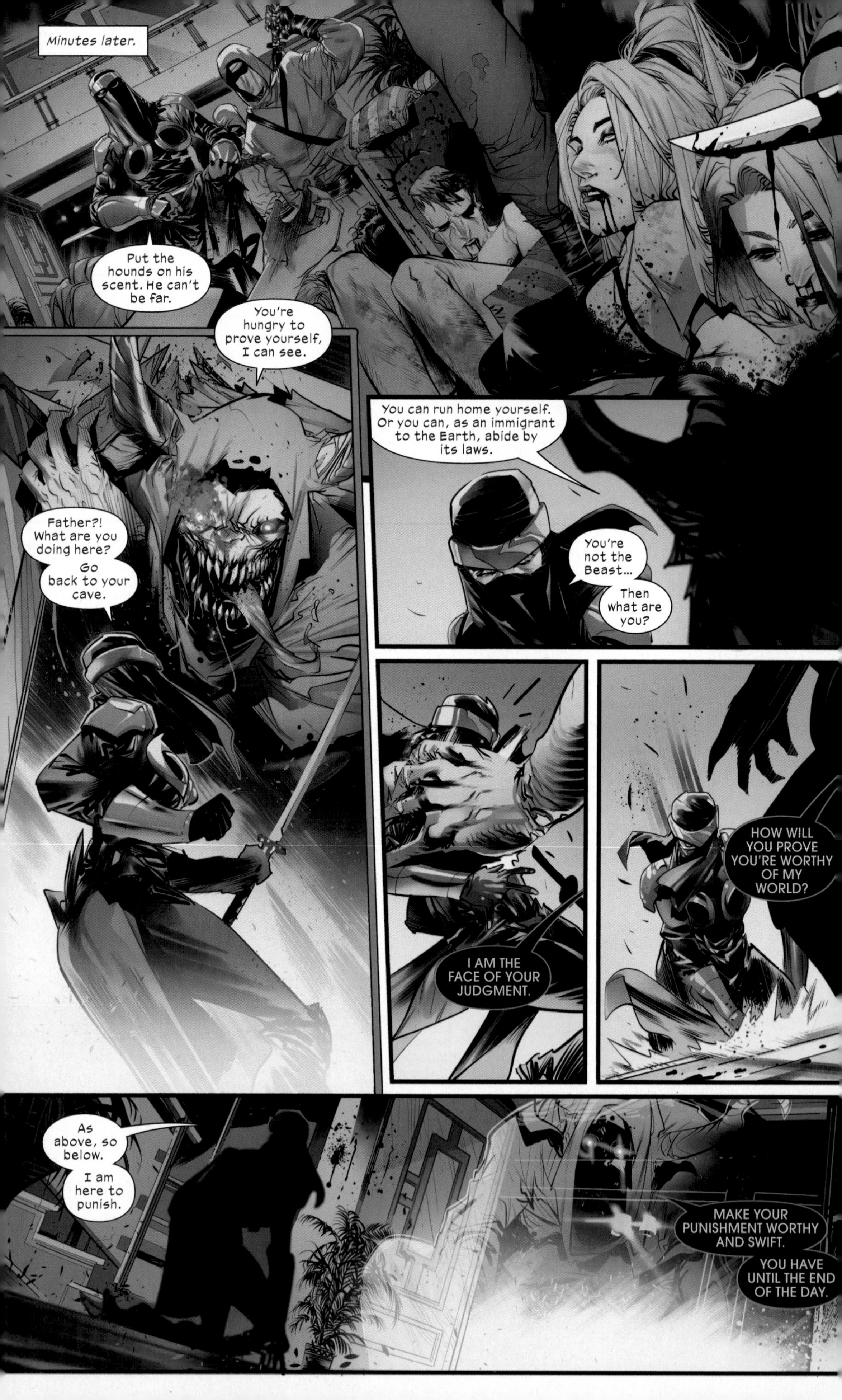
Minutes later.
Put the hounds on his scent. He can't be far.
You're hungry to prove yourself, I can see.
Father?! What are you doing here?
Go back to your cave.
You can run home yourself. Or you can, as an immigrant to the Earth, abide by its laws.
You're not the Beast...
Then what are you?
I AM THE FACE OF YOUR JUDGMENT.
HOW WILL YOU PROVE YOU'RE WORTHY OF MY WORLD?
As above, so below.
I am here to punish.
MAKE YOUR PUNISHMENT WORTHY AND SWIFT.
YOU HAVE UNTIL THE END OF THE DAY.

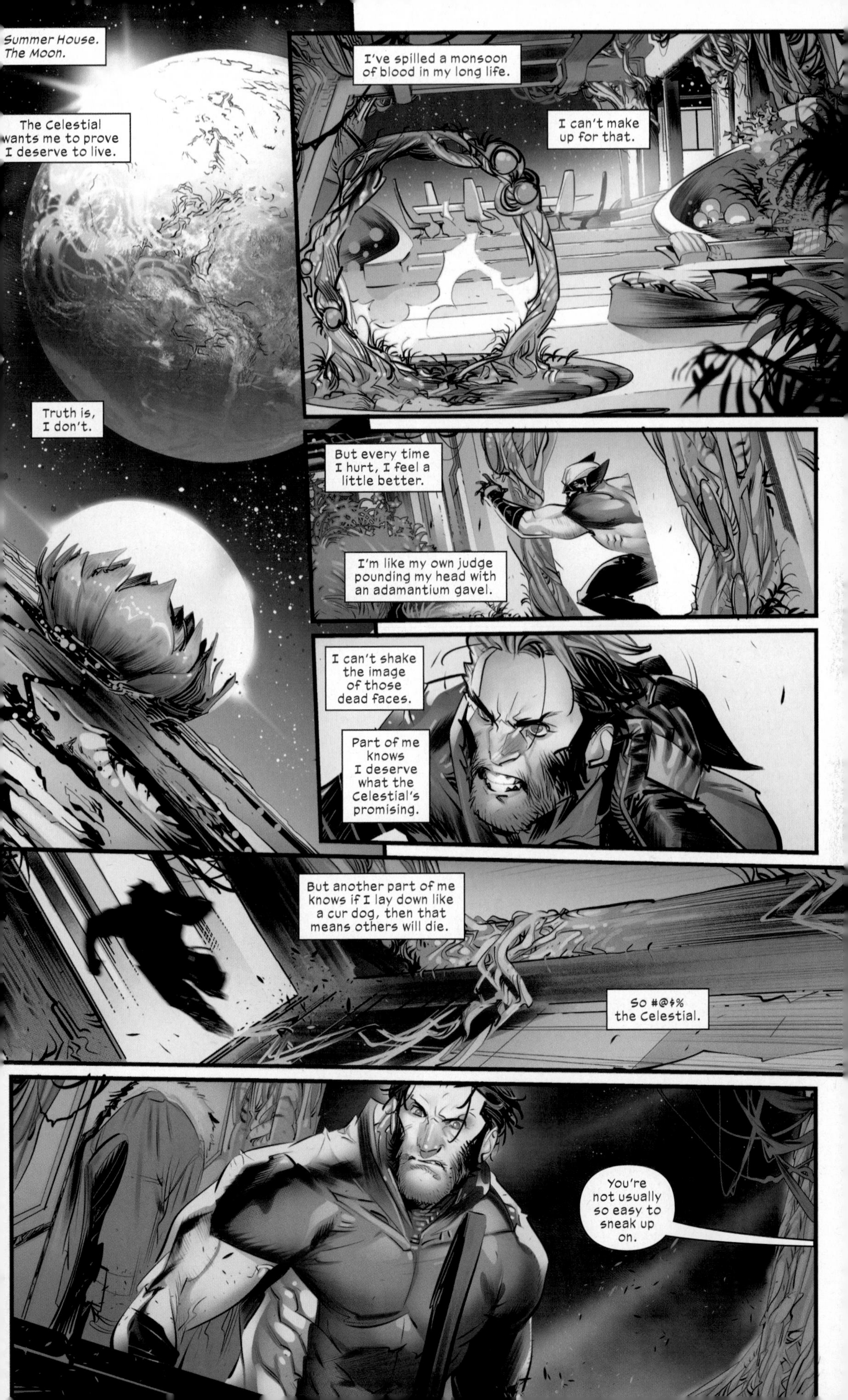
Summer House.
The Moon.
The Celestial wants me to prove I deserve to live.
Truth is, I don't.
I've spilled a monsoon of blood in my long life.
I can't make up for that.
But every time I hurt, I feel a little better.
I'm like my own judge pounding my head with an adamantium gavel.
I can't shake the image of those dead faces.
Part of me knows I deserve what the Celestial's promising.
But another part of me knows if I lay down like a cur dog, then that means others will die.
So #@$% the Celestial.
You're not usually so easy to sneak up on.

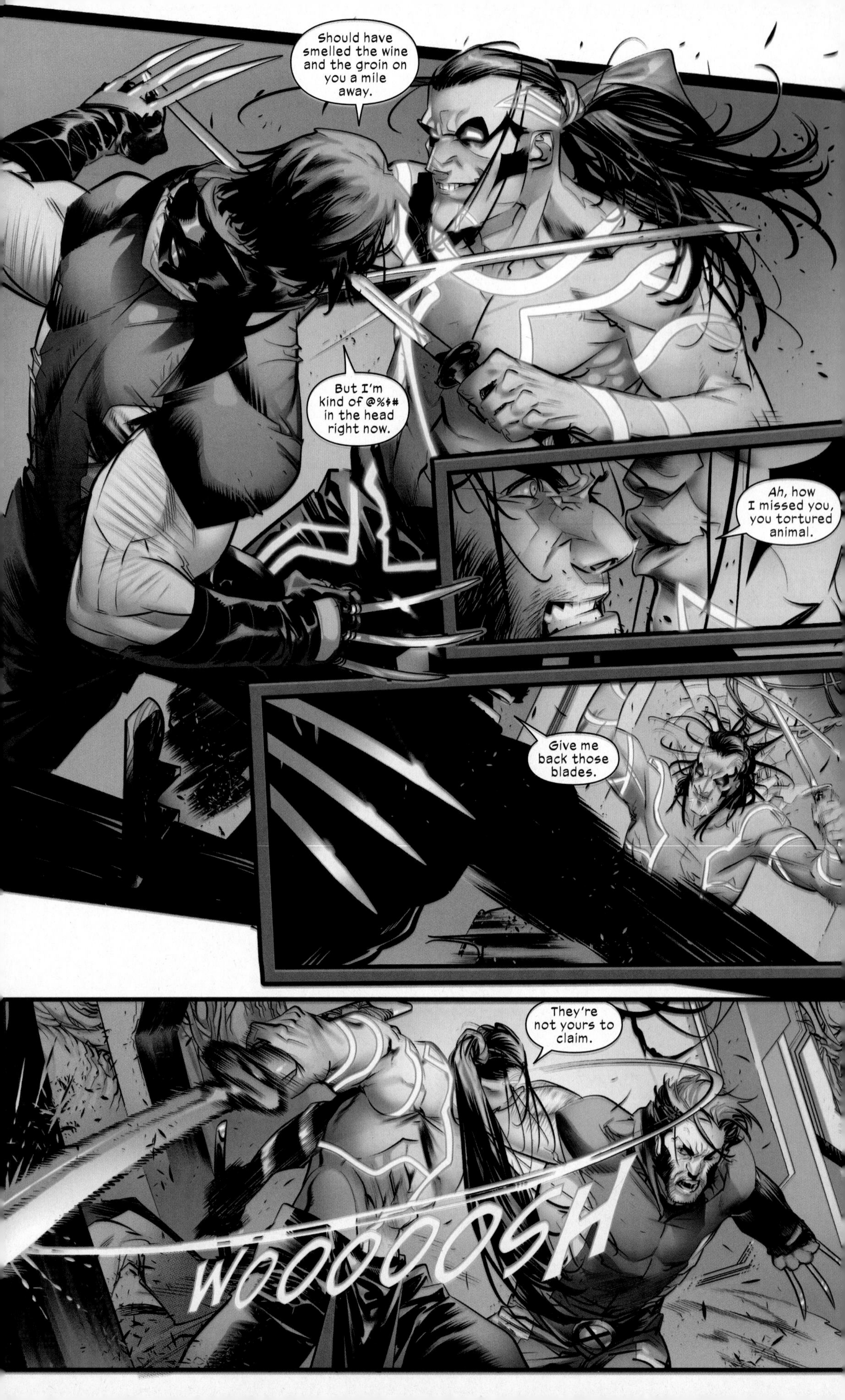
Should have smelled the wine and the groin on you a mile away.
But I'm kind of @%$# in the head right now.
Ah, how I missed you, you tortured animal.
Give me back those blades.
They're not yours to claim.
WOOOOOSH

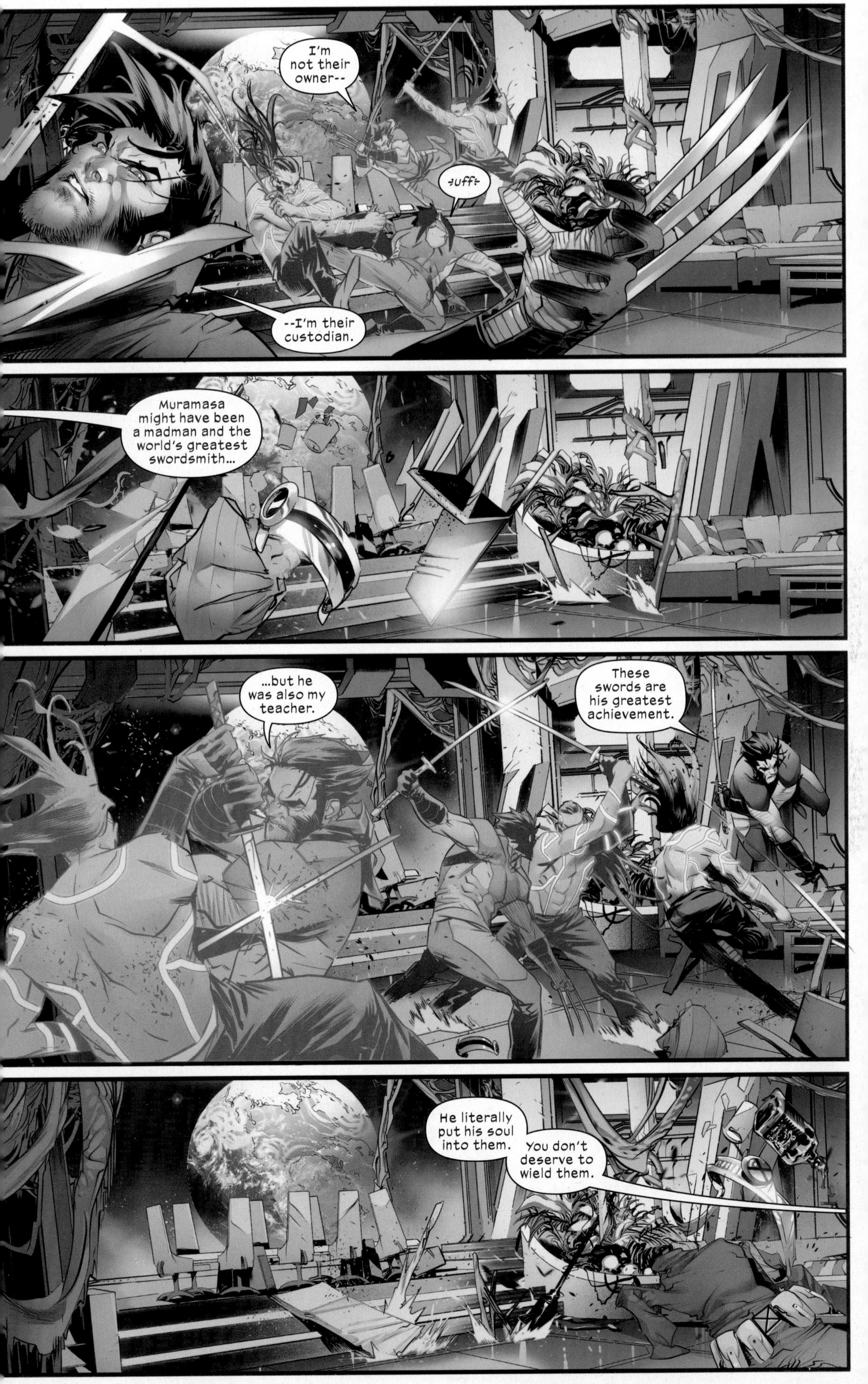
I'm not their owner--
ᵻuffᵻ
--I'm their custodian.
Muramasa might have been a madman and the world's greatest swordsmith...
...but he was also my teacher.
These swords are his greatest achievement.
He literally put his soul into them.
You don't deserve to wield them.

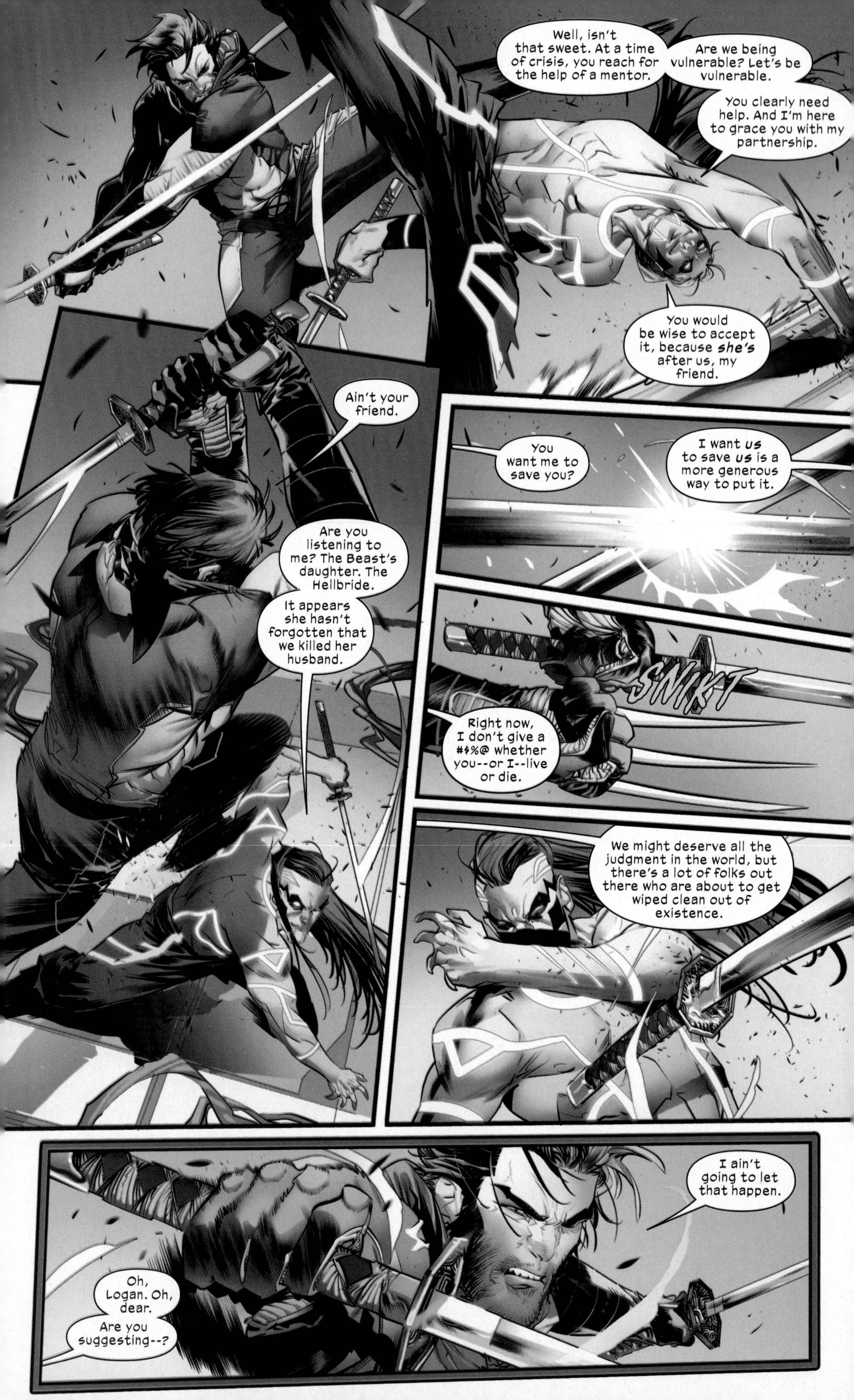
Well, isn't that sweet. At a time of crisis, you reach for the help of a mentor.
Are we being vulnerable? Let's be vulnerable.
You clearly need help. And I'm here to grace you with my partnership.
You would be wise to accept it, because *she's* after us, my friend.
Ain't your friend.
You want me to save you?
I want *us* to save *us* is a more generous way to put it.
Are you listening to me? The Beast's daughter. The Hellbride.
It appears she hasn't forgotten that we killed her husband.
SNIKT
Right now, I don't give a #$%@ whether you--or I--live or die.
We might deserve all the judgment in the world, but there's a lot of folks out there who are about to get wiped clean out of existence.
I ain't going to let that happen.
Oh, Logan. Oh, dear.
Are you suggesting--?

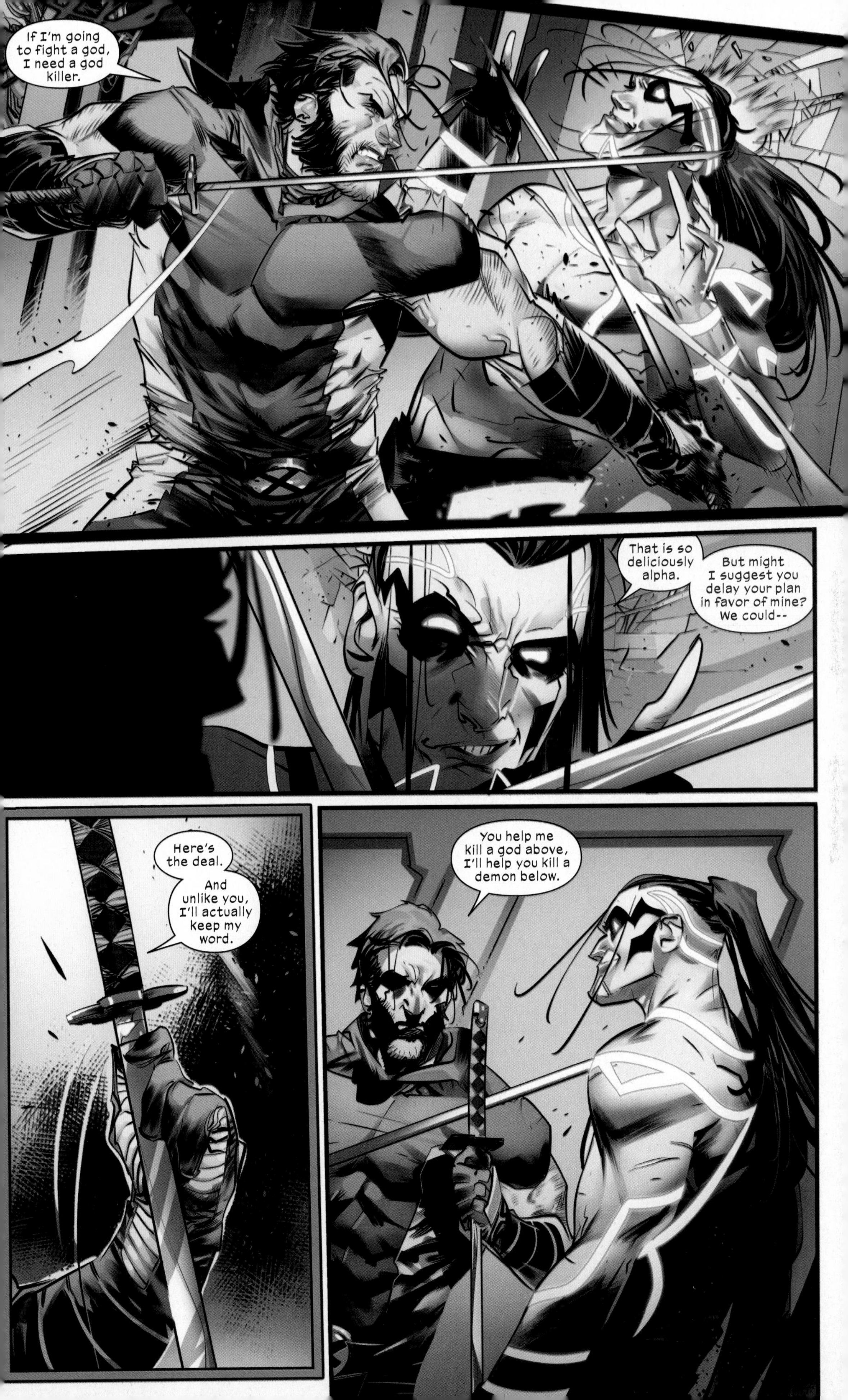
If I'm going to fight a god, I need a god killer.
That is so deliciously alpha.
But might I suggest you delay your plan in favor of mine? We could--
Here's the deal.
And unlike you, I'll actually keep my word.
You help me kill a god above, I'll help you kill a demon below.

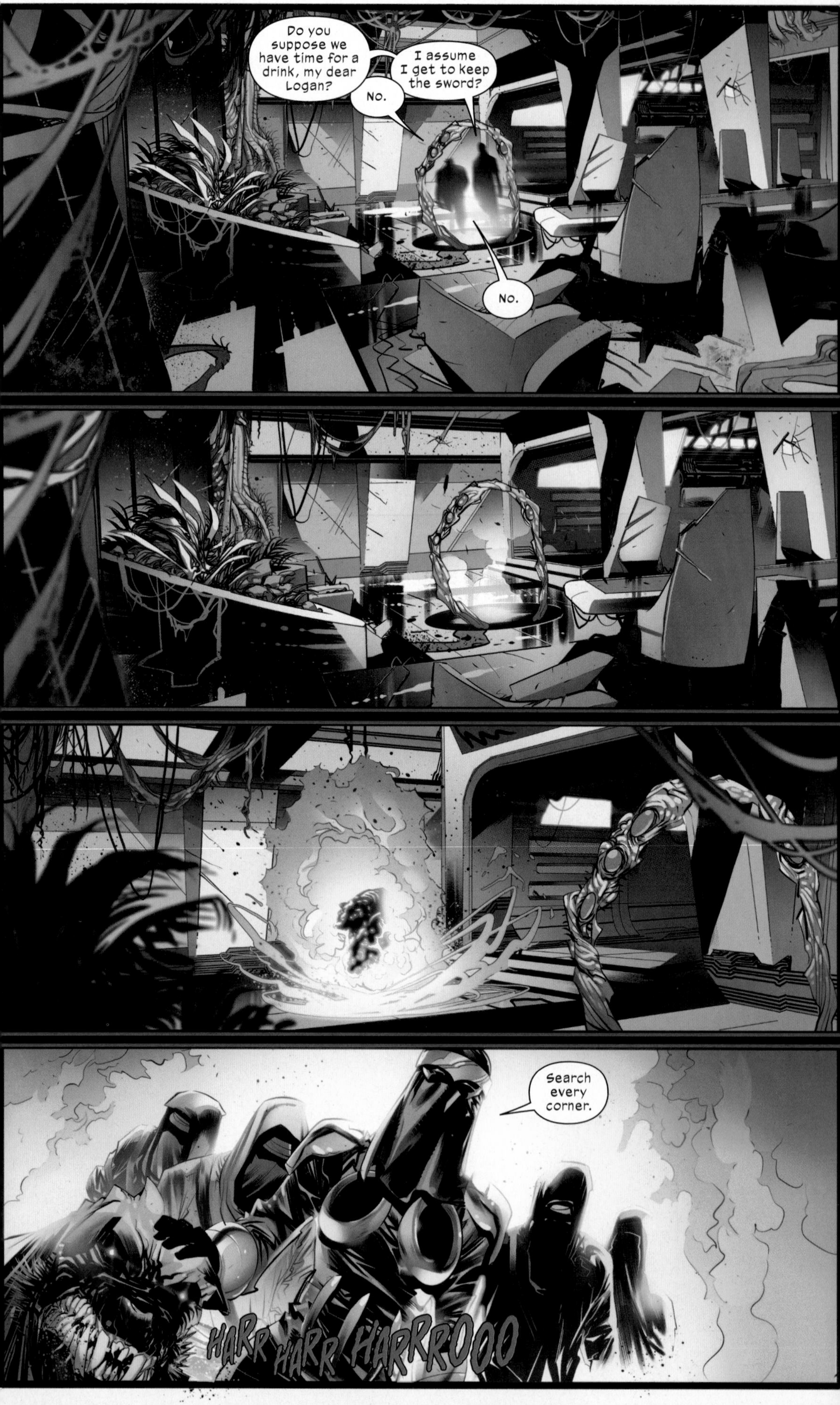
Do you suppose we have time for a drink, my dear Logan?
No.
I assume I get to keep the sword?
No.
Search every corner.
HARR HARR HARRROOO

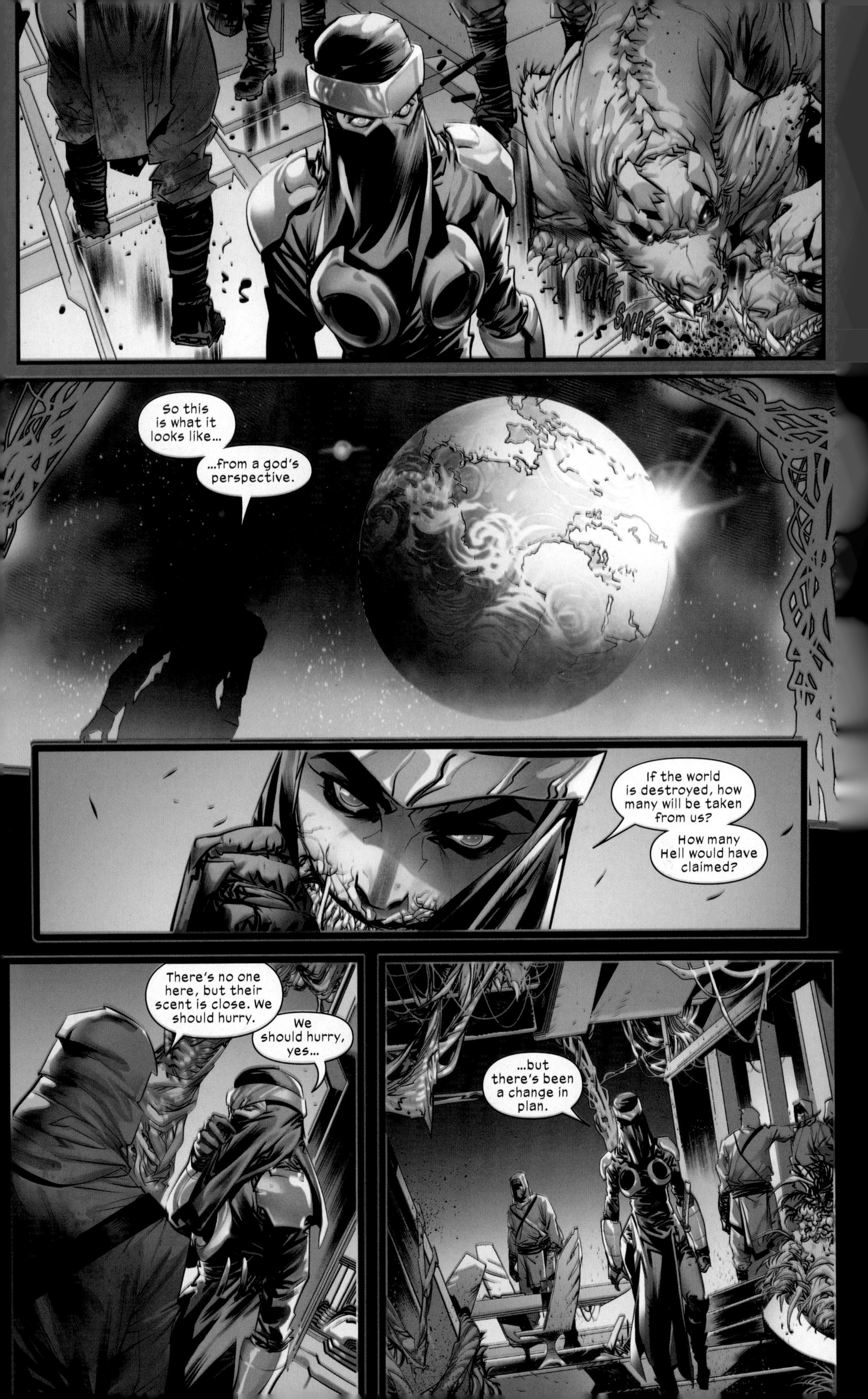
SNAFF
SNIFF
So this is what it looks like...
...from a god's perspective.
If the world is destroyed, how many will be taken from us?
How many Hell would have claimed?
There's no one here, but their scent is close. We should hurry.
We should hurry, yes...
...but there's been a change in plan.

"Folks want badly to believe in something bigger. Because the scariest god you can imagine don't care. It's as cold and indifferent as the blackest corner of space. A god of nothing. That's why somebody's always trying to take control. In a family. In an office. On a court or in a chapel. In a battlefield or a statehouse. Make order and meaning out of all that nothing. And there's no better way to get people to kneel and weep at your altar than punishment. Every would-be god is a punisher."

-- WOLVERINE

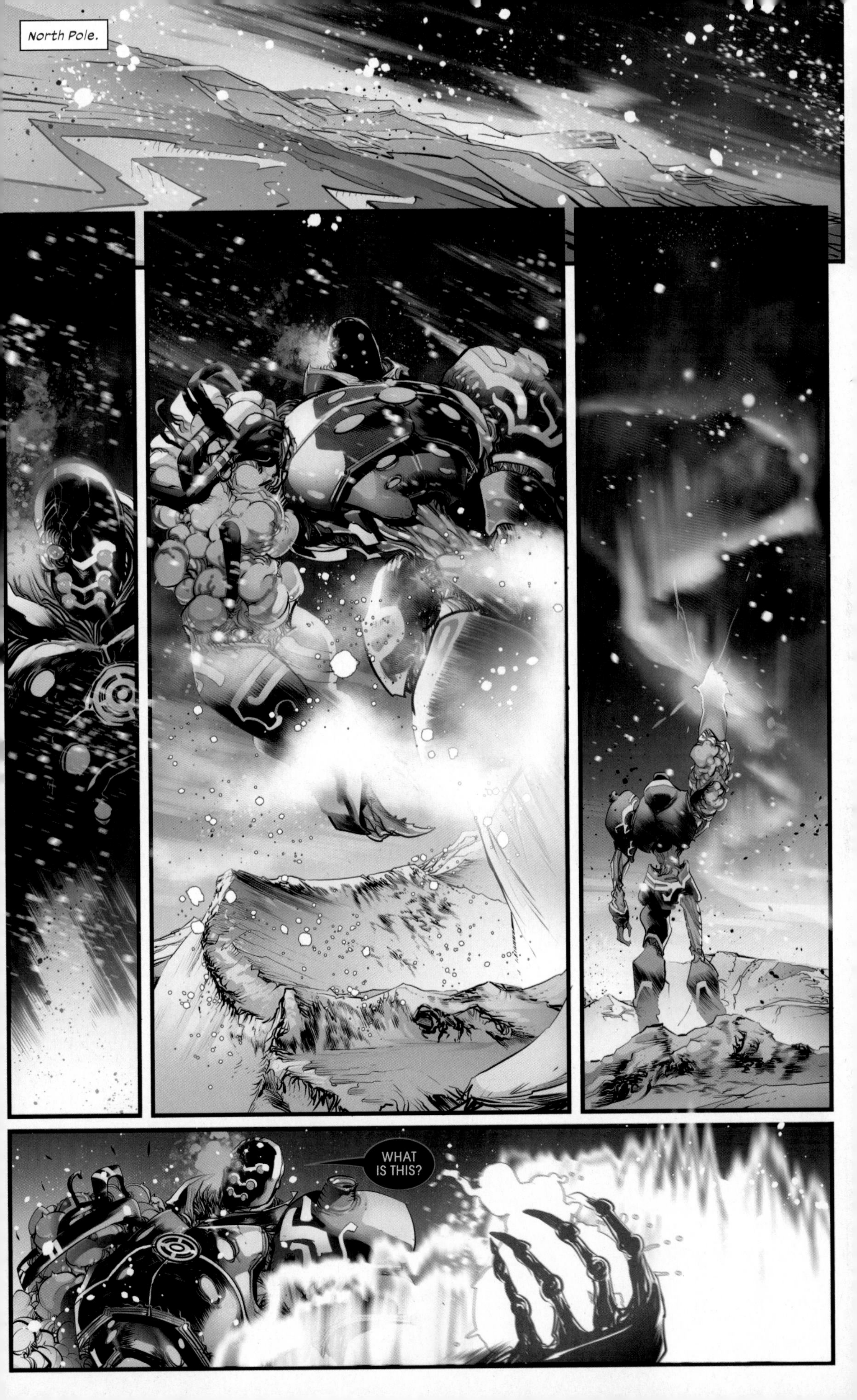
North Pole.
WHAT IS THIS?

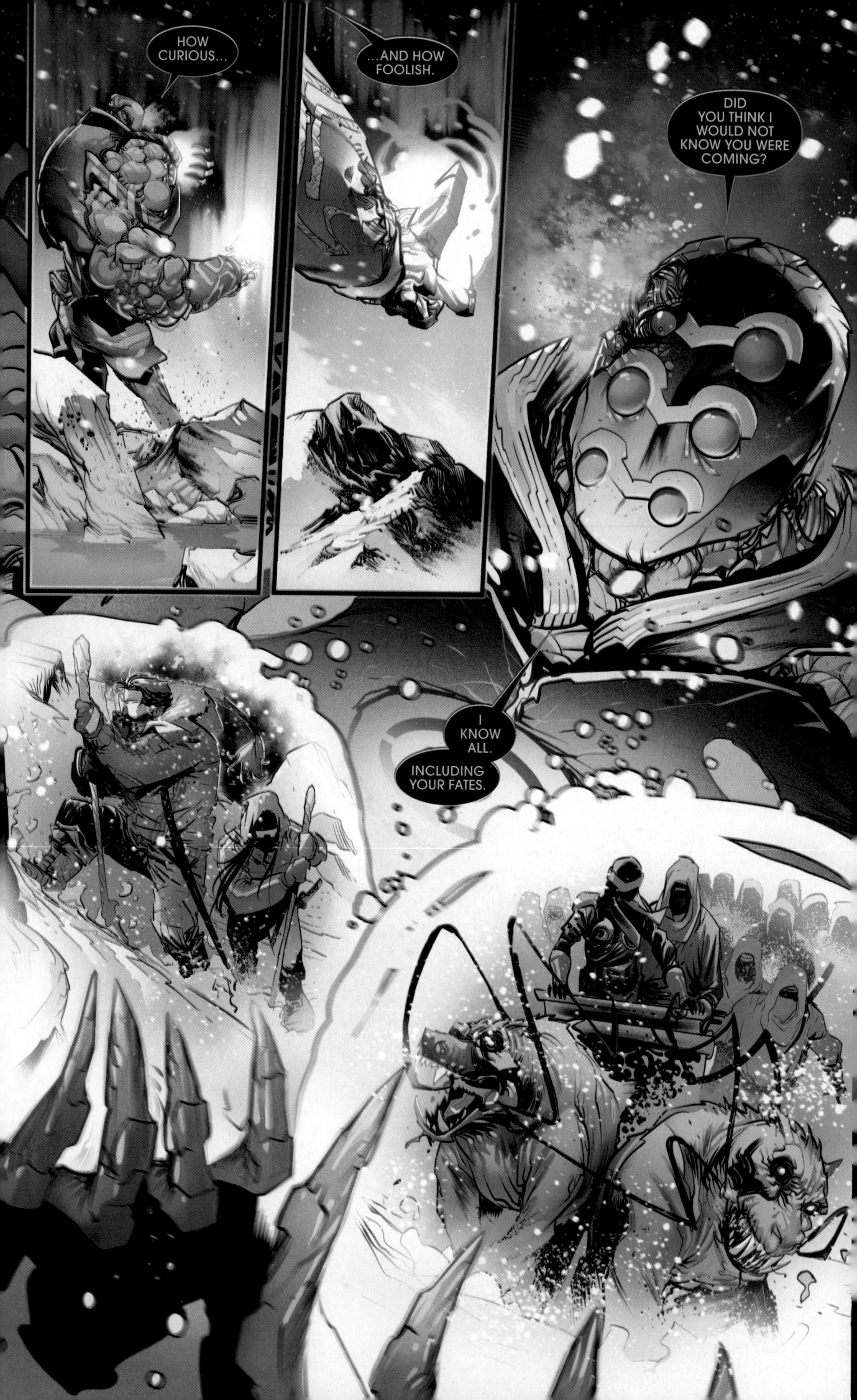
HOW CURIOUS...
...AND HOW FOOLISH.
DID YOU THINK I WOULD NOT KNOW YOU WERE COMING?
I KNOW ALL.
INCLUDING YOUR FATES.

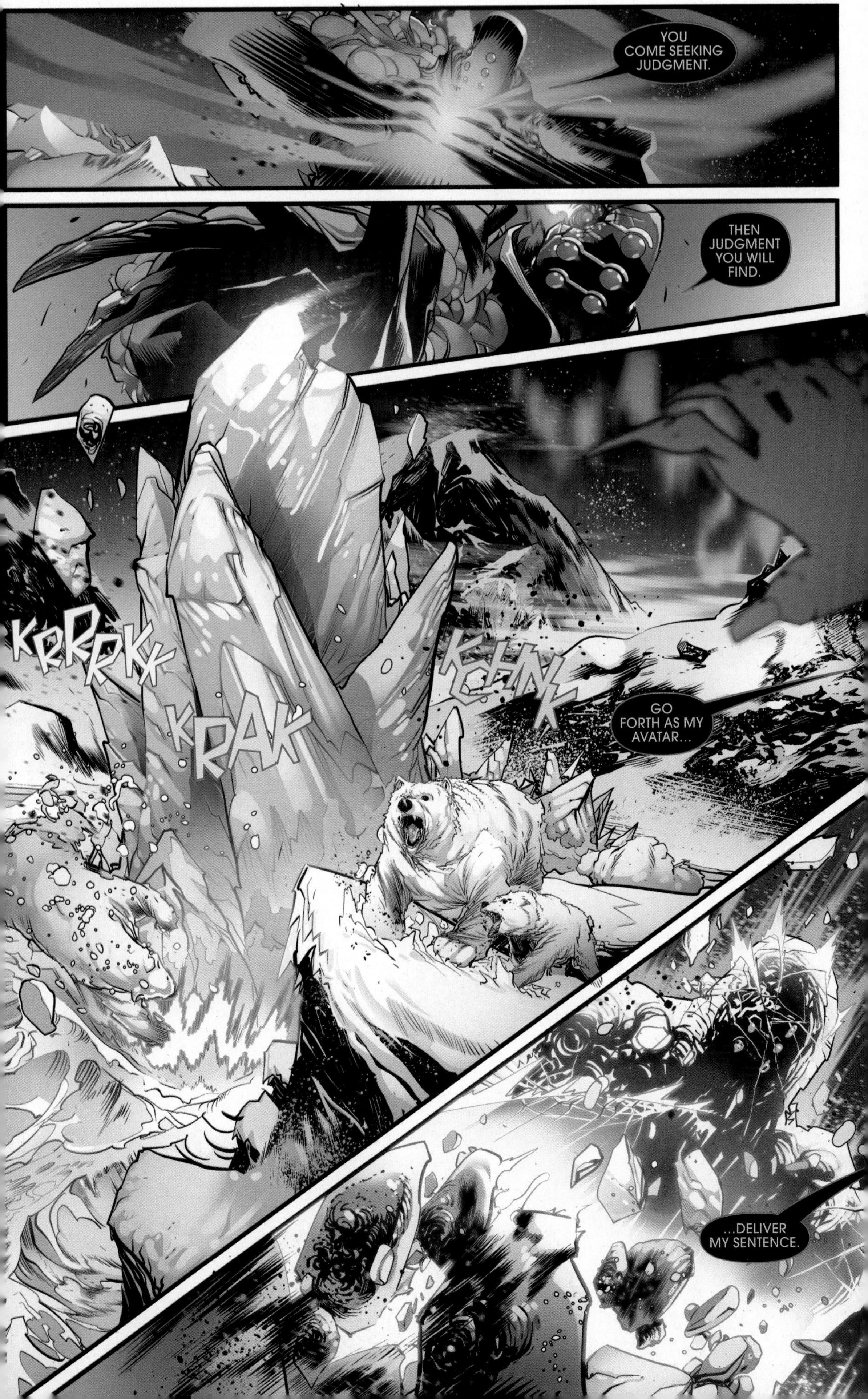
YOU COME SEEKING JUDGMENT.
THEN JUDGMENT YOU WILL FIND.
KRRRKK
KRAK
KCHNK
GO FORTH AS MY AVATAR...
...DELIVER MY SENTENCE.

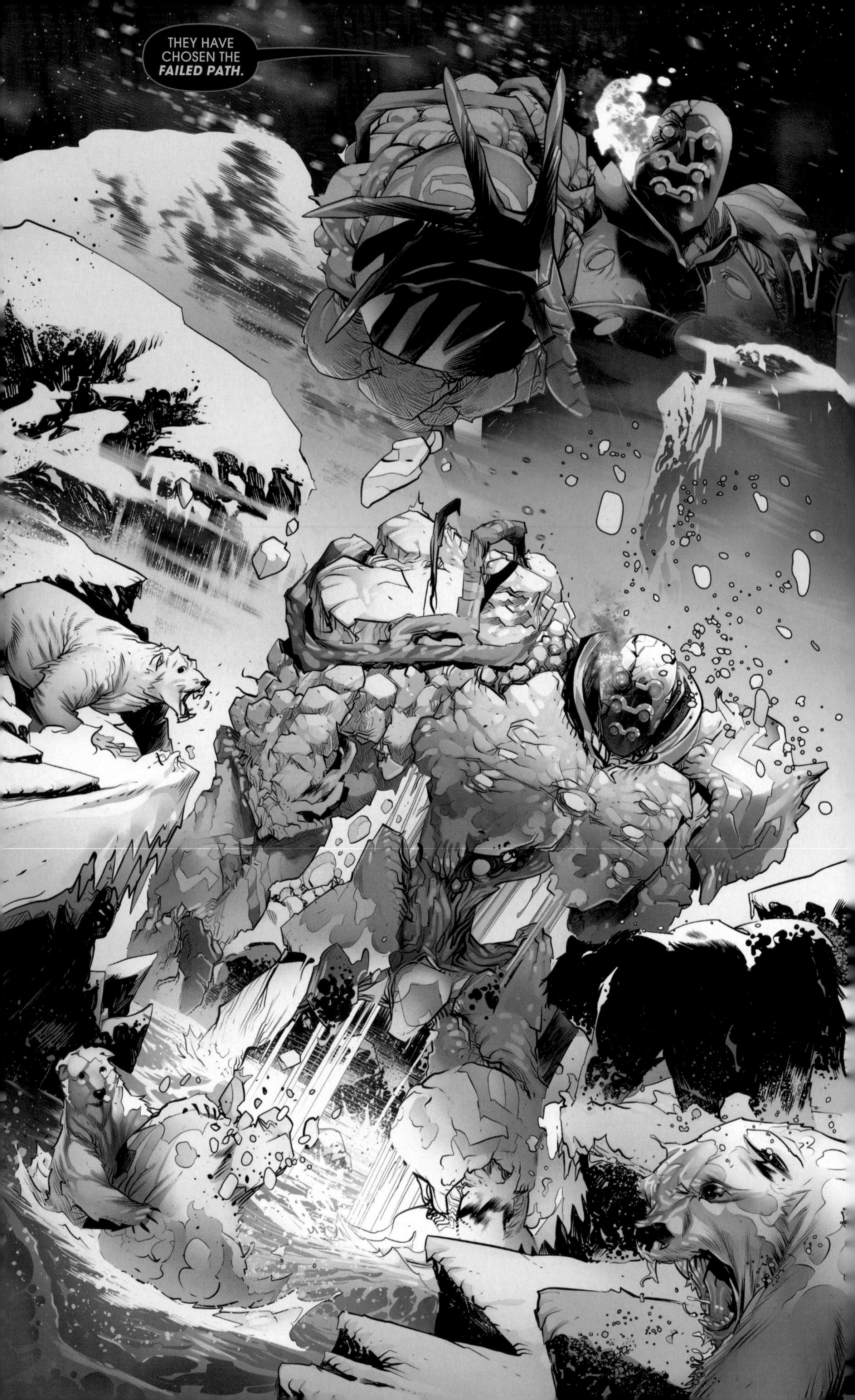
THEY HAVE CHOSEN THE ***FAILED PATH.***

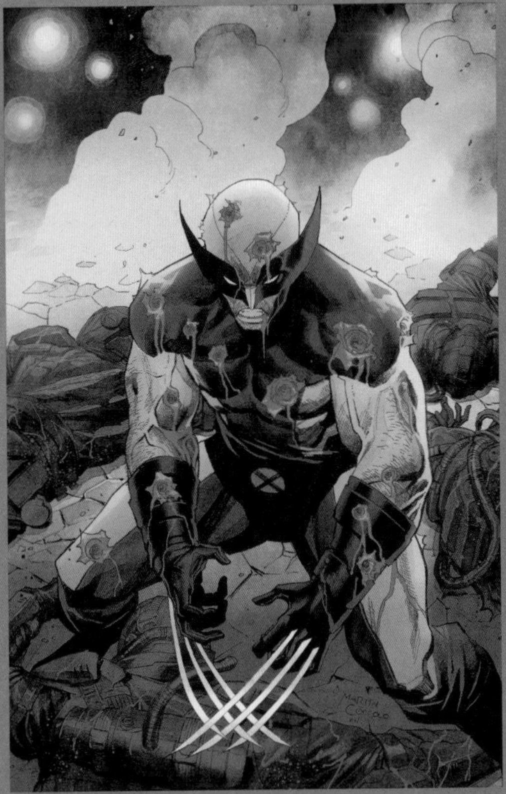

Wolverine #20 Variant
by Martin Coccolo & Matthew Wilson

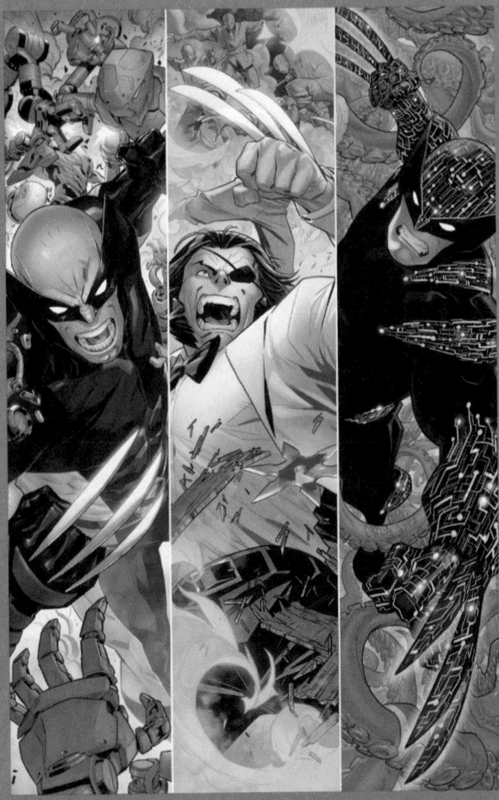

Wolverine #20 Promo Variant
by Carlos Gómez & Jesus Aburtov

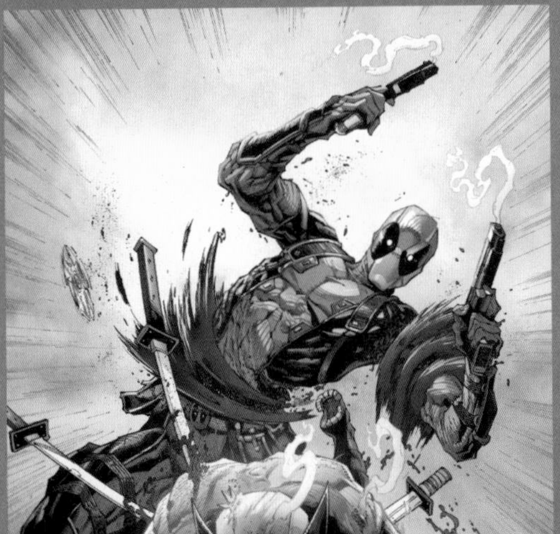

Wolverine #21 Variant
by Ryan Stegman, JP Mayer
& Marte Gracia

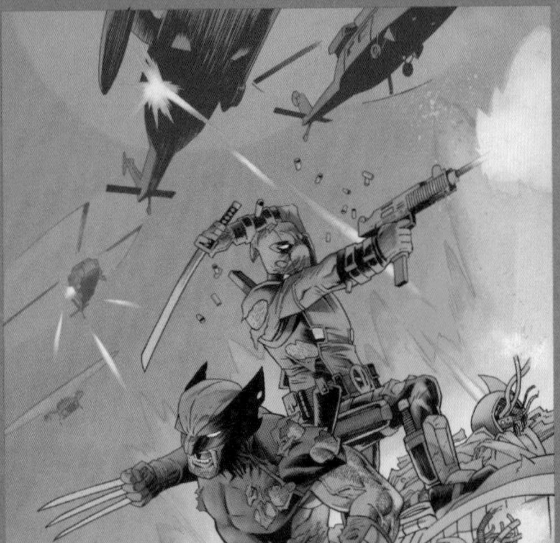

Wolverine #22 Variant
by Declan Shalvey

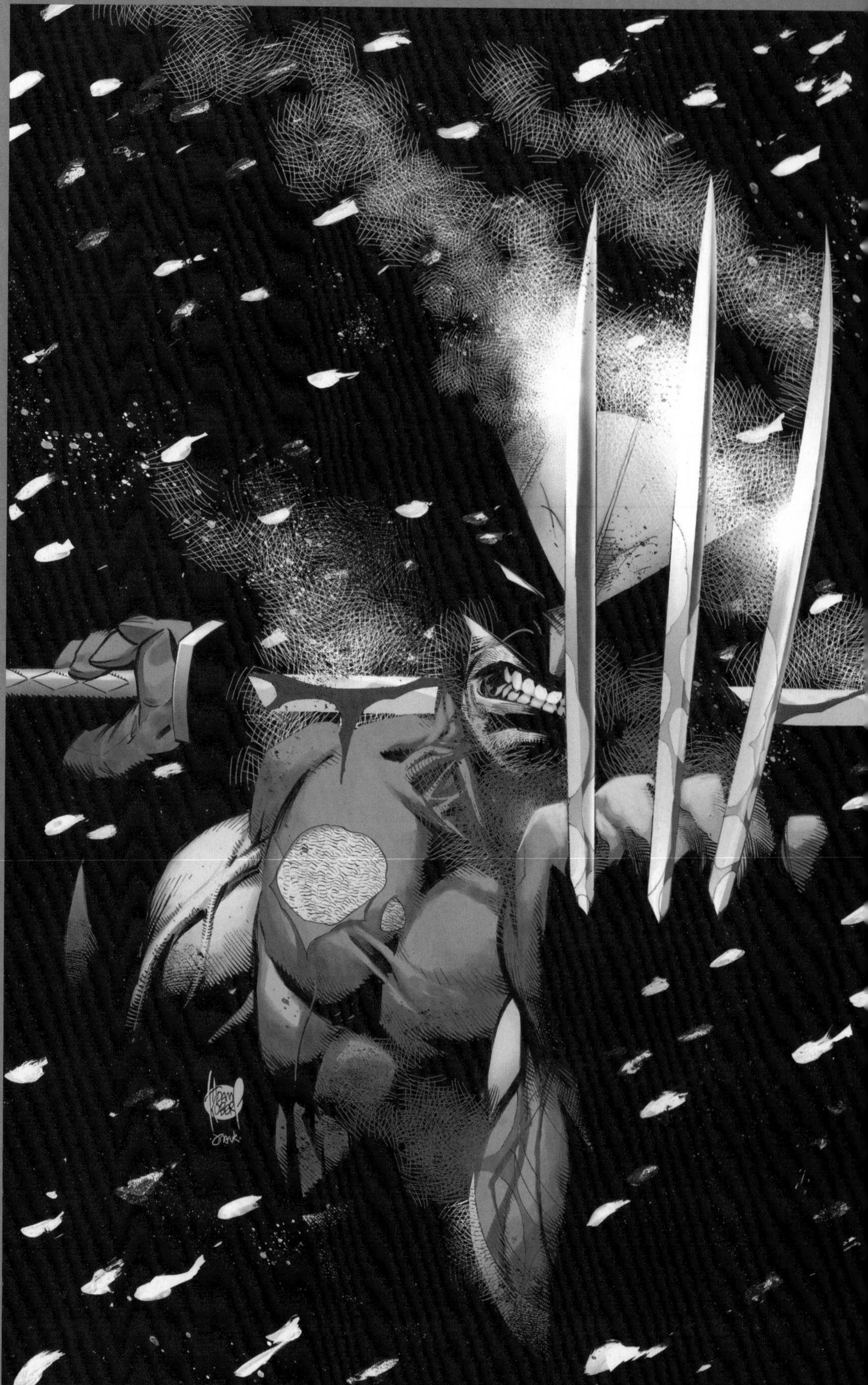

Hell to Pay Part Two

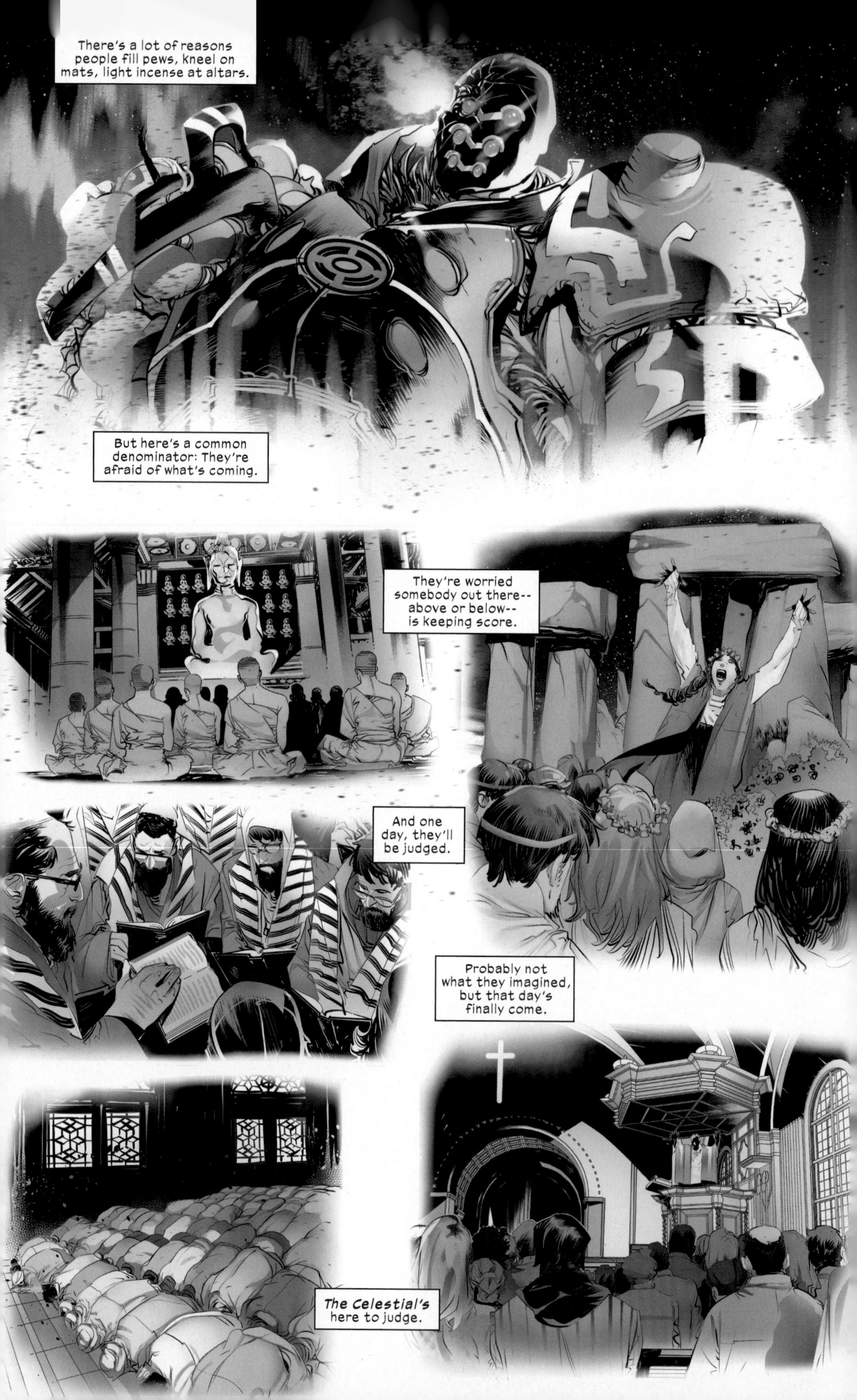
There's a lot of reasons people fill pews, kneel on mats, light incense at altars.
But here's a common denominator: They're afraid of what's coming.
They're worried somebody out there-- above or below-- is keeping score.
And one day, they'll be judged.
Probably not what they imagined, but that day's finally come.
The Celestial's here to judge.

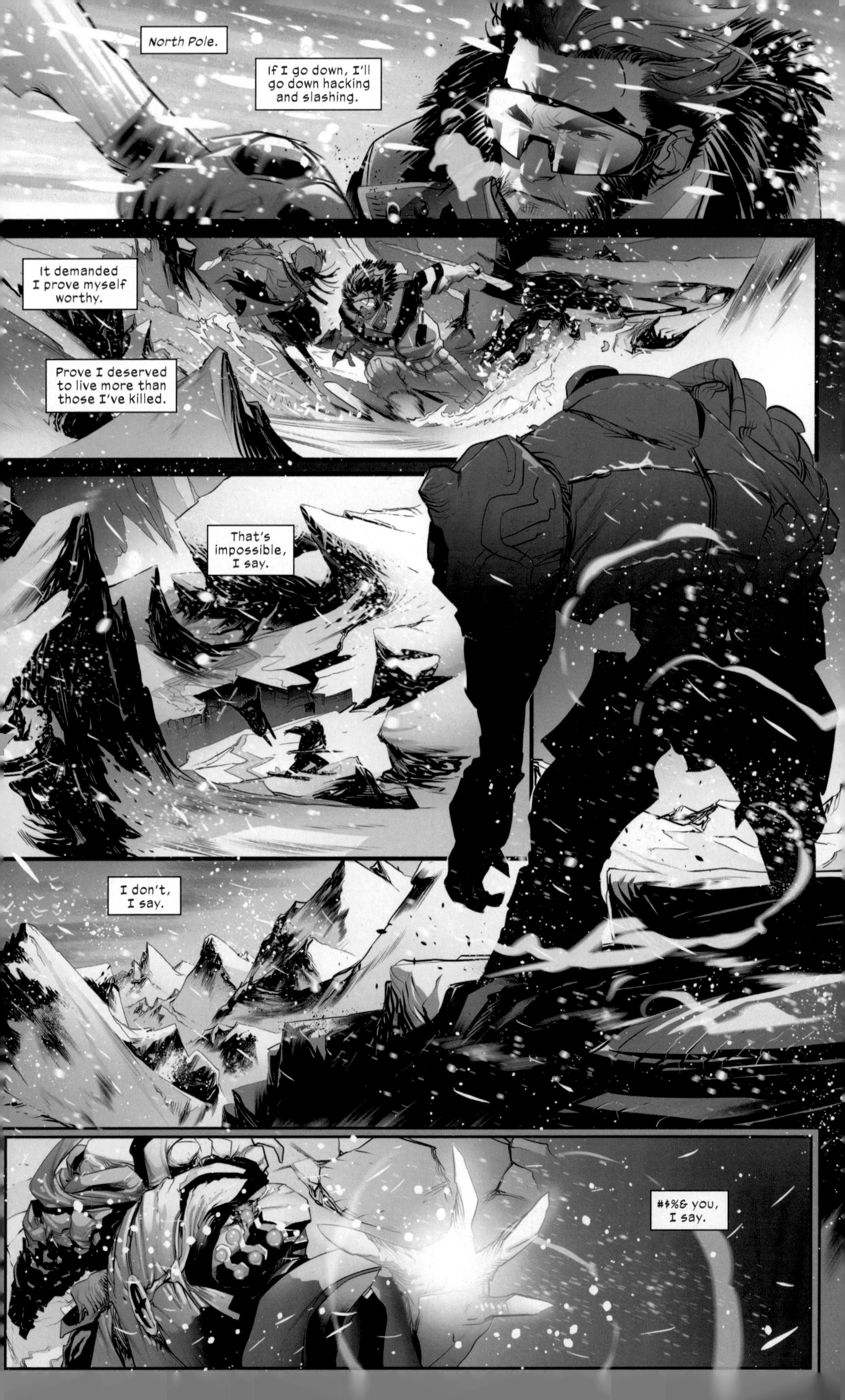
North Pole.
If I go down, I'll go down hacking and slashing.
It demanded I prove myself worthy.
Prove I deserved to live more than those I've killed.
That's impossible, I say.
I don't, I say.
#$%& you, I say.

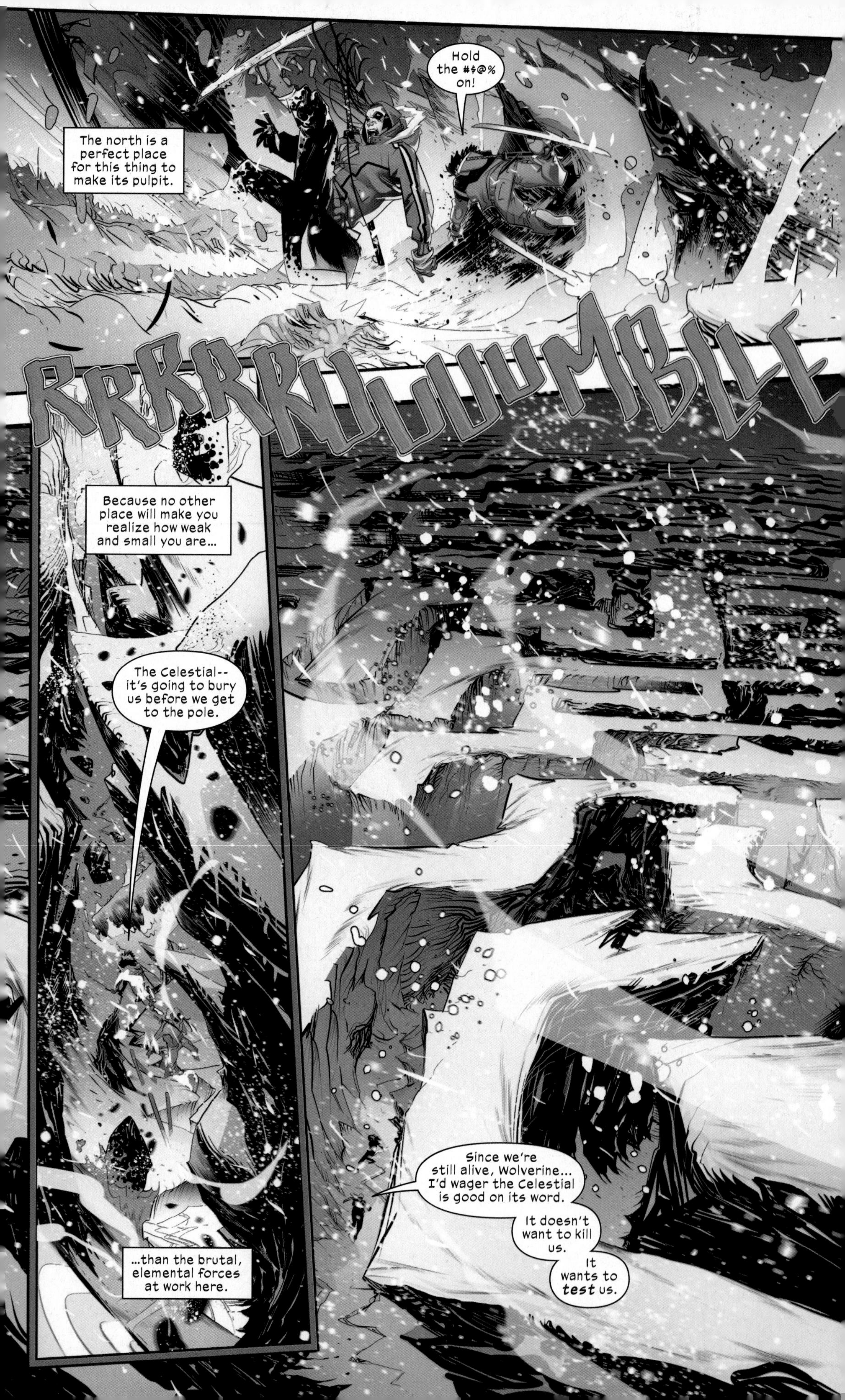

The north is a perfect place for this thing to make its pulpit.
Hold the #$@% on!
RRRRRUUUUMBLE
Because no other place will make you realize how weak and small you are...
The Celestial-- it's going to bury us before we get to the pole.
...than the brutal, elemental forces at work here.
Since we're still alive, Wolverine... I'd wager the Celestial is good on its word.
It doesn't want to kill us.
It wants to *test* us.

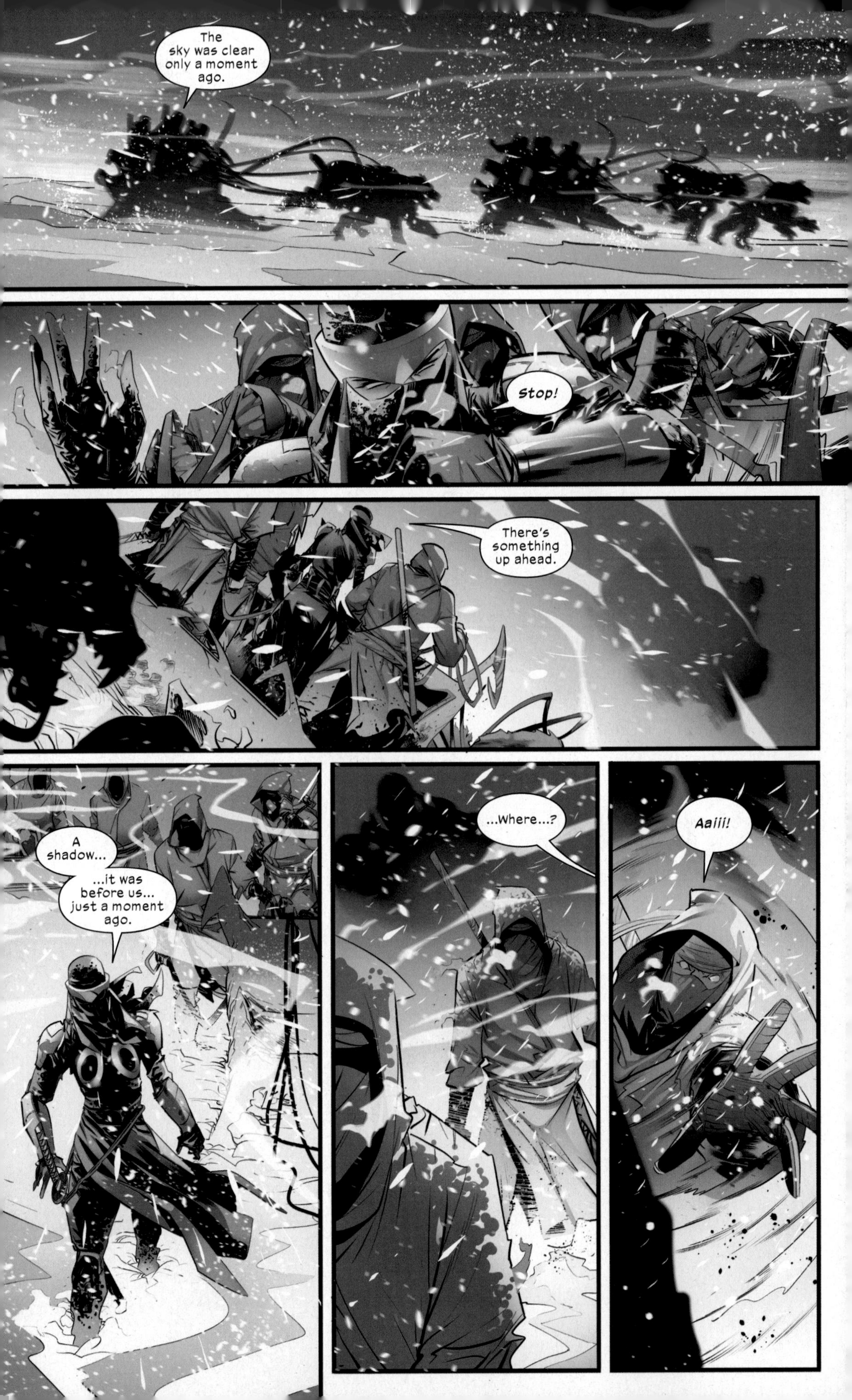
The sky was clear only a moment ago.
Stop!
There's something up ahead.
A shadow...
...it was before us... just a moment ago.
...Where...?
Aaiii!

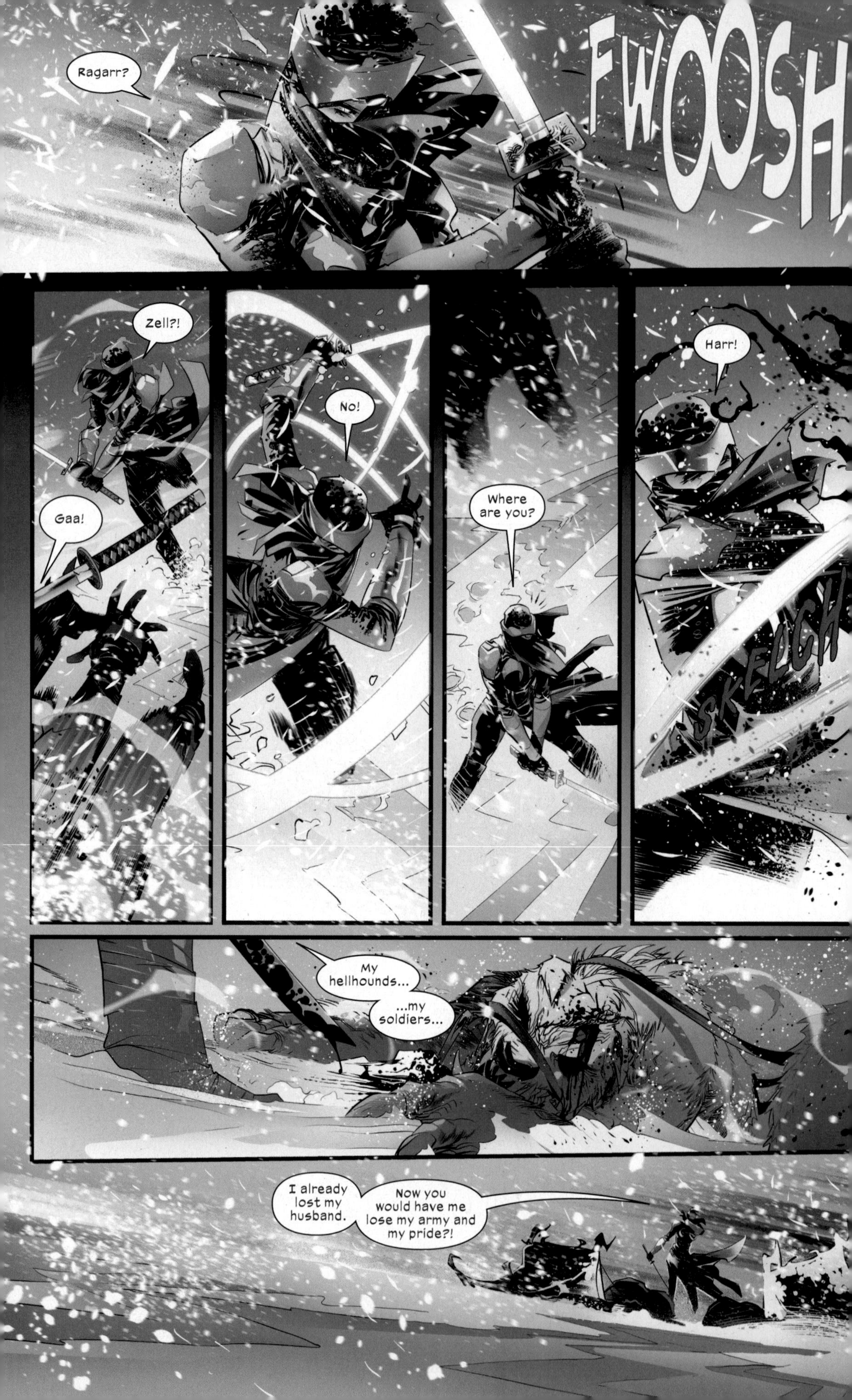
Ragarr?
FWOOSH
Zell?!
Gaa!
No!
Where are you?
Harr!
SKELCH
My hellhounds...
...my soldiers...
I already lost my husband.
Now you would have me lose my army and my pride?!

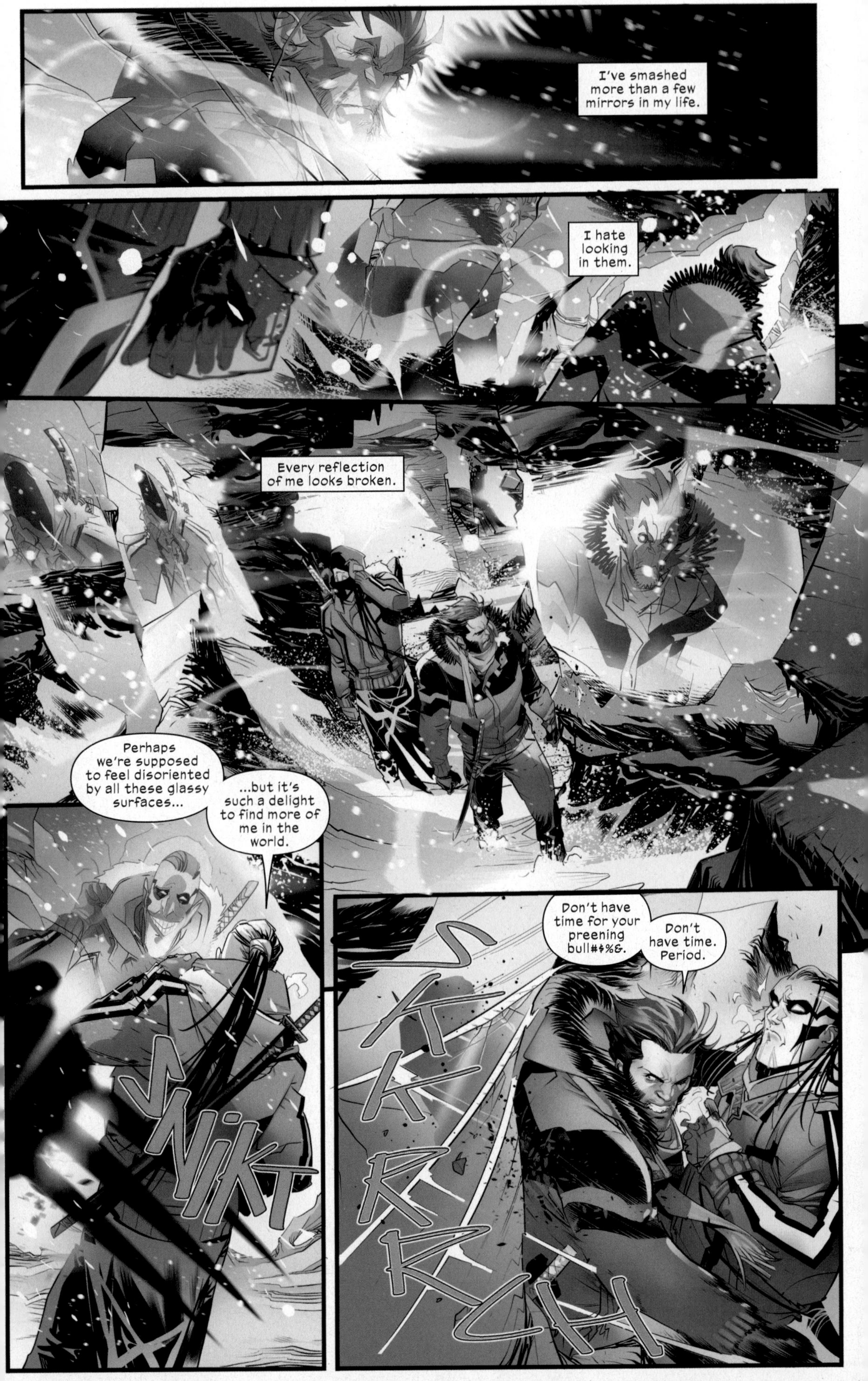
I've smashed more than a few mirrors in my life.
I hate looking in them.
Every reflection of me looks broken.
Perhaps we're supposed to feel disoriented by all these glassy surfaces...
...but it's such a delight to find more of me in the world.
SNIKT
Don't have time for your preening bull#$%&.
Don't have time. Period.
SKKRRRCHH

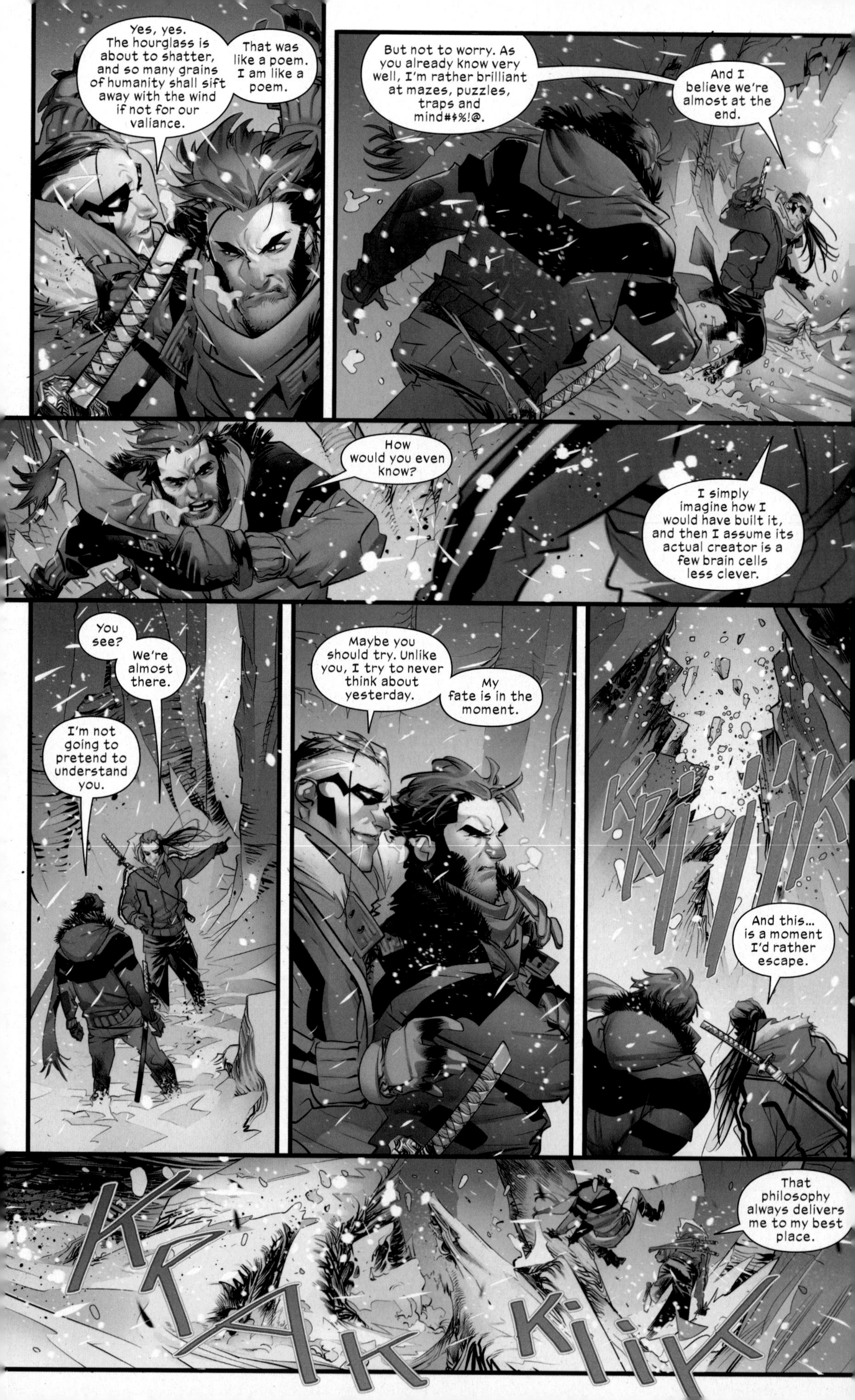

Yes, yes. The hourglass is about to shatter, and so many grains of humanity shall sift away with the wind if not for our valiance.
That was like a poem. I am like a poem.
But not to worry. As you already know very well, I'm rather brilliant at mazes, puzzles, traps and mind#$%!@.
And I believe we're almost at the end.
How would you even know?
I simply imagine how I would have built it, and then I assume its actual creator is a few brain cells less clever.
You see?
We're almost there.
I'm not going to pretend to understand you.
Maybe you should try. Unlike you, I try to never think about yesterday.
My fate is in the moment.
KRIIIIK
And this... is a moment I'd rather escape.
KRAKKIIIK
That philosophy always delivers me to my best place.

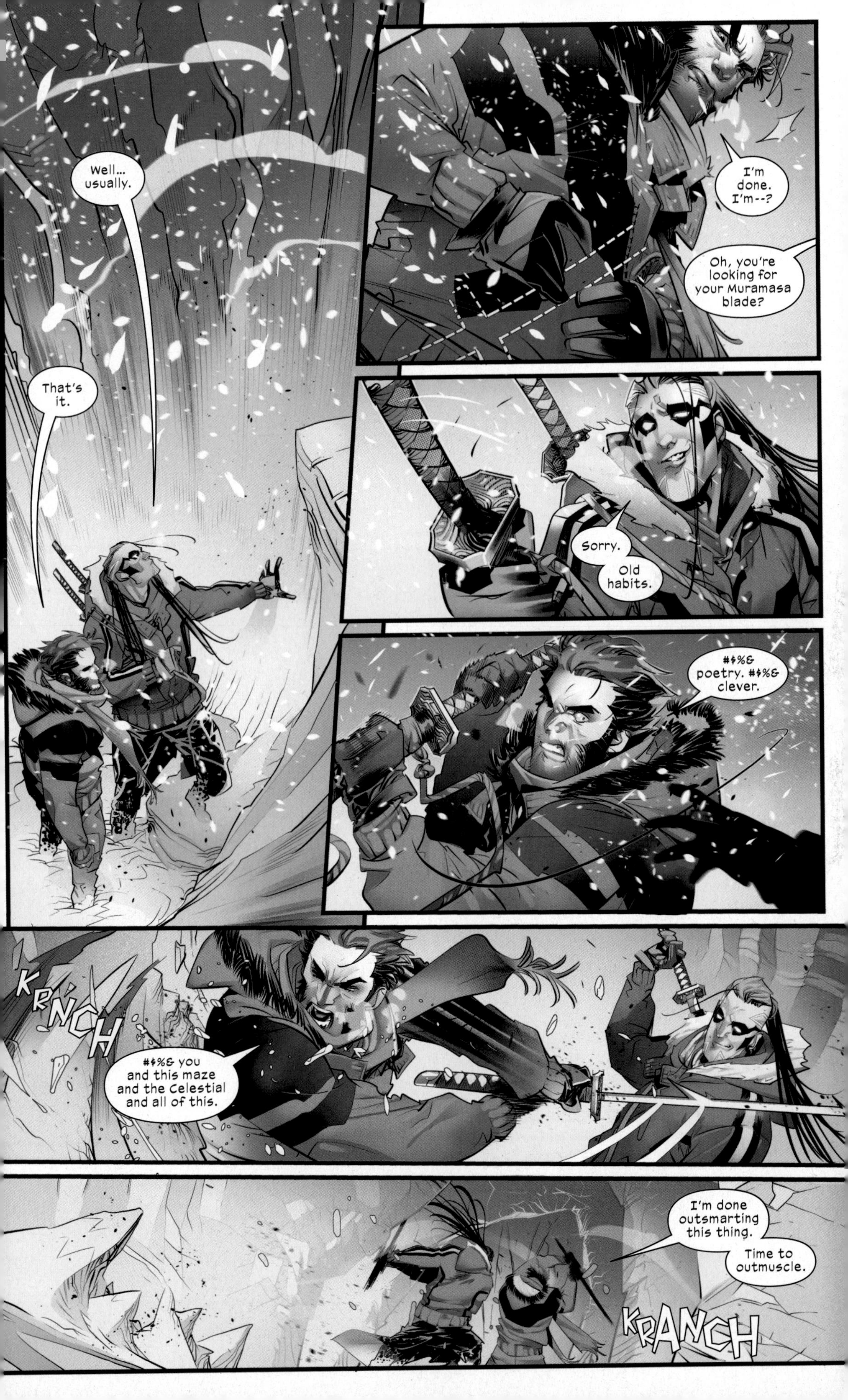

Well... usually.
I'm done. I'm--?
Oh, you're looking for your Muramasa blade?
That's it.
Sorry.
Old habits.
#$%& poetry. #$%& clever.
KRNCH
#$%& you and this maze and the Celestial and all of this.
I'm done outsmarting this thing.
Time to outmuscle.
KRANCH

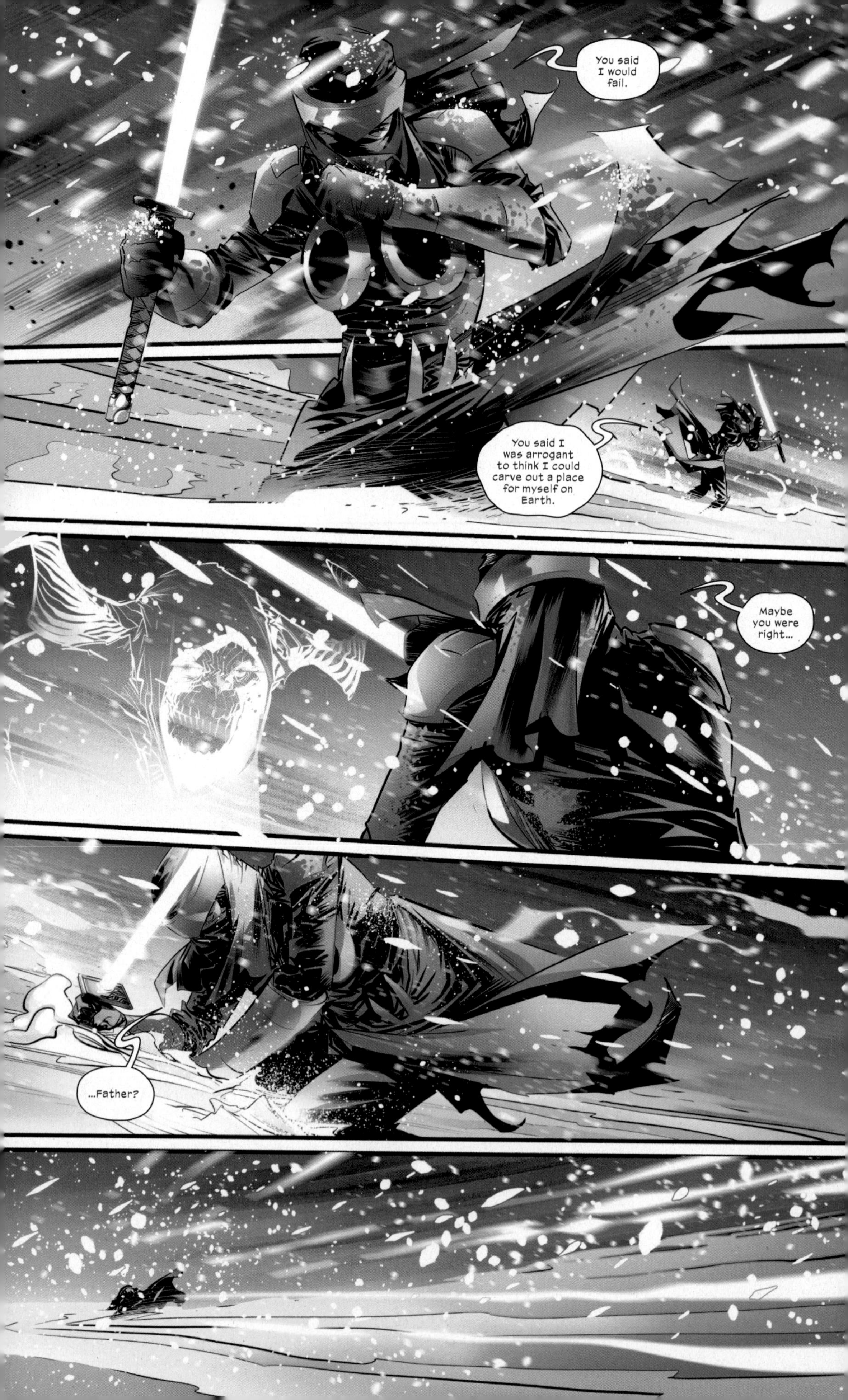
You said I would fail.
You said I was arrogant to think I could carve out a place for myself on Earth.
Maybe you were right...
...Father?

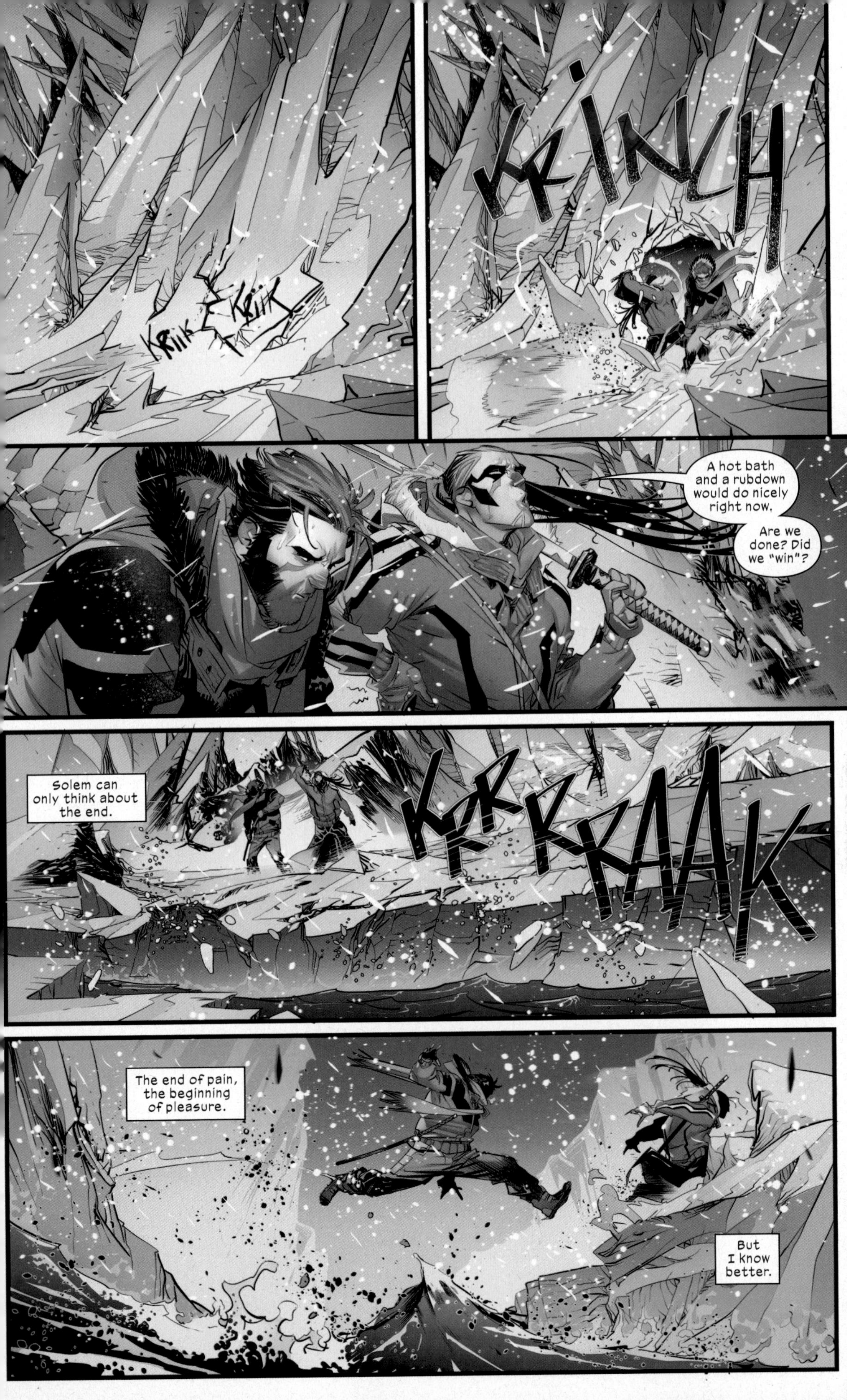
KRIIK KRIIK
KRINCH
A hot bath and a rubdown would do nicely right now.
Are we done? Did we "win"?
Solem can only think about the end.
KRRRAAAK
The end of pain, the beginning of pleasure.
But I know better.

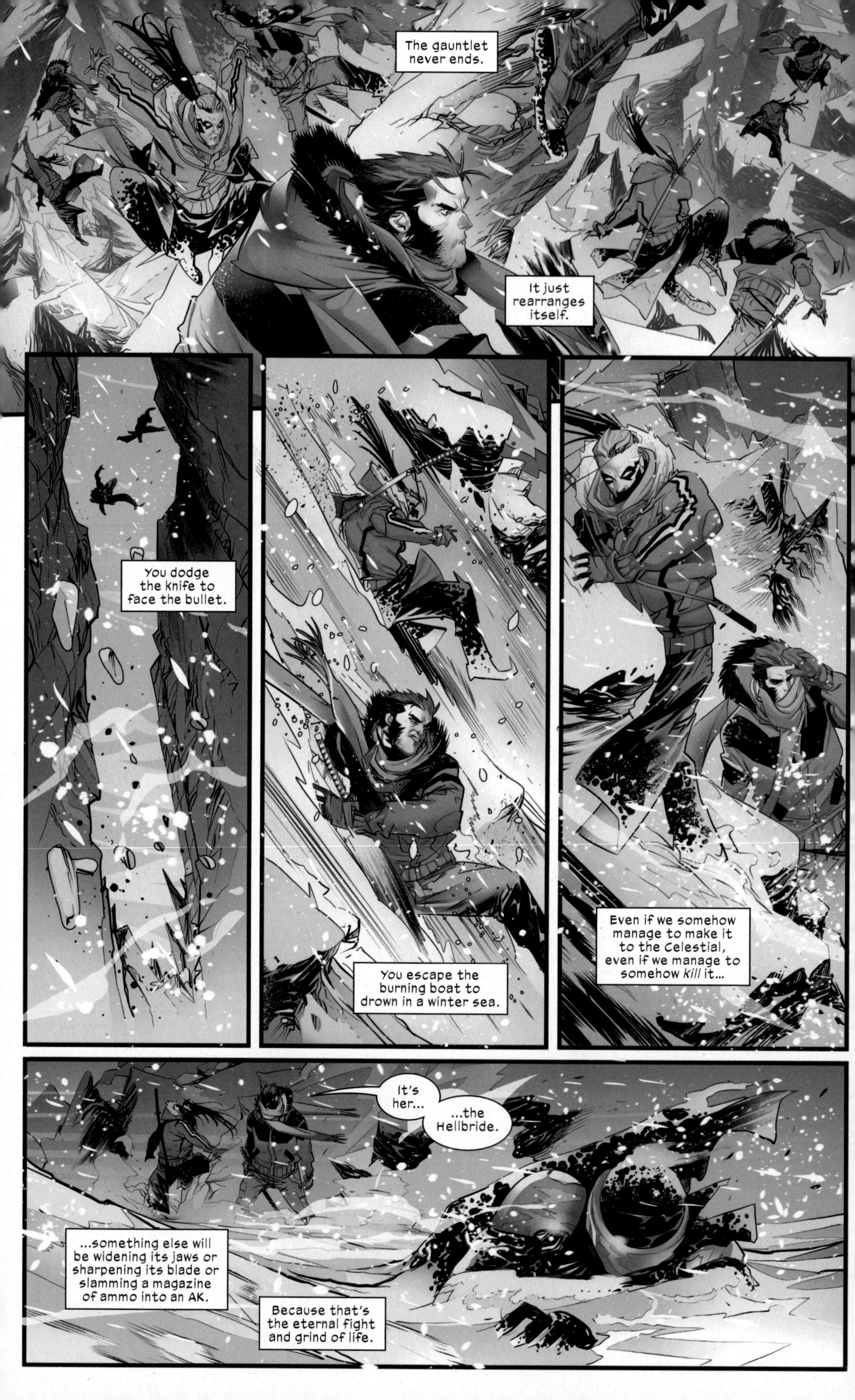
The gauntlet never ends.
It just rearranges itself.
You dodge the knife to face the bullet.
You escape the burning boat to drown in a winter sea.
Even if we somehow manage to make it to the Celestial, even if we manage to somehow *kill* it...
It's her...
...the Hellbride.
...something else will be widening its jaws or sharpening its blade or slamming a magazine of ammo into an AK.
Because that's the eternal fight and grind of life.

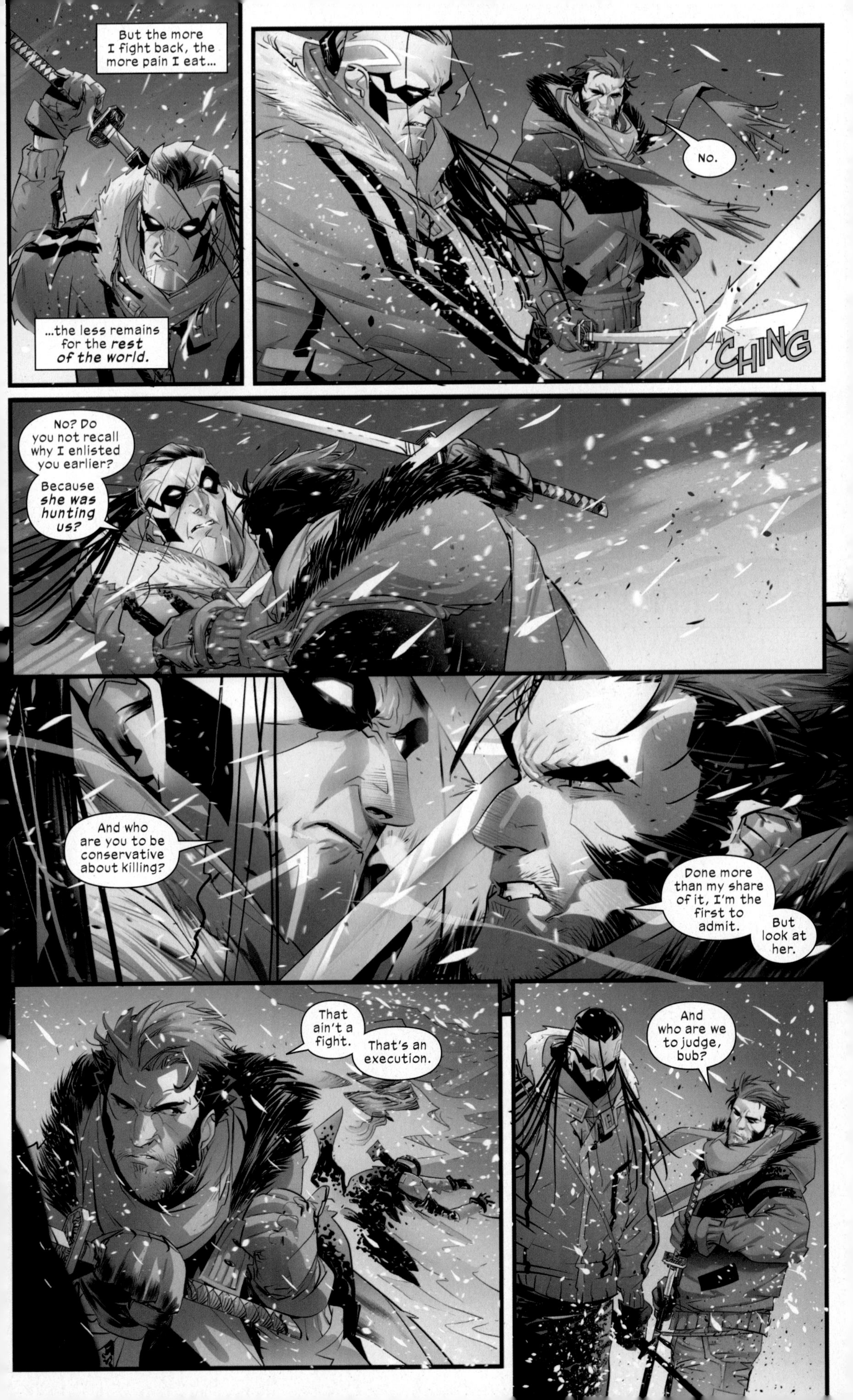
But the more I fight back, the more pain I eat...
...the less remains for the *rest of the world.*
No.
CHING
No? Do you not recall why I enlisted you earlier?
Because *she was hunting us?*
And who are you to be conservative about killing?
Done more than my share of it, I'm the first to admit.
But look at her.
That ain't a fight.
That's an execution.
And who are we to judge, bub?

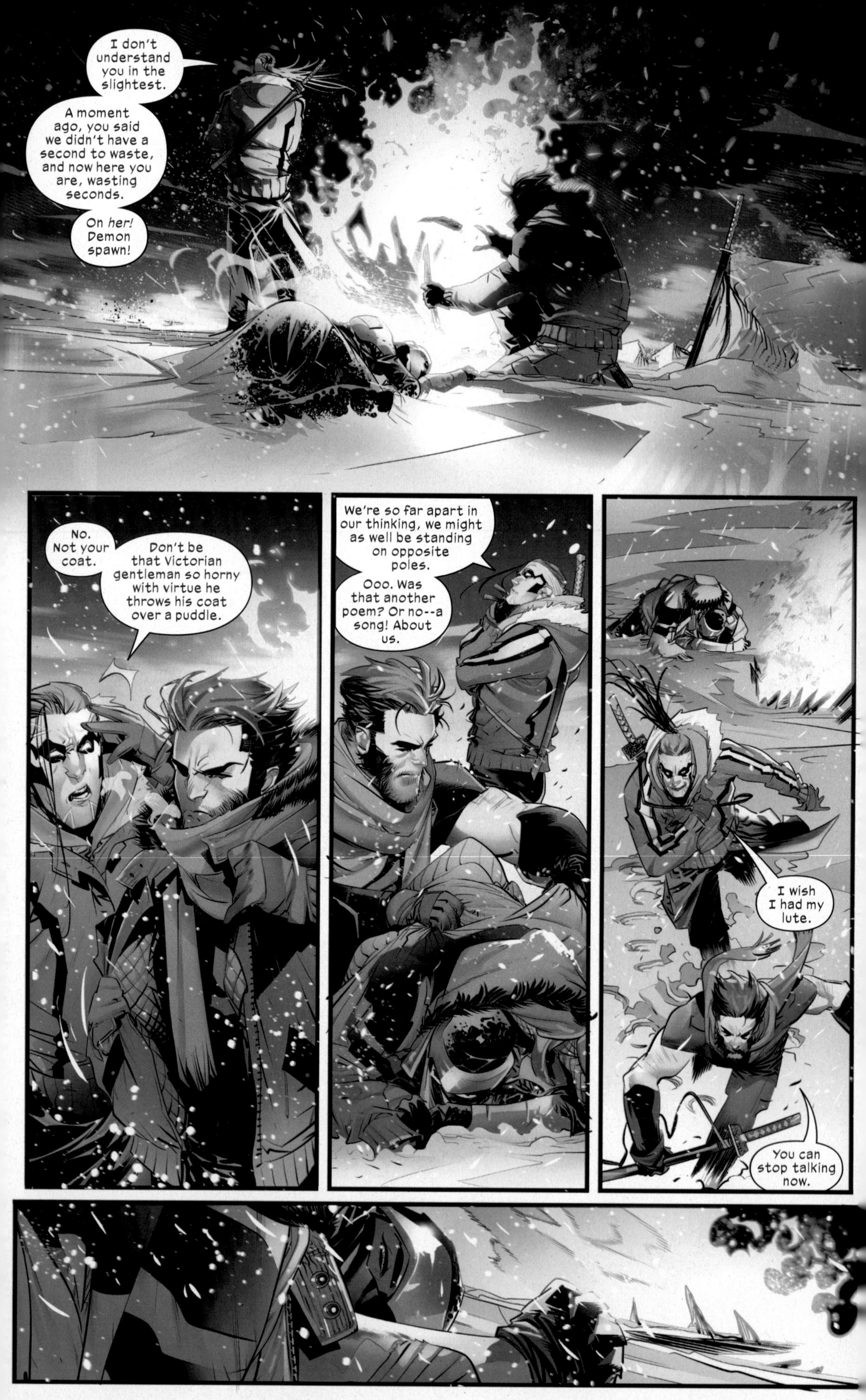
I don't understand you in the slightest.
A moment ago, you said we didn't have a second to waste, and now here you are, wasting seconds.
On her! Demon spawn!
No. Not your coat.
Don't be that Victorian gentleman so horny with virtue he throws his coat over a puddle.
We're so far apart in our thinking, we might as well be standing on opposite poles.
Ooo. Was that another poem? Or no--a song! About us.
I wish I had my lute.
You can stop talking now.

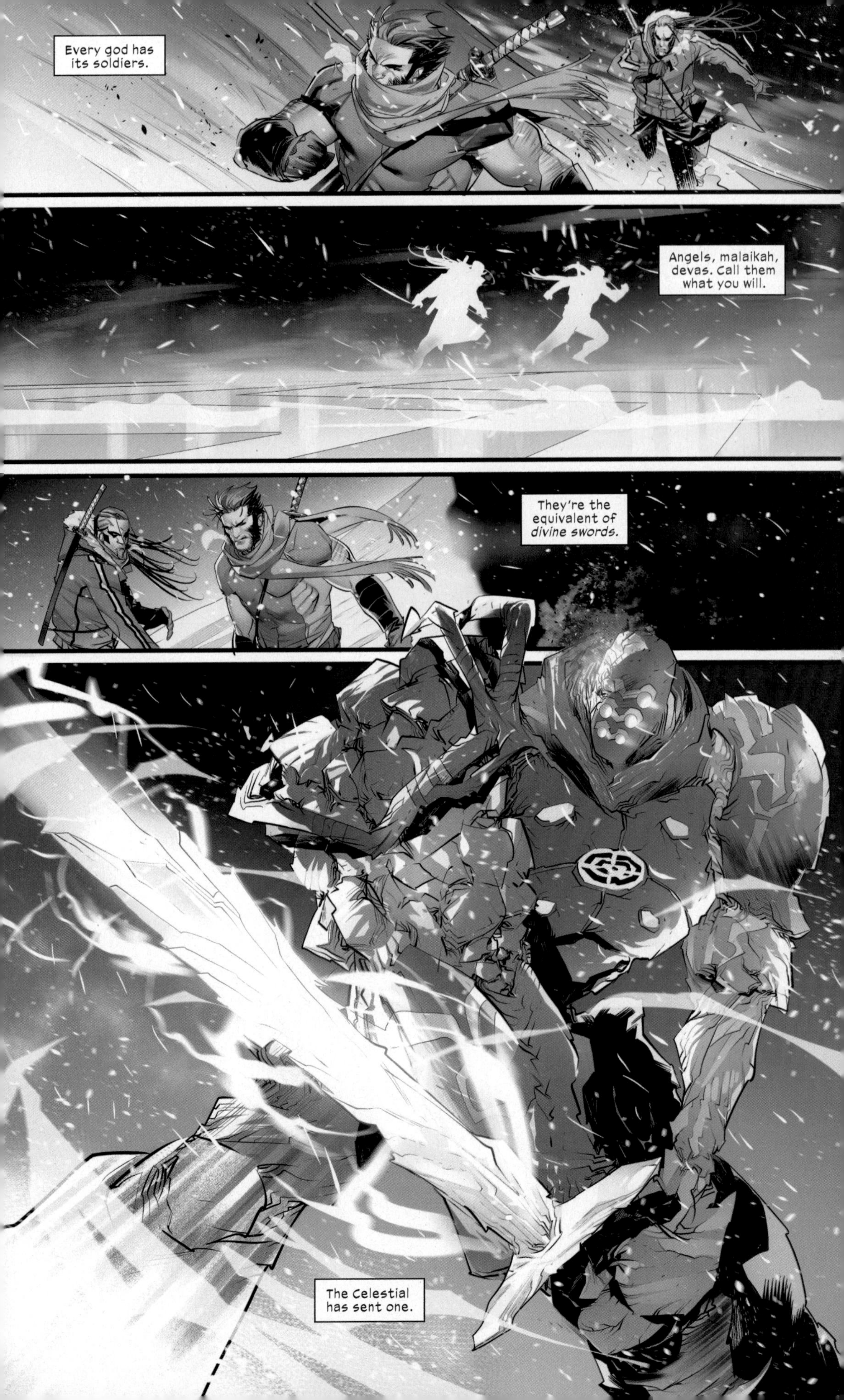
Every god has its soldiers.
Angels, malaikah, devas. Call them what you will.
They're the equivalent of *divine swords.*
The Celestial has sent one.

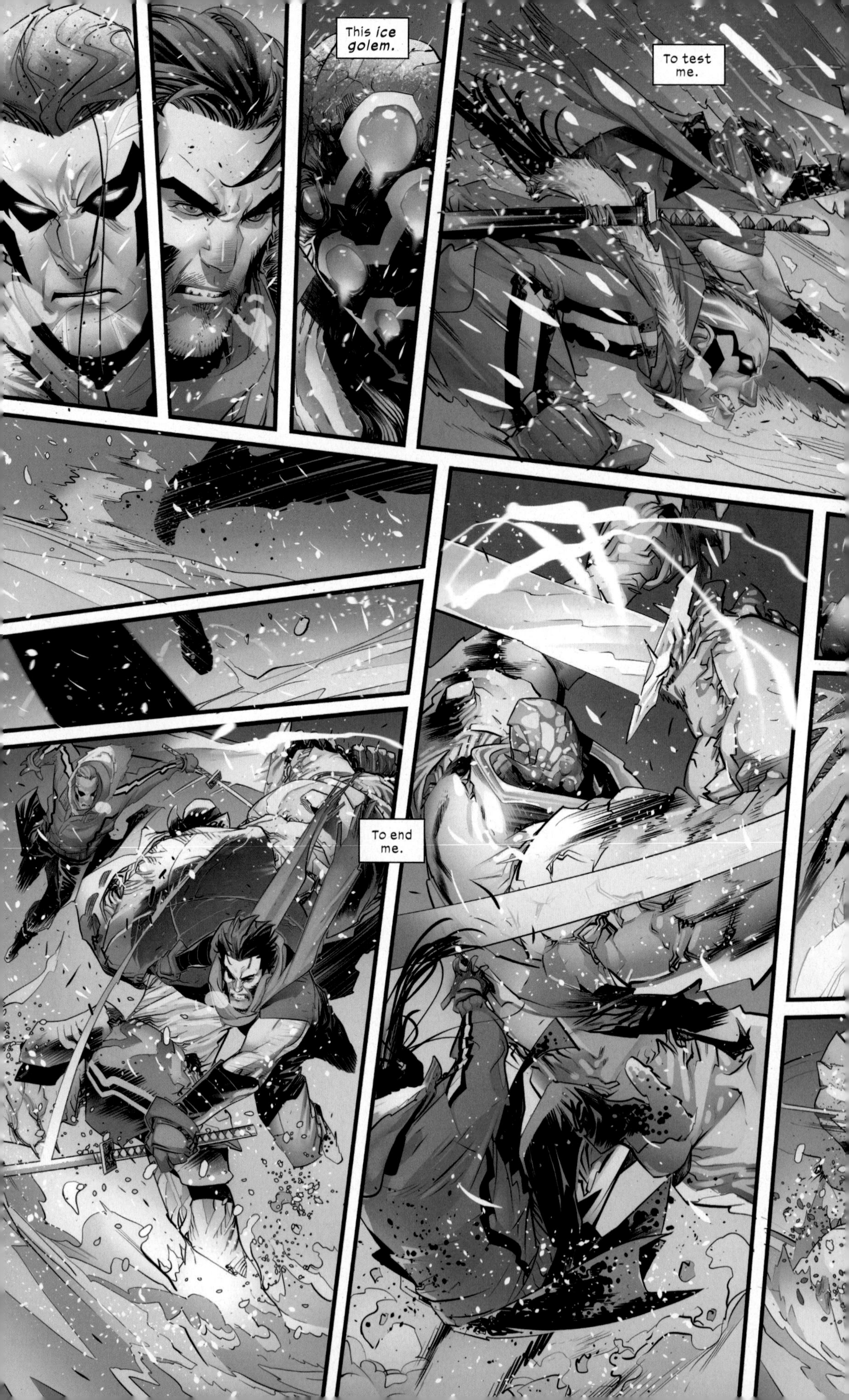
This *ice golem.*
To test me.
To end me.

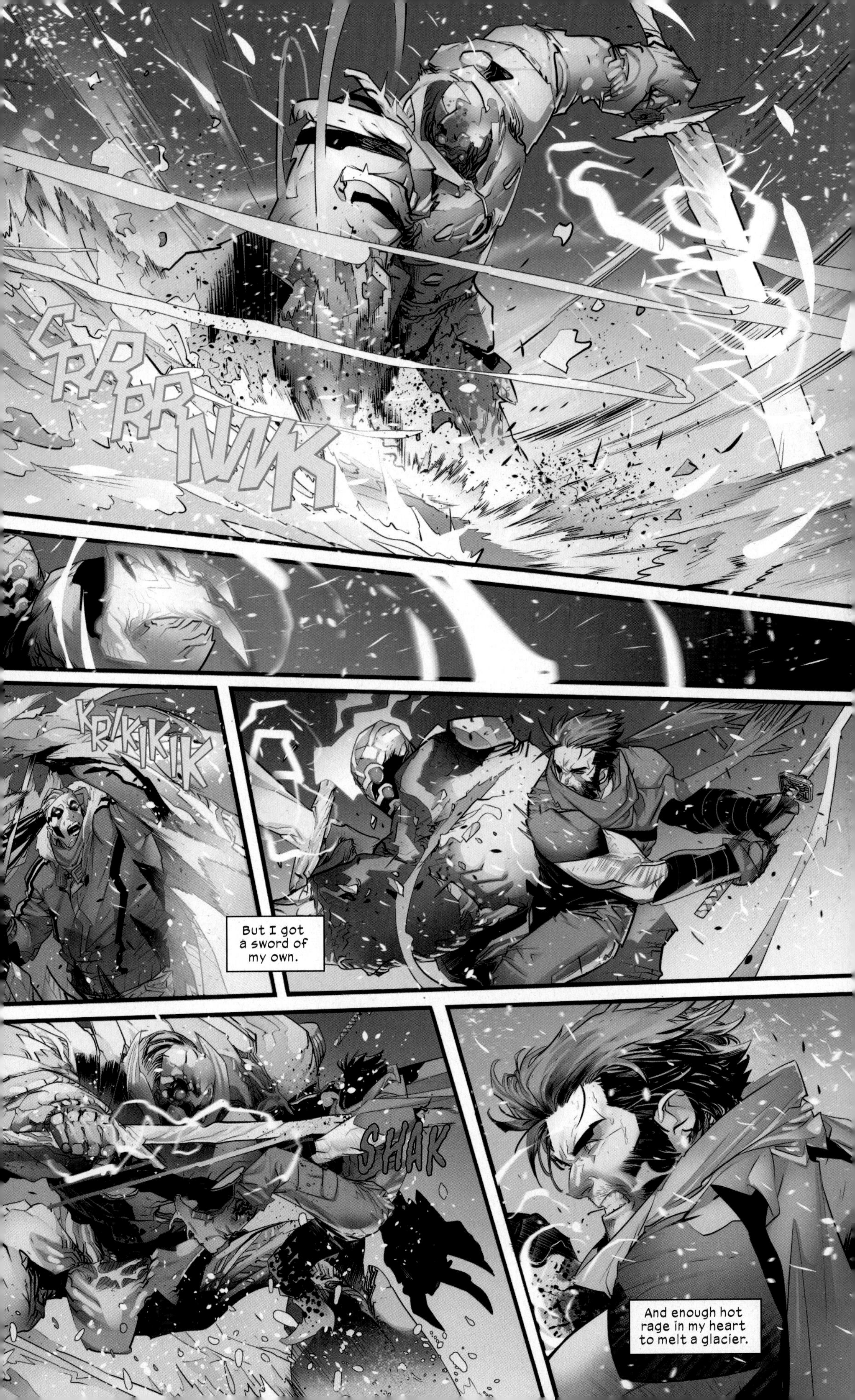
CRRRRNNK
KRIKIKIK
But I got a sword of my own.
SHAK
And enough hot rage in my heart to melt a glacier.

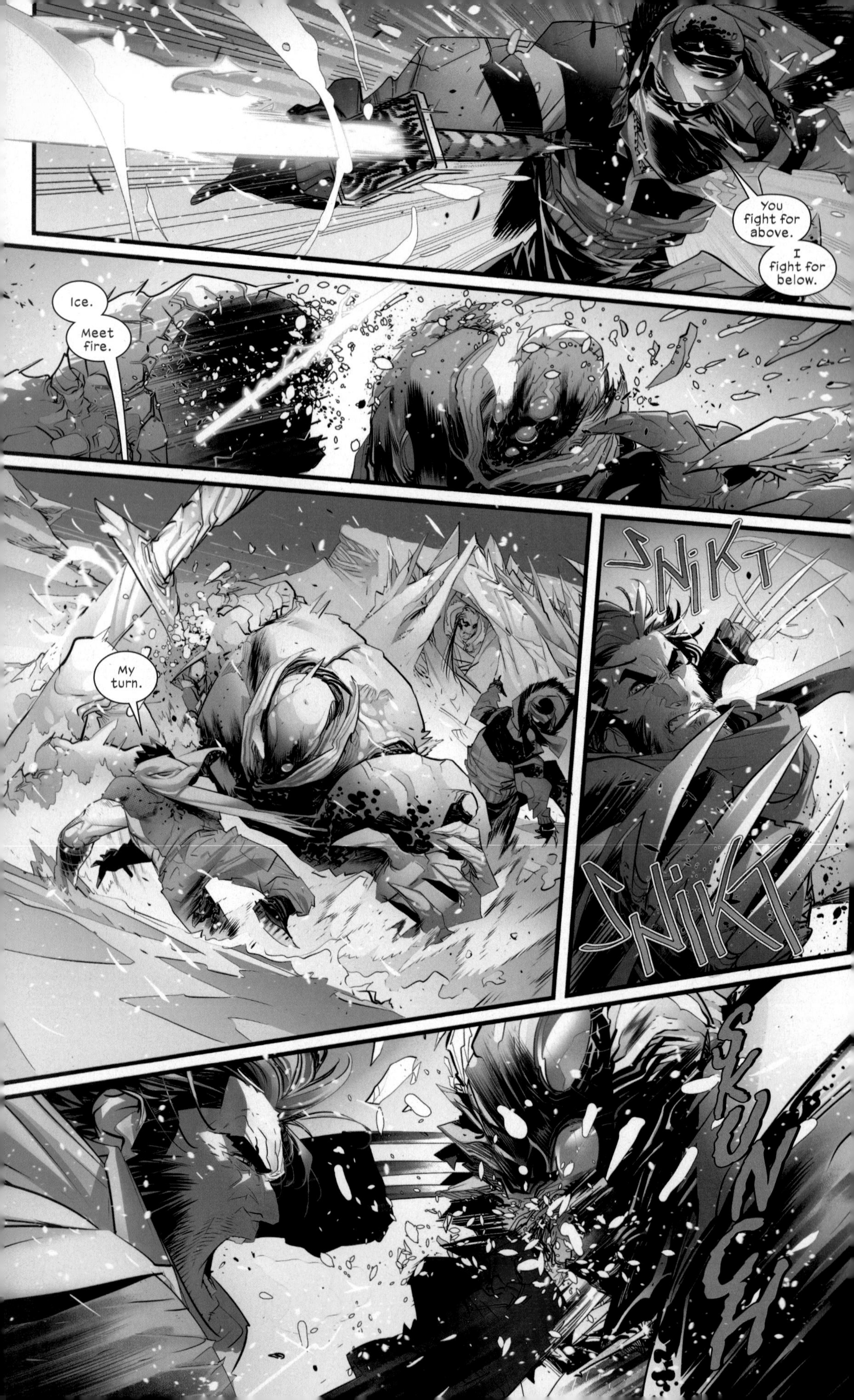
You fight for above.
I fight for below.
Ice.
Meet fire.
My turn.
SNIKT
SNIKT
SKUNCH

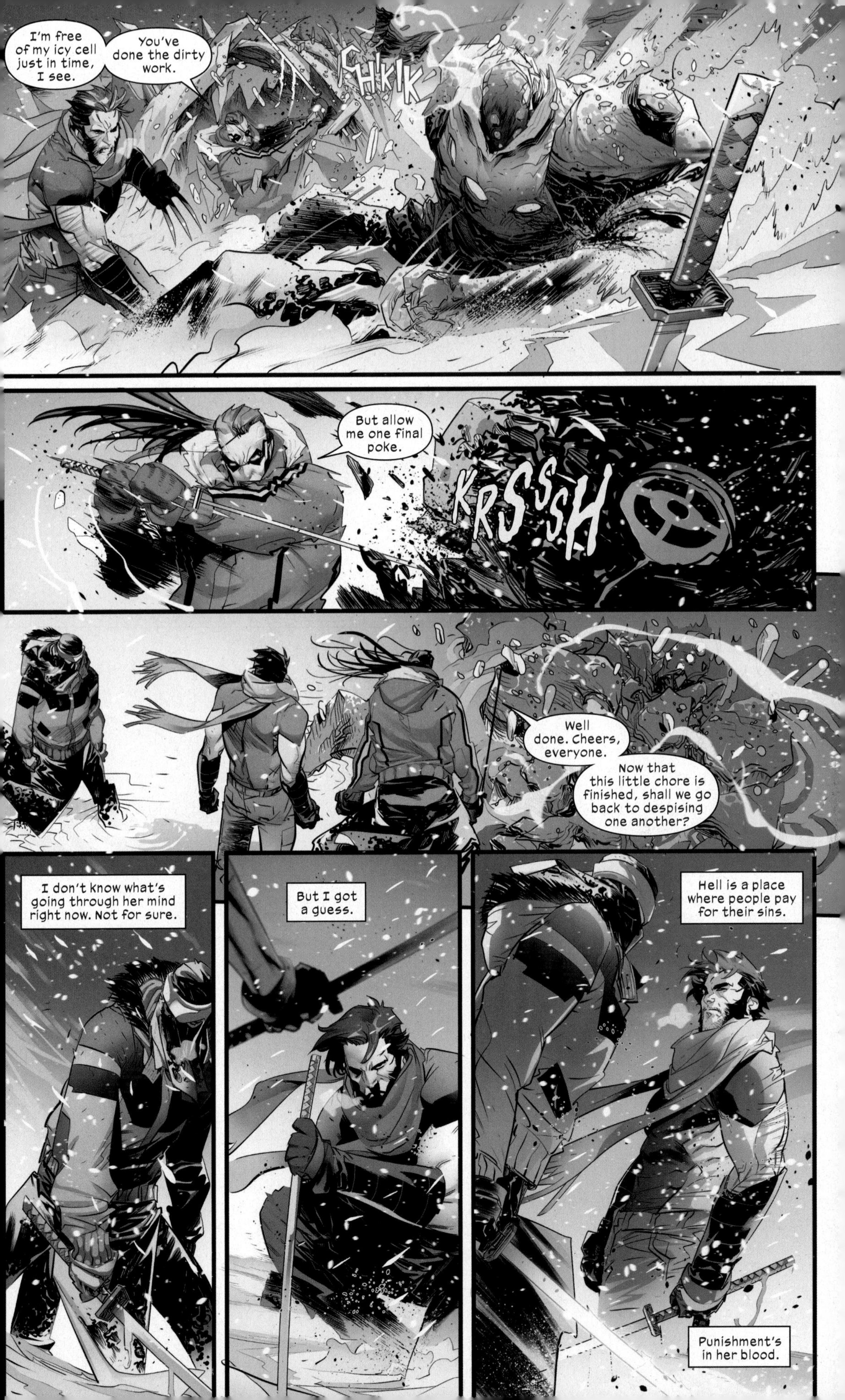
I'm free of my icy cell just in time, I see.
You've done the dirty work.
CHKIK
But allow me one final poke.
KRSSSH
Well done. Cheers, everyone.
Now that this little chore is finished, shall we go back to despising one another?
I don't know what's going through her mind right now. Not for sure.
But I got a guess.
Hell is a place where people pay for their sins.
Punishment's in her blood.

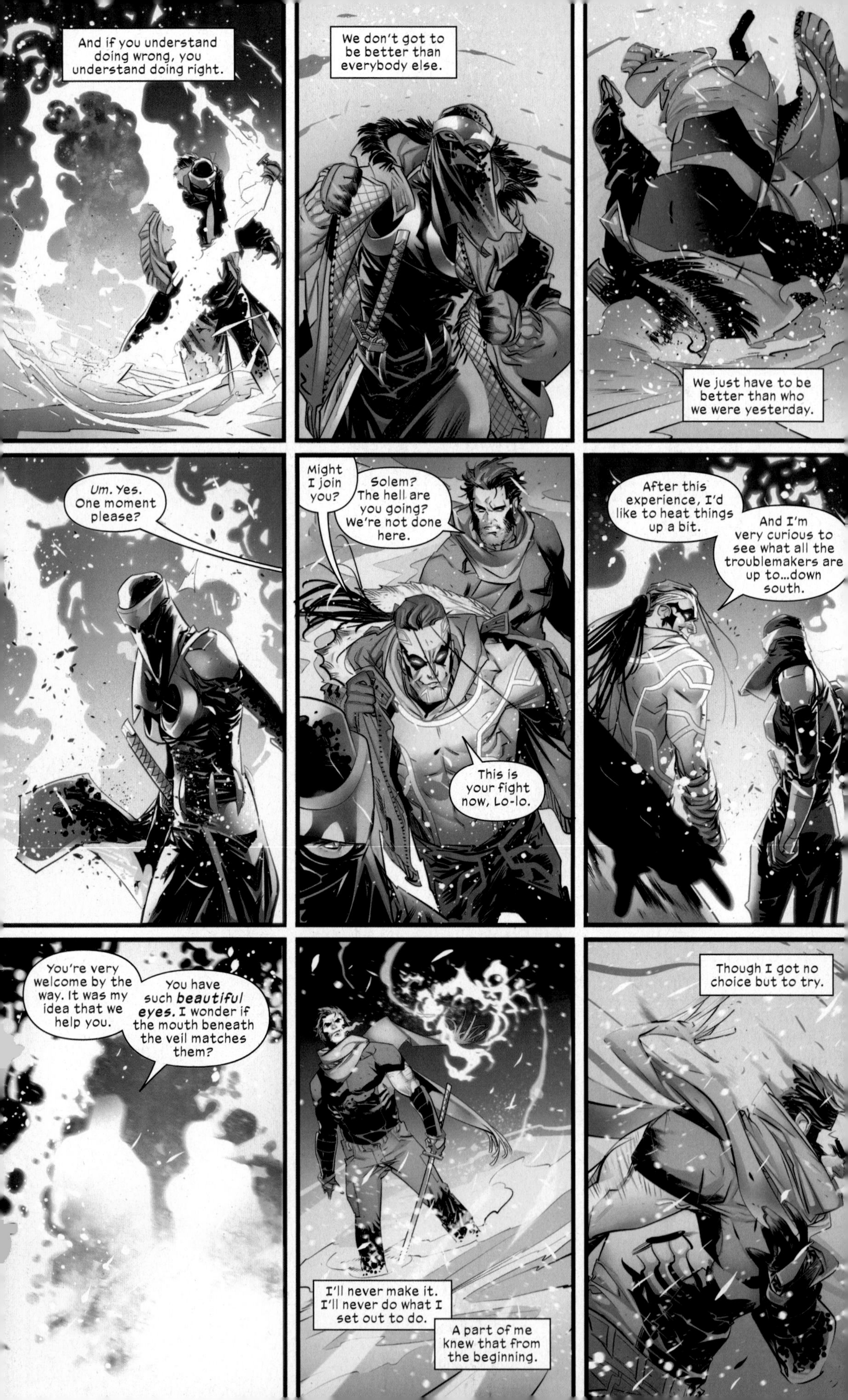

And if you understand doing wrong, you understand doing right.
We don't got to be better than everybody else.
We just have to be better than who we were yesterday.
Um. Yes. One moment please?
Might I join you?
Solem? The hell are you going? We're not done here.
This is your fight now, Lo-lo.
After this experience, I'd like to heat things up a bit.
And I'm very curious to see what all the troublemakers are up to...down south.
You're very welcome by the way. It was my idea that we help you.
You have such beautiful eyes. I wonder if the mouth beneath the veil matches them?
I'll never make it. I'll never do what I set out to do.
A part of me knew that from the beginning.
Though I got no choice but to try.

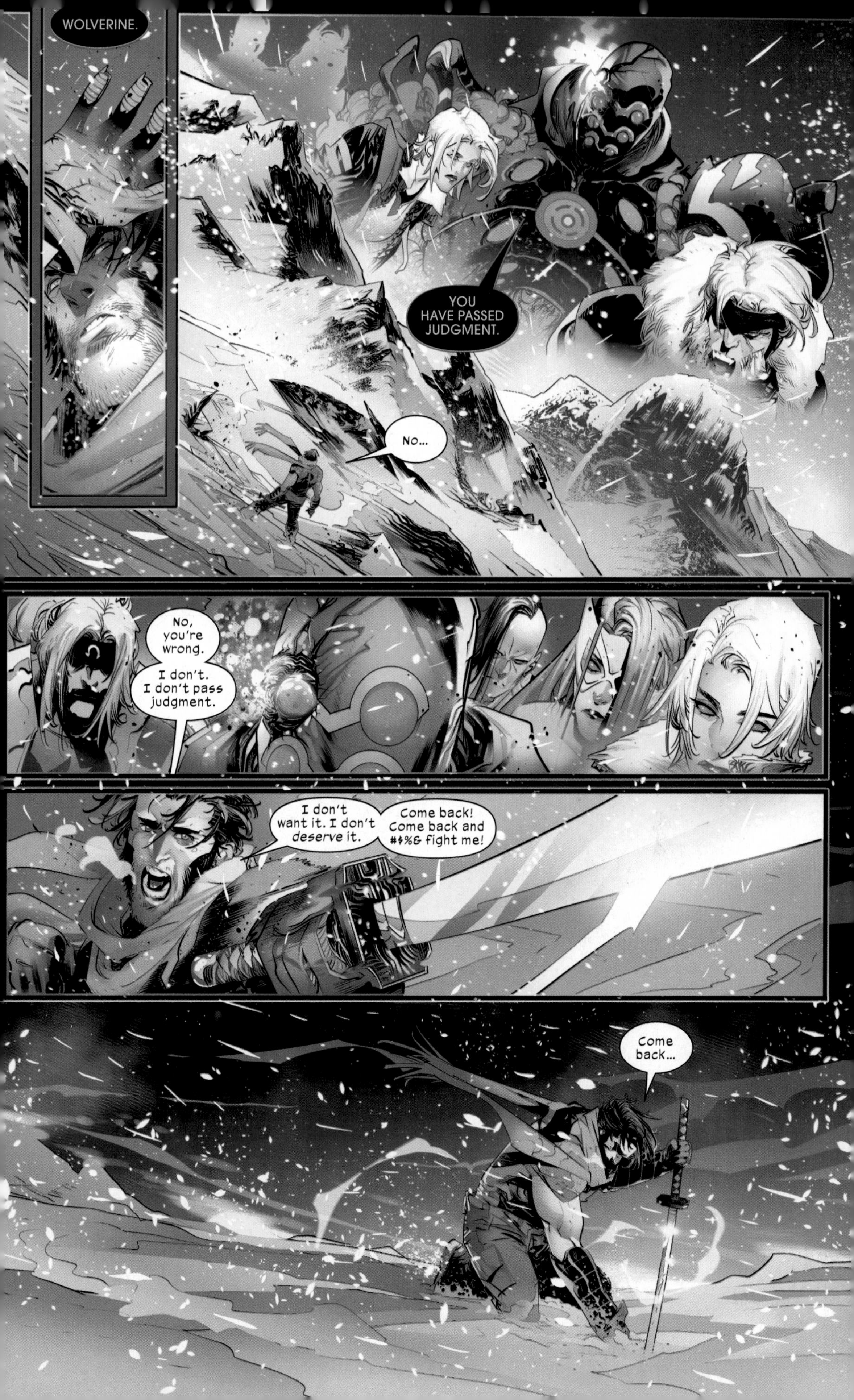
WOLVERINE.
YOU HAVE PASSED JUDGMENT.
NO...
No, you're wrong.
I don't. I don't pass judgment.
I don't want it. I don't *deserve* it.
Come back! Come back and #$%& fight me!
Come back...

[sol...[0.0]
[em....[0.0]

"There would be no Wolverine without pain. Or whiskey."

-- SOLEM

[sol...[0.0]
[em....[0.0]

[wolverine_25]

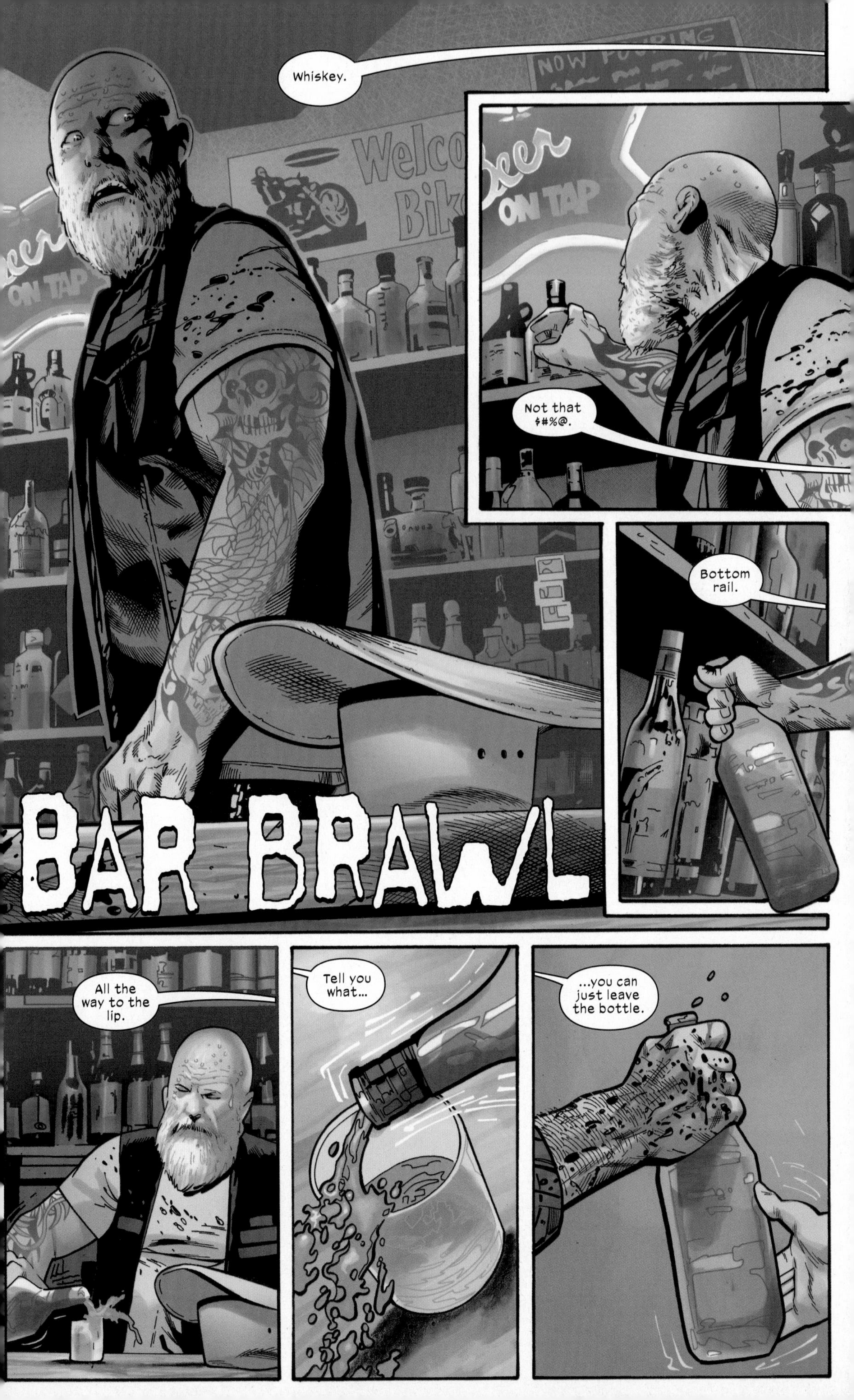
Whiskey.
Not that $#%@.
Bottom rail.
BAR BRAWL
All the way to the lip.
Tell you what...
...you can just leave the bottle.

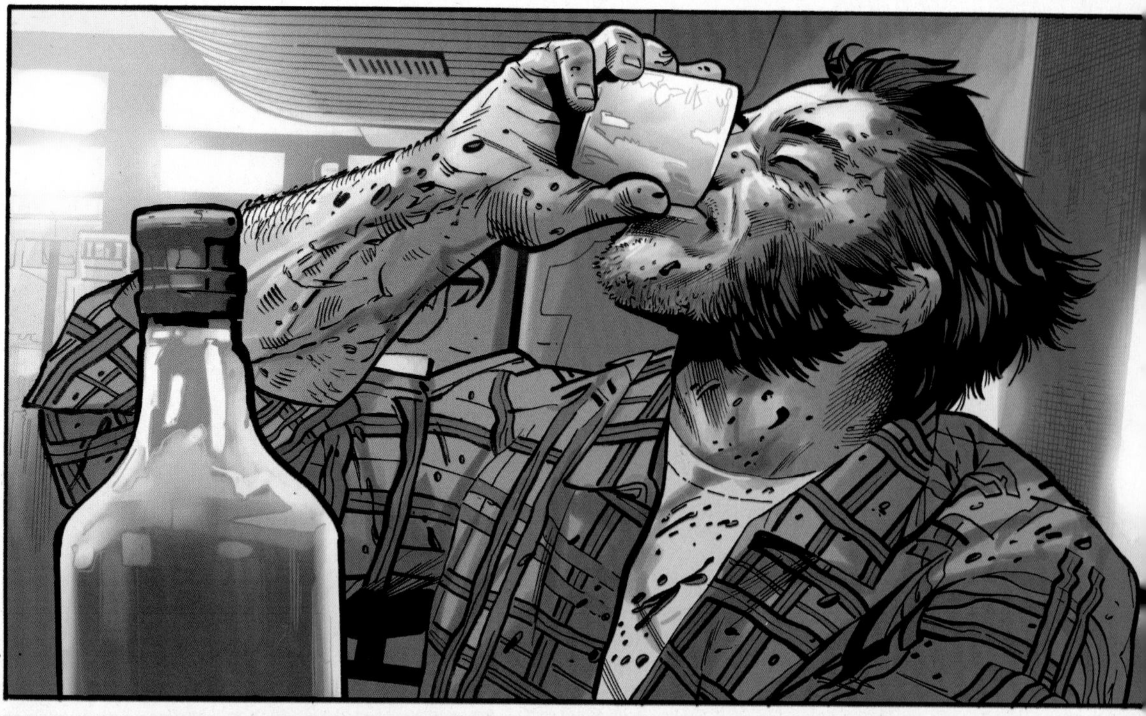

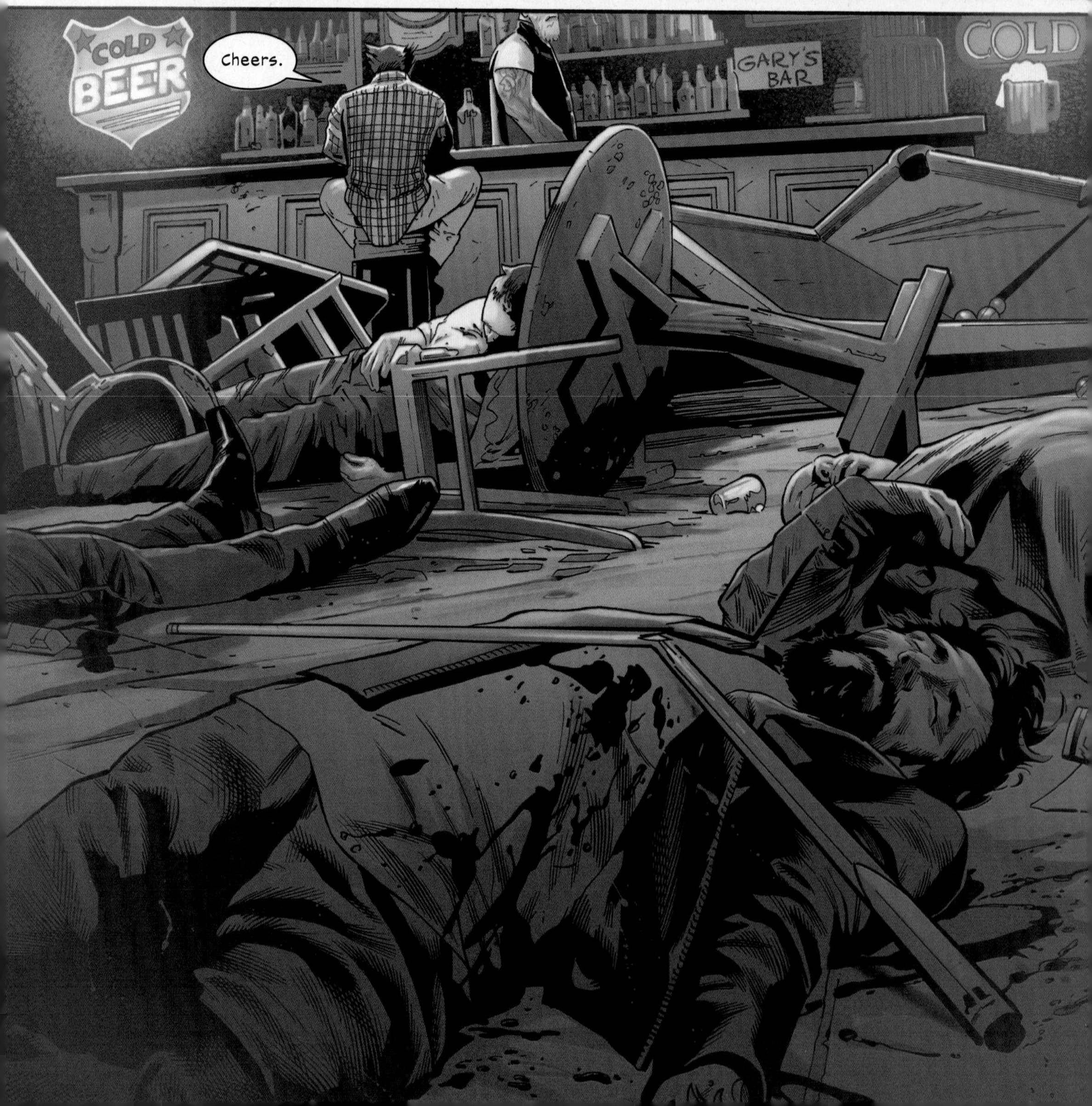
COLD BEER
Cheers.
GARY'S BAR
COLD

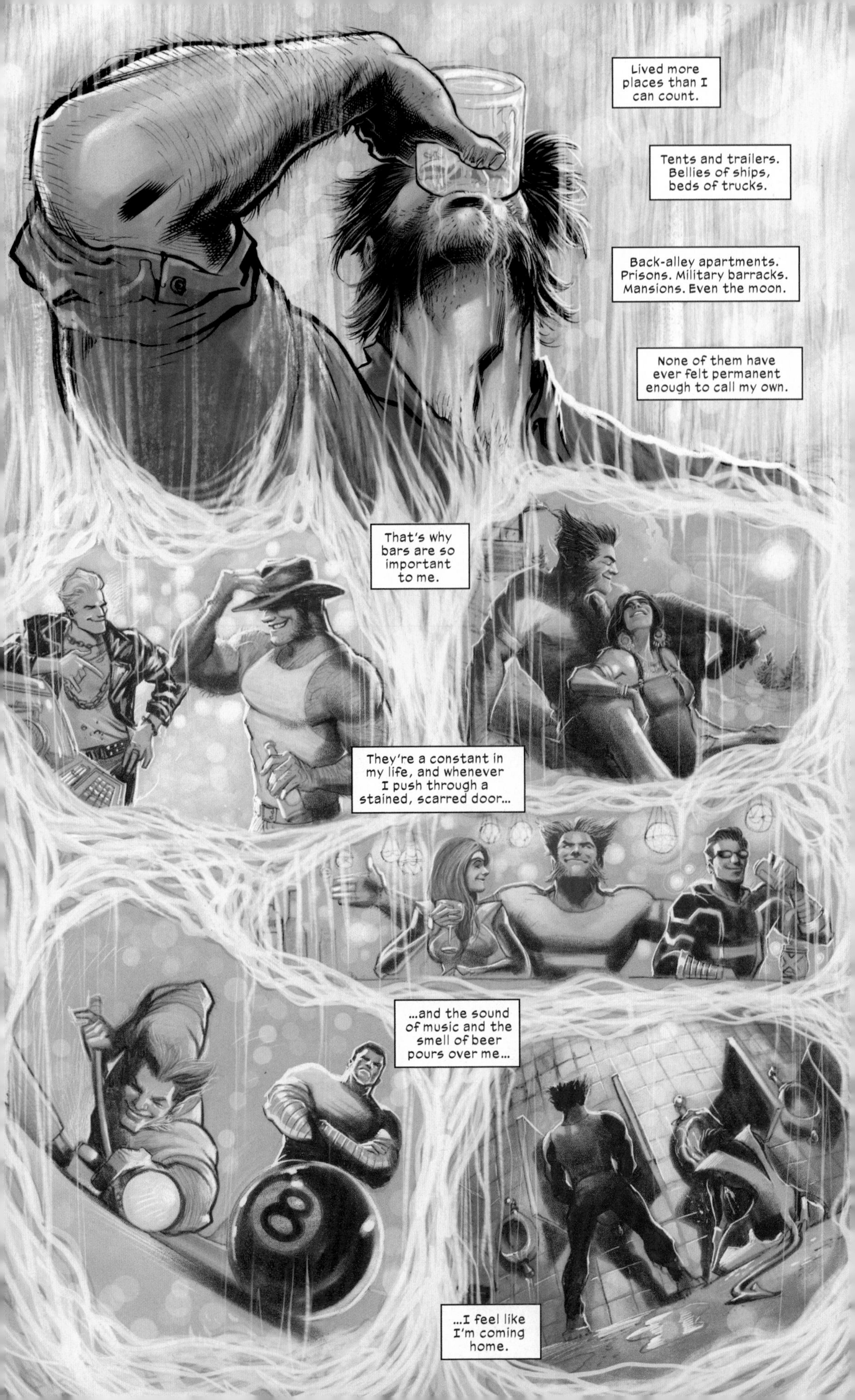
Lived more places than I can count.
Tents and trailers. Bellies of ships, beds of trucks.
Back-alley apartments. Prisons. Military barracks. Mansions. Even the moon.
None of them have ever felt permanent enough to call my own.
That's why bars are so important to me.
They're a constant in my life, and whenever I push through a stained, scarred door...
...and the sound of music and the smell of beer pours over me...
...I feel like I'm coming home.

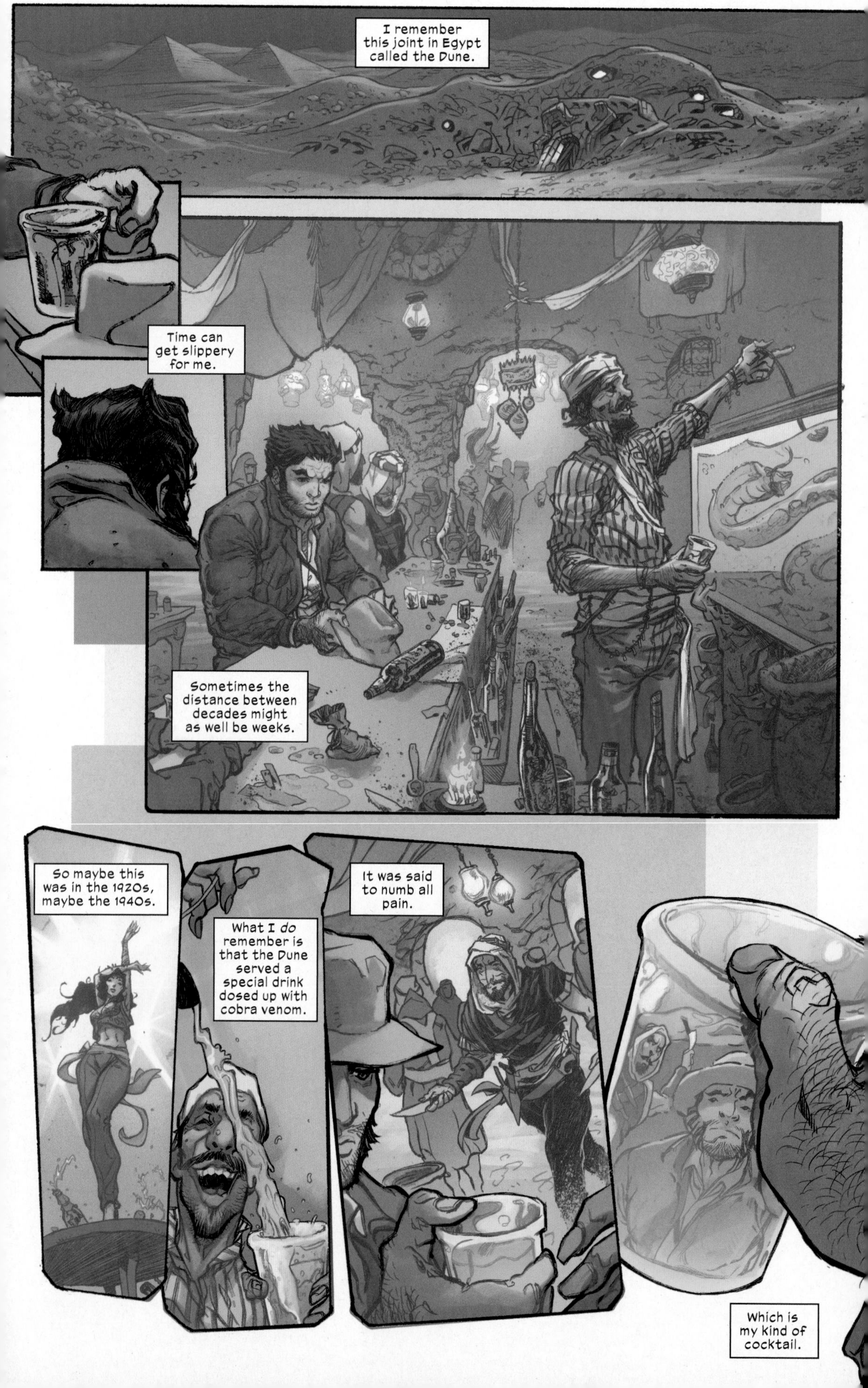
I remember this joint in Egypt called the Dune.
Time can get slippery for me.
Sometimes the distance between decades might as well be weeks.
So maybe this was in the 1920s, maybe the 1940s.
What I *do* remember is that the Dune served a special drink dosed up with cobra venom.
It was said to numb all pain.
Which is my kind of cocktail.

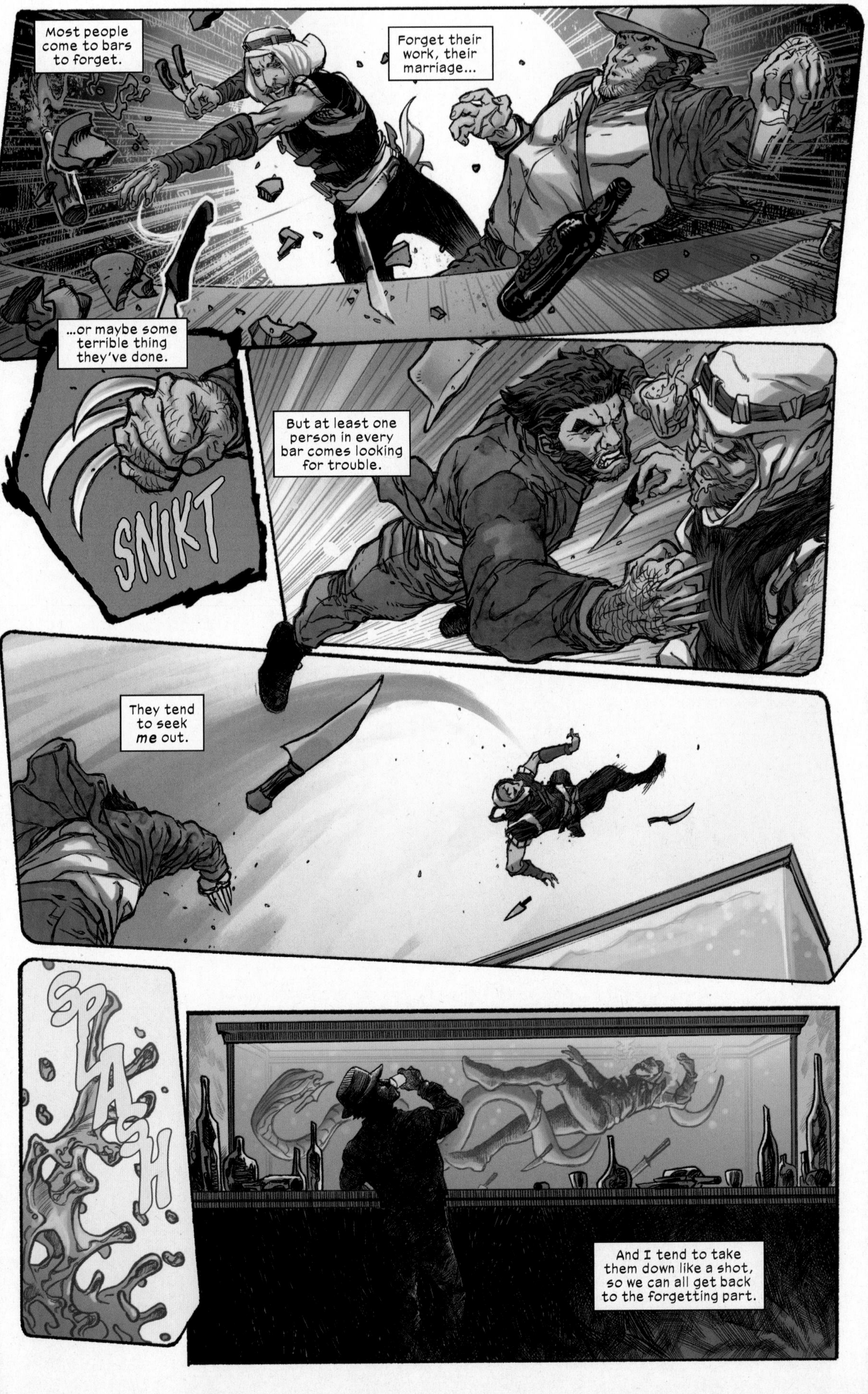
Most people come to bars to forget.
Forget their work, their marriage...
...or maybe some terrible thing they've done.
SNIKT
But at least one person in every bar comes looking for trouble.
They tend to seek *me* out.
SPLASH
And I tend to take them down like a shot, so we can all get back to the forgetting part.

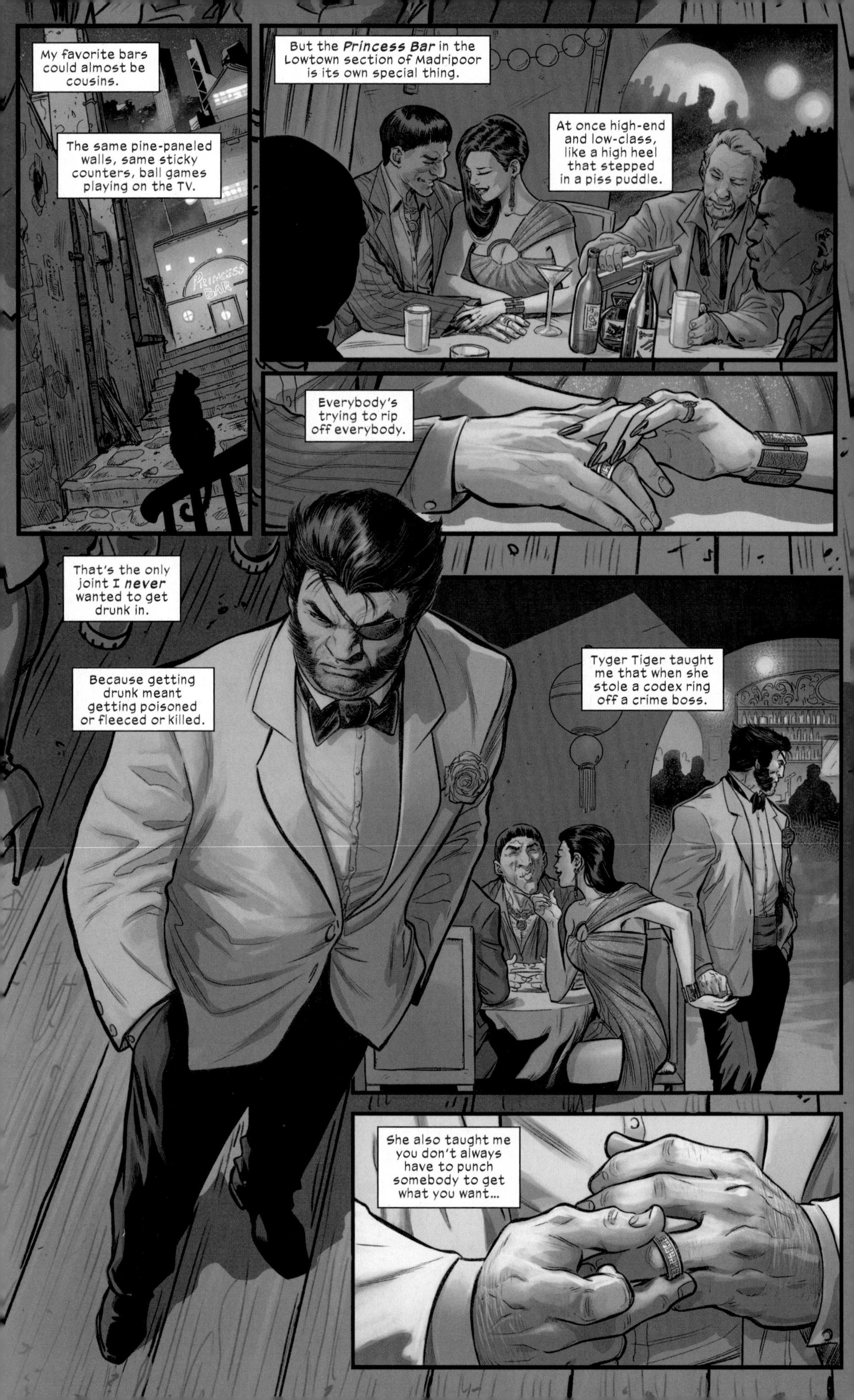
My favorite bars could almost be cousins.
The same pine-paneled walls, same sticky counters, ball games playing on the TV.
But the Princess Bar in the Lowtown section of Madripoor is its own special thing.
At once high-end and low-class, like a high heel that stepped in a piss puddle.
PRINCESS BAR
Everybody's trying to rip off everybody.
That's the only joint I never wanted to get drunk in.
Because getting drunk meant getting poisoned or fleeced or killed.
Tyger Tiger taught me that when she stole a codex ring off a crime boss.
She also taught me you don't always have to punch somebody to get what you want...

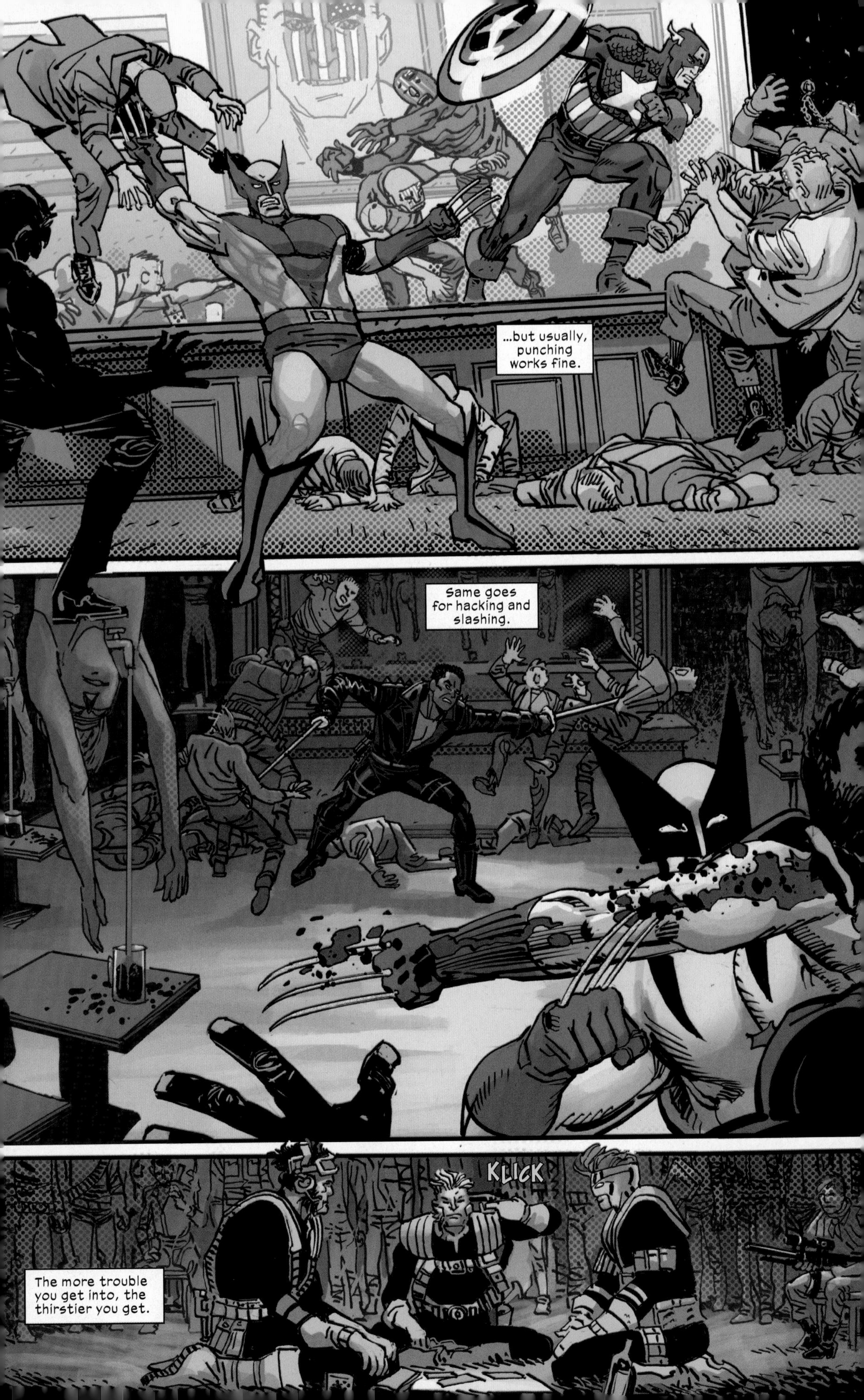
...but usually, punching works fine.
Same goes for hacking and slashing.
KLICK
The more trouble you get into, the thirstier you get.

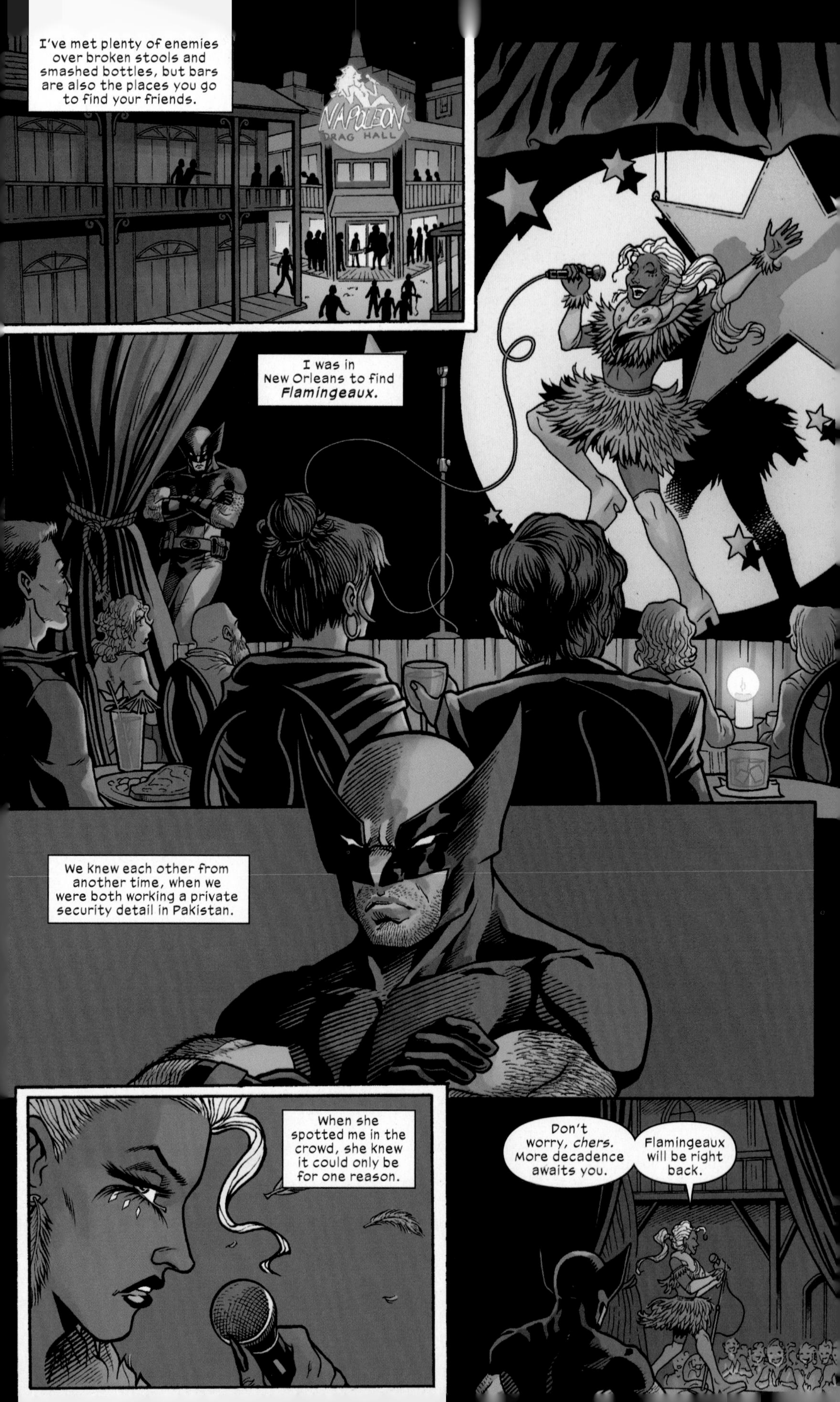
I've met plenty of enemies over broken stools and smashed bottles, but bars are also the places you go to find your friends.
NAPOLEON DRAG HALL
I was in New Orleans to find Flamingeaux.
We knew each other from another time, when we were both working a private security detail in Pakistan.
When she spotted me in the crowd, she knew it could only be for one reason.
Don't worry, chers. More decadence awaits you.
Flamingeaux will be right back.

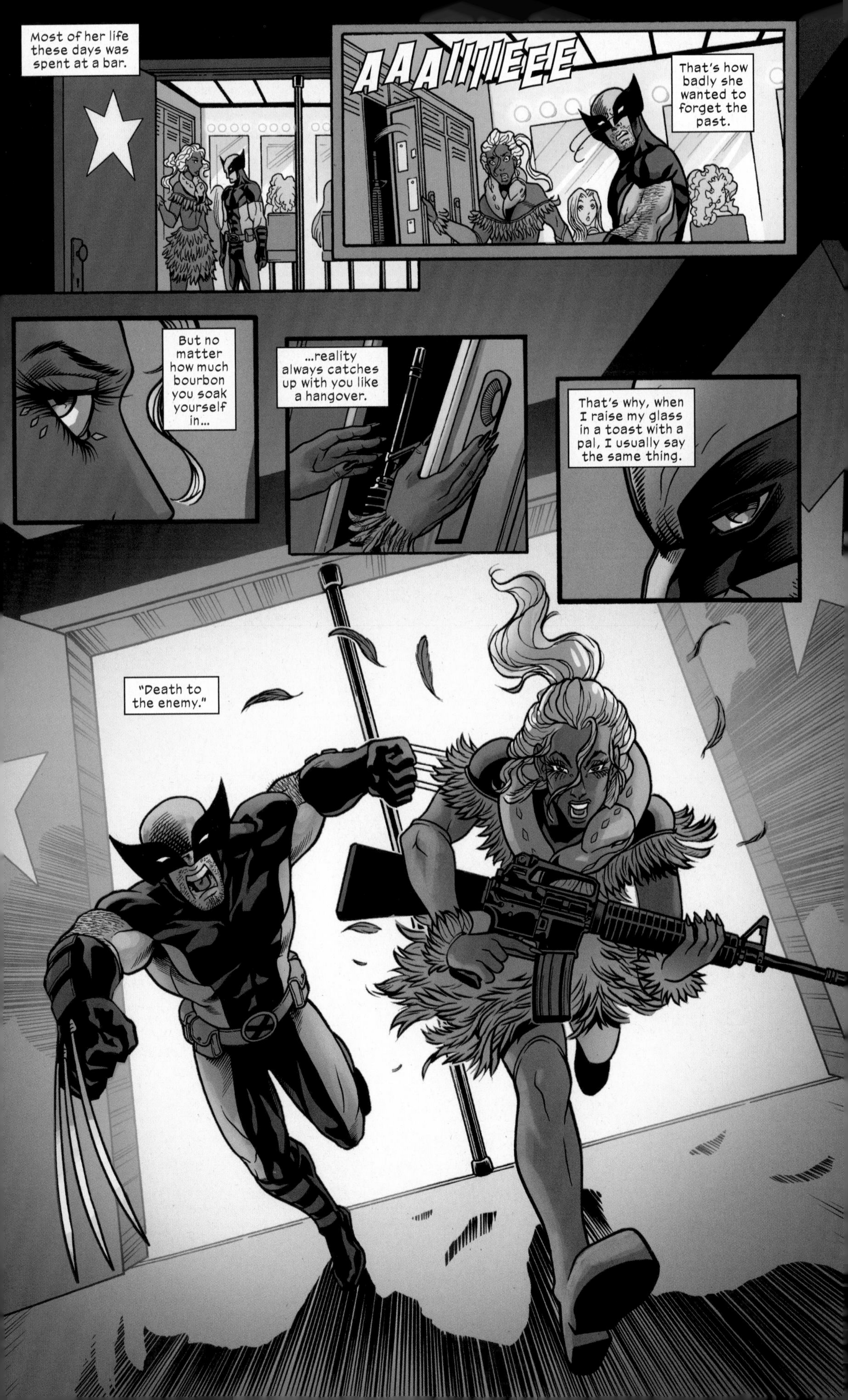
Most of her life these days was spent at a bar.
AAAIIIIIEEE
That's how badly she wanted to forget the past.
But no matter how much bourbon you soak yourself in...
...reality always catches up with you like a hangover.
That's why, when I raise my glass in a toast with a pal, I usually say the same thing.
"Death to the enemy."

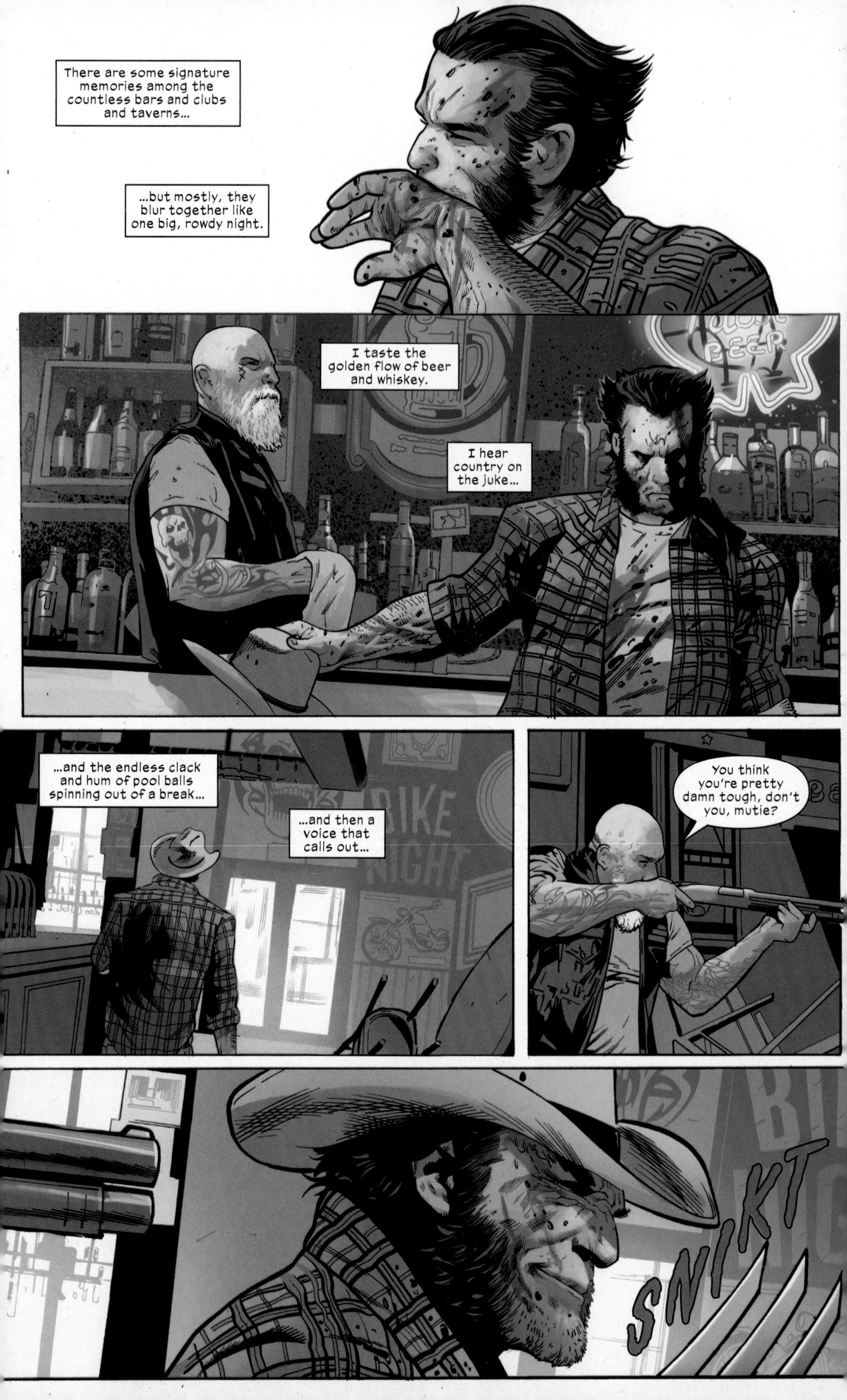

There are some signature memories among the countless bars and clubs and taverns...
...but mostly, they blur together like one big, rowdy night.
I taste the golden flow of beer and whiskey.
I hear country on the juke...
...and the endless clack and hum of pool balls spinning out of a break...
BIKE NIGHT
...and then a voice that calls out...
You think you're pretty damn tough, don't you, mutie?
SNIKT

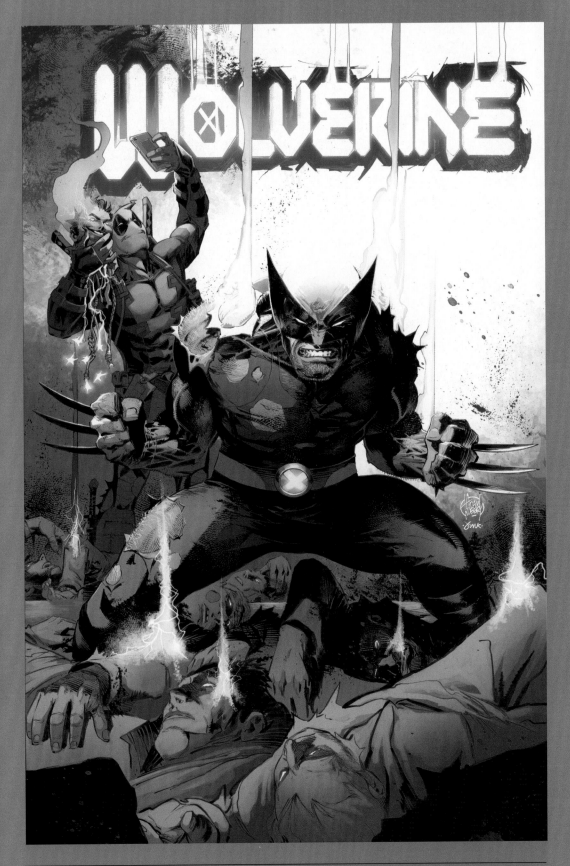

Wolverine #20

by Adam Kubert
& Frank Martin

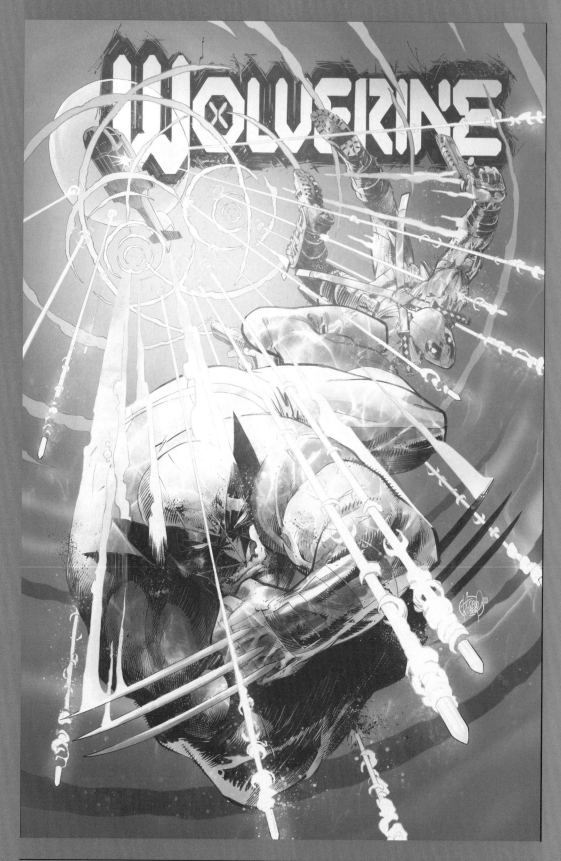

Wolverine #21

by Adam Kubert
& Frank Martin

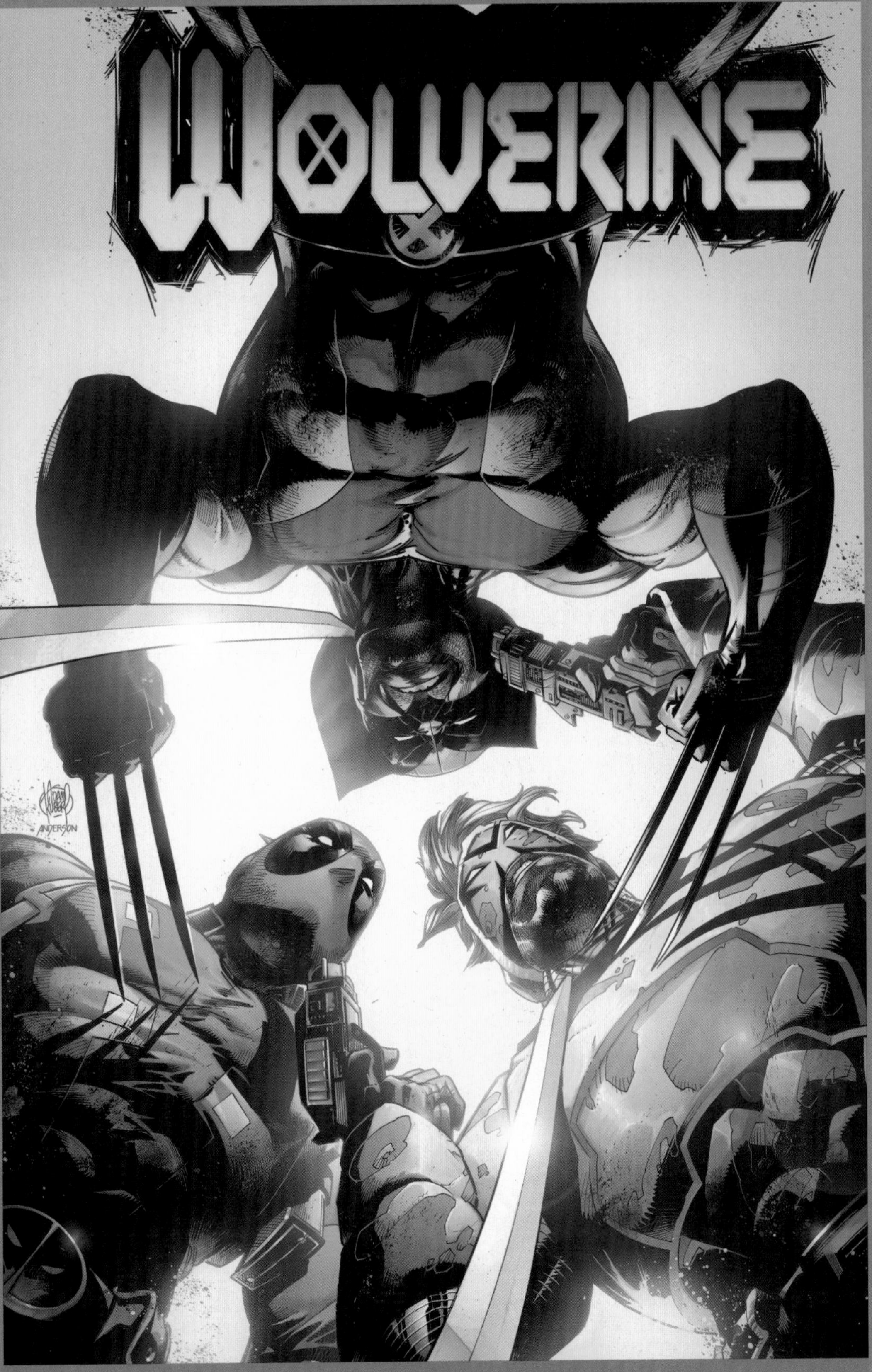
WOLVERINE
ANDERSON

Wolverine #22

by Adam Kubert
& Frank Martin

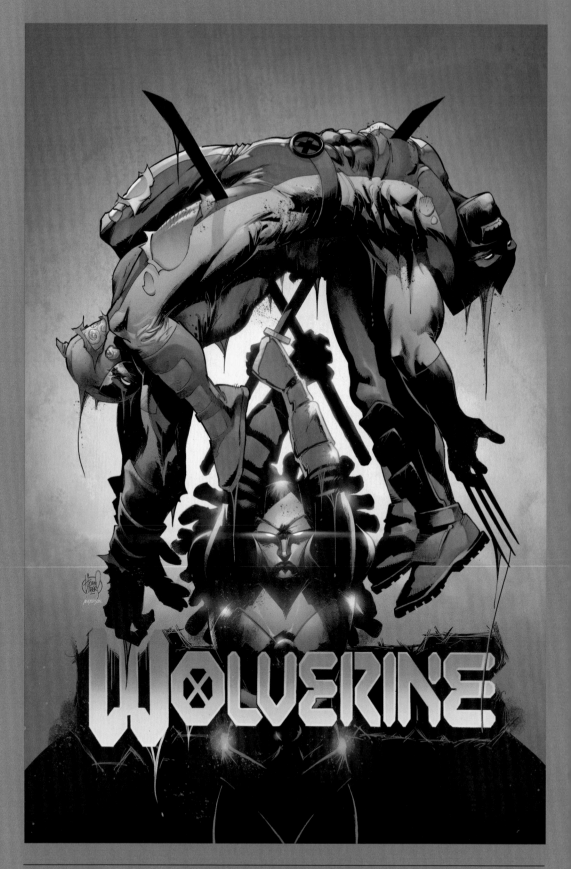

Wolverine #23

by Adam Kubert
& Frank Martin

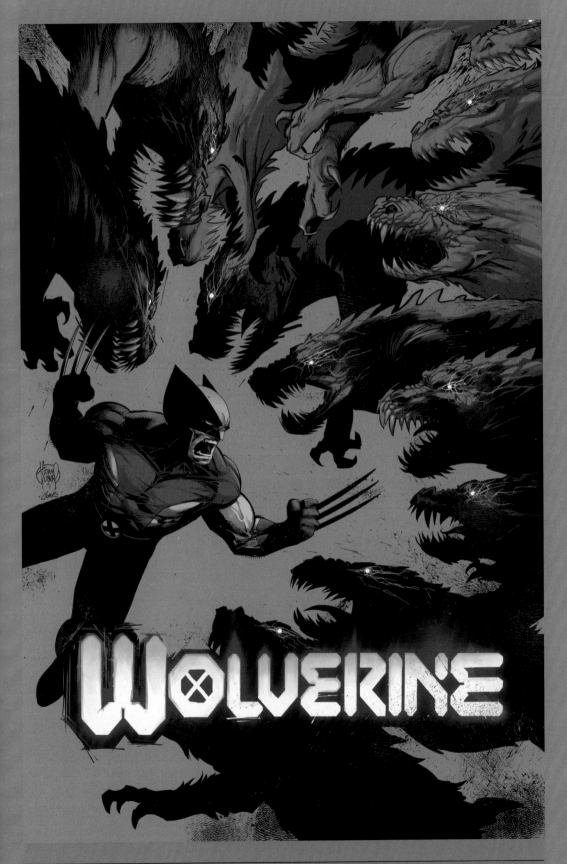

Wolverine #24

by Adam Kubert
& Frank Martin

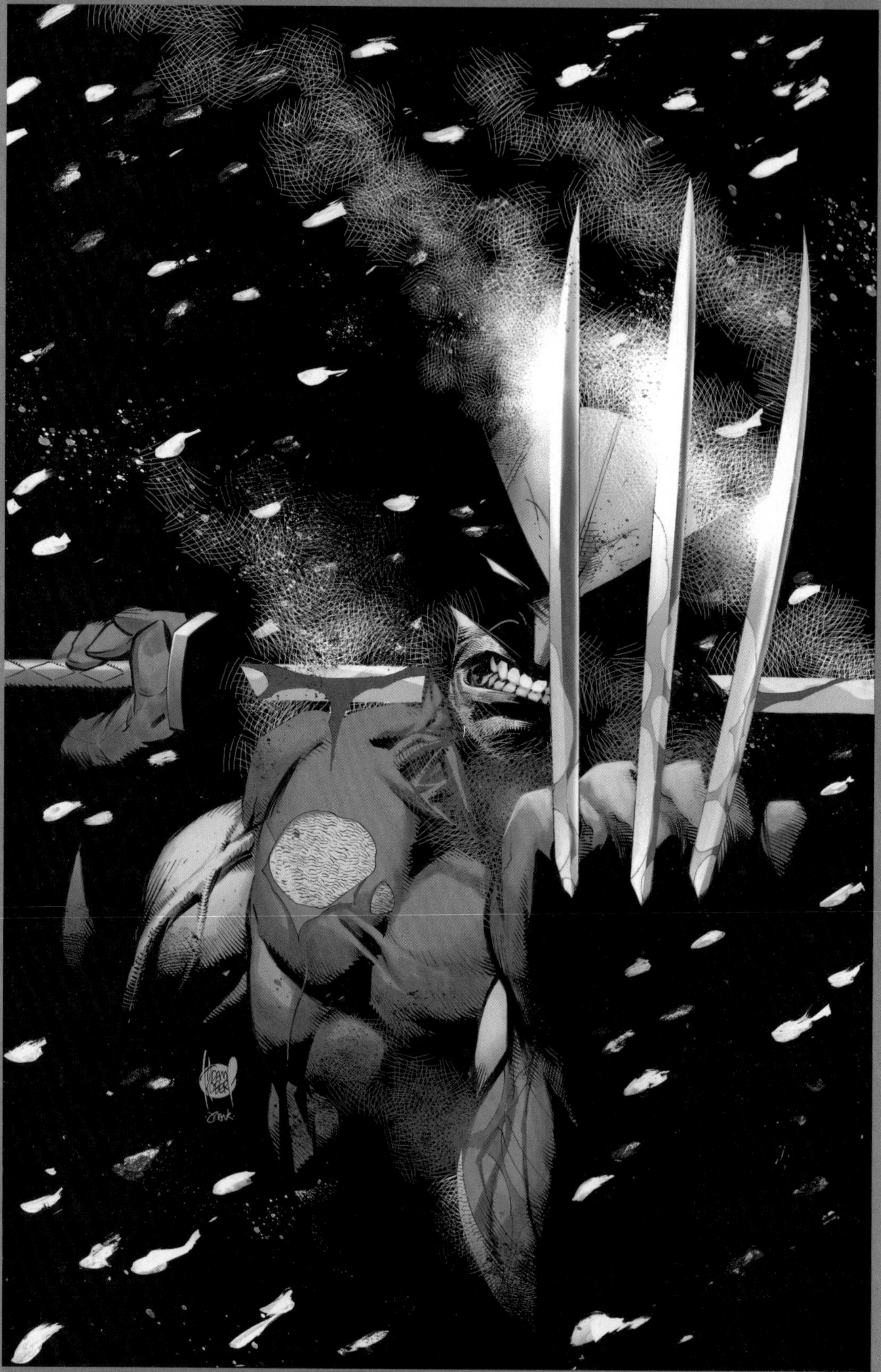

Wolverine #25

by Adam Kubert
& Frank Martin

Wolverine #23 SDCC Variant
by Salvador Larroca & Frank D'Armata

Wolverine #24 Variant
by David Nakayama

Wolverine #24 Variant
by Lucio Parrillo

Wolverine #24 Variant
by Chrissie Zullo

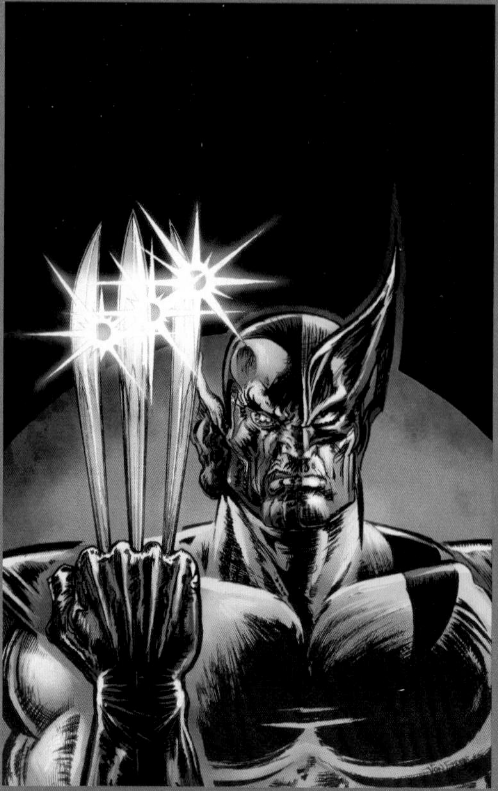

Wolverine #21 Skrull Variant
by Trevor von Eeden
& Rachelle Rosenberg

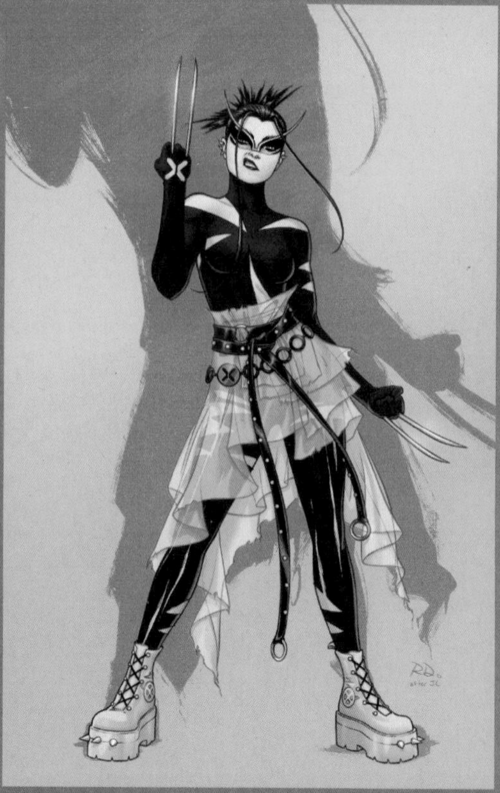

Wolverine #22 Hellfire Gala Variant
by Russell Dauterman
& Matthew Wilson

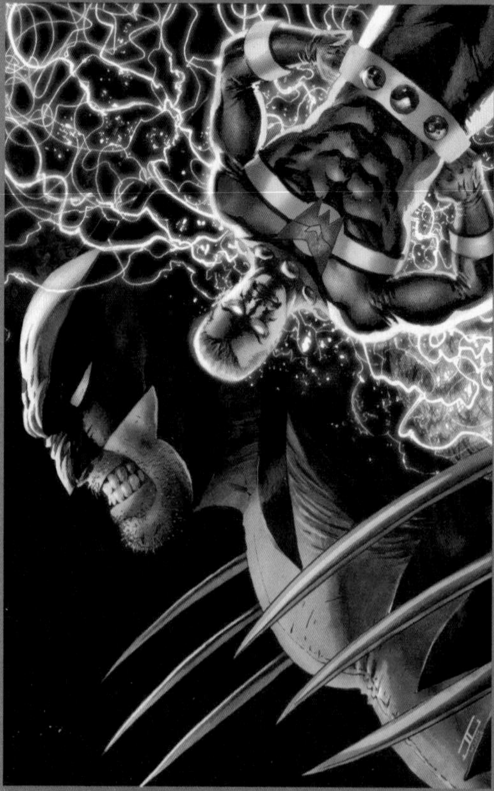

Wolverine #25 Miracleman Variant
by John Cassaday & Paul Mounts